Storytelling and Collecti[...]

"Darren Kelsey takes us on a powerful and erudite exploration of the role of narrative, myth and collective psychology in helping us to make sense of the world, our place in it and above all our own sense of who we are. As Kelsey sets out, the work of the illusionist Derren Brown is a fascinating example of how popular culture has taken on some of the important roles traditionally played by storytellers, orators and performers."
—Alex Evans, *Founder of Larger Us and best-selling author of* The Myth Gap

"This is a book about the psychological importance of the philosophical tradition of Stoicism, and its place and value within wider discourses of popular culture. It has two key figures from which it draws its examples and case studies: the author's own story (as a kind of 'everyman'), and the work of Derren Brown (as a kind of 'overman'). It argues for a reconfiguration of the understanding of the meaning of 'self-help' according to a version of Stoicism whose contours can be traced in such places as Cognitive Behavioural Therapy (CBT) in the medical/therapeutic world, and magician-turned-psychological illusionist and creative conjurer, Derren Brown.

Storytelling and Collective Psychology seeks to build bridges across disciplines. Via a range of fascinating and stimulating examples and case studies – most prominently, the psychological illusionist Derren Brown – Kelsey connects Stoic philosophy and modern psychology, revealing astonishing connections between Stoicism and Cognitive Behavioural Therapy (CBT). The book argues that Stoicism offers valuable ways to live life 'more philosophically'."
—Paul Bowman, *Professor of Cultural Studies, Cardiff University*

"*Storytelling and Collective Psychology* is an original and timely book which combines popular and academic elements. Using examples from Brown's shows and books, the book merges his philosophy with Jungian Analytical Psychology and delves into the nature of what it means to be human in today's world."
—Helena Bassil-Morozow, *Lecturer in Media and Journalism, Glasgow School for Business and Society*

Darren Kelsey

Storytelling and Collective Psychology

Ancient Wisdom, Modern Life and the Work of Derren Brown

Dear Jules

Philosophy for Life was great. Many thanks!

Enjoy.

palgrave macmillan

Darren Kelsey
School of Arts and Cultures
Newcastle University
Newcastle upon Tyne, UK

ISBN 978-3-030-93659-4   ISBN 978-3-030-93660-0 (eBook)
https://doi.org/10.1007/978-3-030-93660-0

© The Editor(s) (if applicable) and The Author(s), under exclusive licence to Springer Nature Switzerland AG 2022

This work is subject to copyright. All rights are solely and exclusively licensed by the Publisher, whether the whole or part of the material is concerned, specifically the rights of translation, reprinting, reuse of illustrations, recitation, broadcasting, reproduction on microfilms or in any other physical way, and transmission or information storage and retrieval, electronic adaptation, computer software, or by similar or dissimilar methodology now known or hereafter developed.

The use of general descriptive names, registered names, trademarks, service marks, etc. in this publication does not imply, even in the absence of a specific statement, that such names are exempt from the relevant protective laws and regulations and therefore free for general use.

The publisher, the authors and the editors are safe to assume that the advice and information in this book are believed to be true and accurate at the date of publication. Neither the publisher nor the authors or the editors give a warranty, expressed or implied, with respect to the material contained herein or for any errors or omissions that may have been made. The publisher remains neutral with regard to jurisdictional claims in published maps and institutional affiliations.

This Palgrave Macmillan imprint is published by the registered company Springer Nature Switzerland AG.
The registered company address is: Gewerbestrasse 11, 6330 Cham, Switzerland

Everything has its wonders, even darkness and silence, and I learn, whatever state I may be in, therein to be content.
Helen Keller

Being honest and publicly vulnerable is not the only way to be, but it's certainly a brave and deeply humane way to be.
Elizabeth Day

Courage is not something that you already have that makes you brave when the tough times start. Courage is what you earn when you've been through the tough times and you discover they aren't so tough after all.
Malcolm Gladwell

In loving memory of Brian Cole

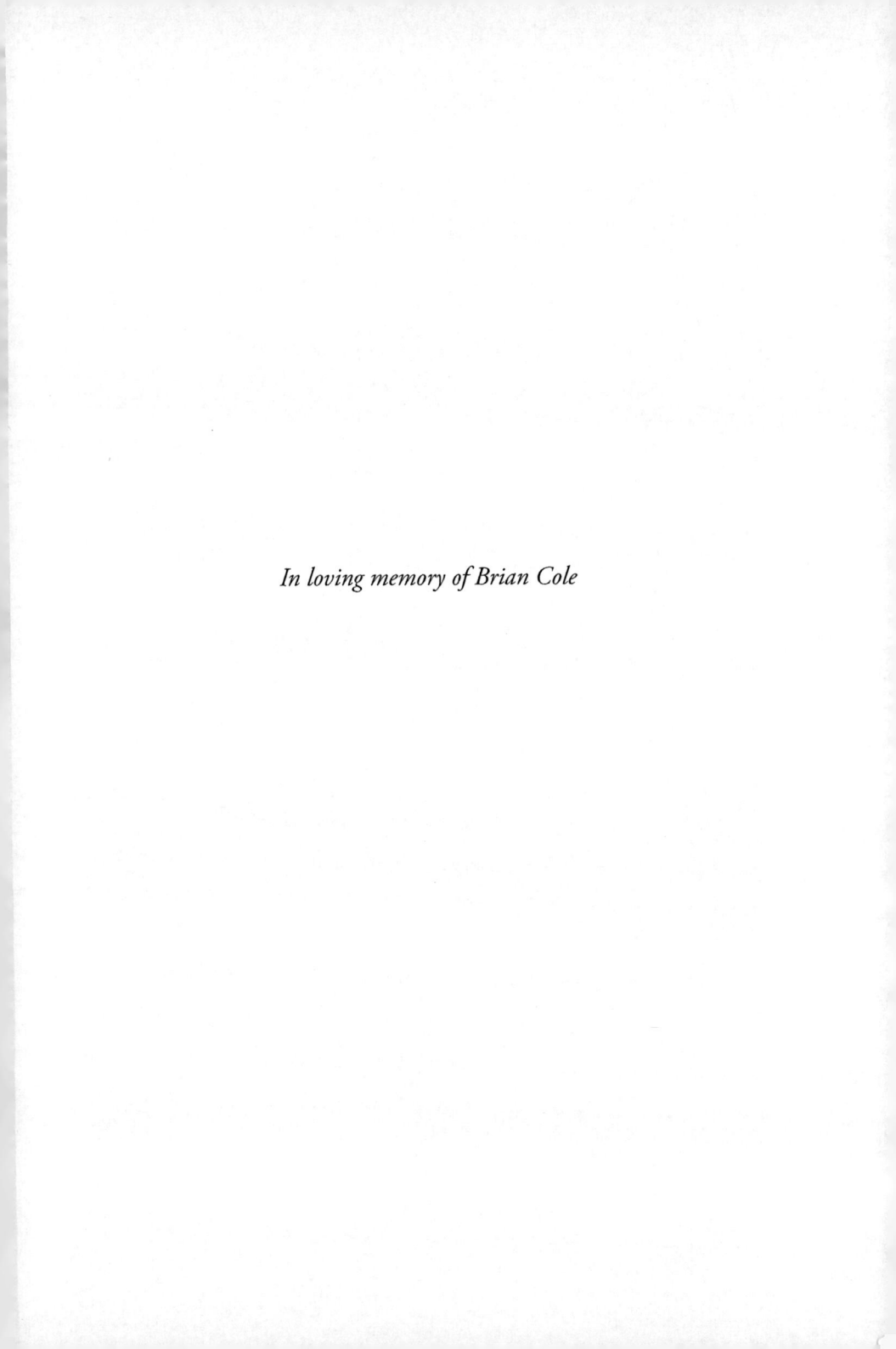

Preface: Help!

Life often seems chaotic. As individuals we can feel bewildered and anxious. As collectives we can feel disparate and divided. But troublesome times are not unique to modern life. For centuries, humans have looked for advice on how to live well and find tranquillity amidst adversity, while striving to take better care of each other.

Sometimes we need a little bit of wisdom to get us back on track. Like the troubled heroes in popular stories that we know and love, we all need figures who offer some light in the darkness—those magicians and wise elders who enlighten us, help us overcome our flaws and fears and guide us on our journey. This is a book about a figure who plays that role in popular culture today.

When I started writing this book I had just recovered from a crippling bout of anxiety. For many years of my life I had struggled to enjoy success or achievements and seldom would I feel calm or content in any circumstances. I endured regular periods of obsessive thought patterns that stimulated all-consuming fears and worries about hypothetical catastrophes and impending doom. Even as a child, I was a compulsive worrier, and I would often obsess over losing things or having things taken away from me. As I grew up, these compulsions became a recurring pattern in the stories I told myself. They shaped my perception of the world around me and my place in it.

In hindsight, relative to my age, my worries were often trivial, even if they felt serious at the time. But as my life responsibilities became increasingly less trivial, so did my worries. By the time I had my dream life—my wife, my daughter, my house, my job—my worries deepened. Either I would lose those things I adored the most or, somehow, they would lose me. As always, no matter what my circumstances were, or how privileged I was, gratitude fell victim to fear.

I was a terrible storyteller. My internal stories began to have a physical effect on me as I became increasingly convinced that they were true and I regularly functioned on high alert. One day, I decided to get help. Through a combination of serendipity, curiosity and perseverance, my experience motivated me to write a book about a magician whose work resonated with me on my road to recovery.

While receiving Cognitive Behavioural Therapy (CBT), I read a book called *Happy: Why More or Less Everything Is Absolutely Fine* by the magician and psychological illusionist Derren Brown. In response to some of the unhelpful messages on happiness that we are often fed by the self-help industry, Brown had turned his attention to the ancient Greek philosophy of Stoicism to rethink how we approach happiness in modern life and what advice the Stoics can offer us today.

When I discovered that the foundations of CBT were based on the core principles of Stoicism, *Happy* became a recurring talking point with my therapist. I found countless similarities between my thought patterns and Brown's examples of the stories we tell ourselves and how they affect us. *Happy* nudged me into a reading marathon on Stoic philosophy: I had soon read the works of Marcus Aurelius, Seneca and Epictetus followed by more recent Stoic endorsements from the likes of Massimo Pigliucci, Donald Robertson, William Irvine and Ryan Holiday.

I then caught up on the TV and stage shows that Brown had discussed on a number of podcasts and media appearances during his marketing of *Happy*.[1] Here, I found further overlaps between the themes in Brown's work and my research interests in storytelling and collective psychology.

So many disturbances in life—personally, socially and politically—stem from the stories we conjure up about our lives and the lives of others. Some of our greatest qualities and potentials get left out of our stories about who we think we are, what we should be and how we should live as individuals and collectives.

Like those archetypal magicians who appear in popular stories and fairy tales, in Brown I saw a conjuror, creator and performer who sought to guide us on our collective journey through the messy trials and tribulations that life throws at us. Brown's work is not simply about magic. It's about the stories, beliefs, philosophies, morals and behaviours that shape our personal and collective lives. His work is as much about our conjuring minds as an audience, as it is about his own conjuring on stage.

So, who is this book for? Anyone. We are all storytellers, and this book is all about stories. There are many reasons why different readers might enjoy this book—whether they are interested in psychology, self-help, philosophy, politics, society, popular culture or any other timely themes and issues that are covered throughout. We all need stories—they help us to make sense of the noise and confusion of daily life—and we can all benefit from advice on how to tell better stories for ourselves and society.

This book is written as part of my research and teaching, but it should appeal to readers both within and beyond academia. Whether readers are familiar with Brown's work or not, this book provides thought-provoking insights designed to give readers more confidence to critically reflect on the personal and social role of storytelling in their lives.

My previous research has critically analysed the political, economic and cultural factors of media and mythological storytelling.[2] Myths aren't always about lies or untruth; they're often stories that simplify the complexities of life and events and they resonate with us because they help us to understand something about our culture or identity.[3]

Myths are stories that serve social purposes—they feel as if they are true without even thinking about it. These types of stories have fascinated me in my research—the war on terror, Brexit, the financial crisis, political protests, institutional scandals, populism, the far-right, political personas, celebrity culture and martial arts have provided an eclectic landscape of cultural mythologies that reflect many of the narrative traits that have been appearing in human societies for centuries.

What I have become most interested in are those underlying psychological dynamics that operate through our stories, which continually recreate familiar narrative conventions. The role that popular culture plays in this mythological landscape is like a narrative hub for our collective storytelling—influencing how we think and feel and relate to each other as a society.

When I published my previous monograph on affective mythologies, I had tried to finish that project with an optimistic mindset—despite some of the darker topics covered, I believed we could create a better future for our society. But in amongst the social and political chaos and polarisation of recent times, it felt like we were missing something, and I couldn't work out what it was. At around that time, I read a book by Alex Evans.[4]

In *The Myth Gap*, Evans proposes that collective storytelling is crucial to how we tackle future challenges for our society and the planet. He argues that in the past we were able to understand ourselves and the world through a rich selection of myths that united us and pulled us together through a sense of common purpose. In current times, however, he suggests that we are suffering from a myth gap, in which our stories do not serve that crucial purpose of helping us navigate towards a better collective future that will ensure the survival of humanity or the planet.

Through his experience as a climate change adviser to the British government and the United Nations, Evans learnt that on some matters no amount of data and indisputable evidence would be enough to influence government policy. Instead, what truly influences people are powerful stories.

In 2018 Evans established the Collective Psychology Project—the predecessor to a network currently known as Larger Us, whose work I refer to throughout this book. Larger Us began a collaborative inquiry to see how psychology and politics could be synergised to create innovative ways of bringing people together beyond a culture of them-and-us thinking.[5]

I became increasingly convinced that this principle applies in our personal stories about our own lives as much as the larger collective stories we share as a society. These elements are entwined on a mass scale, forming the social fabric that determines the state of our collective psychology—shaping our inner world of feeling and perception as much as the outer world and the social conditions in which we live.

Likewise, Evans argues that we need to become better storytellers in our personal *and* collective lives. This is not just about the grand narratives of our society and how we create myths as a civilisation; it is as much about the personal stories that we tell, how we understand ourselves as individuals, how we perceive the world around us and how we relate to each other.

This approach to storytelling and collective psychology influenced how I conducted the research project that led to this book. The material I cover in this study resonates with these principles, and the conclusions I draw provide some optimism for the future.

On the one hand, I have become increasingly concerned that if we do not consider the psychological foundations and implications of our stories then it is more likely that we will overlook the close links between those inner and outer crises that we face as individuals and societies. However, I am also optimistic that we can identify healthy forms of storytelling that are conducive to collective wellbeing, and we can build on the lessons we learn from those stories and the people and communities that create them.

My current focus on collective psychology continues to develop this line of inquiry. Throughout this book, I will return to the work of Evans and the Larger Us team (among other literature and insights) to help guide us through this concept of collective psychology, its compatibility with other philosophical perspectives and its relevance in our daily lives. In doing so, we can look to popular culture as one area that might help us understand more about the state of our collective psychology.

I enjoyed writing this book more than anything else I have written. I always know that I am going to enjoy a project if friends or colleagues frown (or smile politely) when I share a new idea. But this project felt particularly exciting. Magic? Derren Brown? Collective psychology? Stoic philosophy? What's all that about? My peers could be forgiven for thinking I was drifting slightly off topic. But to me it all made sense, and I hope it makes sense to you. I hope you enjoy this book.

Newcastle upon Tyne, UK   Darren Kelsey

Notes

1. The following sources formed the media sample for this project (full references can be found in the bibliography): Brown, 2006, 2011a, 2011b, 2012a, 2012b, 2012c, 2016a, 2016b, 2016c, 2017, 2018a, 2018b, 2018c, 2018d, 2018e, 2019a, 2019b, 2019c, 2019d, 2020a, 2020b, 2020c, 2021a, 2021b.
2. Kelsey, 2015, 2017, 2018, 2020.
3. Barthes, 1993; Lule, 2001; Flood, 2002; Campbell, 1949.
4. Evans, 2017.
5. Larger Us, 2018. The Larger Us website can be found here: https://larger.us/

Bibliography

Barthes, R. (1993). *Mythologies*. Vintage.
Brown, D. (2006, January 4). *The Heist*. Channel 4.
Brown, D. (2011a). *Confessions of a conjuror*. Transworld.
Brown, D. (2011b, April 25). *Miracles for Sale*. Channel 4.
Brown, D. (2012a, November 2). *Apocalypse*. Channel 4.
Brown, D. (2012b). *Apocalypse Q&A*. https://derrenbrown.co.uk/apocalypse-qa/
Brown, D. (2012c). *Steven and Karl*. https://www.youtube.com/watch?v=AqAqhaa0DhE
Brown, D. (2016a). *Happy: Why more or less everything is absolutely fine*. Penguin.
Brown, D. (2016b). New Derren Brown "Happy" book interview. *BBC Breakfast*. https://www.youtube.com/watch?v=ay7IyqQLjtg
Brown, D. (2016c). Derren Brown: 'Performers can be shy and despite my dramatic stunts, in reality, I truly do not like the attention'. *The Belfast Telegraph*. https://www.belfasttelegraph.co.uk/entertainment/news/derren-brown-performers-can-be-shy-and-despite-my-dramatic-stunts-in-reality-i-truly-do-not-like-the-attention-35064763.html
Brown, D. (2017). *Renowned illusionist Derren Brown on stoicism and why more or less everything is absolutely fine*. https://dailystoic.com/derren-brown/
Brown, D. (2018a). Joe Rogan & Derren Brown – The idea of happiness. *The Joe Rogan experience #1198*. https://www.youtube.com/watch?v=E3DigsvZCXo
Brown, D. (2018b). *The Push*. Netflix.
Brown, D. (2018c). *Sacrifice*. Netflix.
Brown, D. (2018d). *Miracle*. Netflix.

Brown, D. (2018e). #143 Keys to the mind: A conversation with Derren Brown. *Making sense with Sam Harris.* https://samharris.org/podcasts/143-keys-mind/

Brown, D. (2019a, May 31). Desert Island Discs. *BBC Radio 4.* https://www.bbc.co.uk/programmes/m0005dyb

Brown, D. (2019b). An illusionist reacts to movies and TV shows about illusions. *Vulture.* https://www.vulture.com/2019/08/derren-brown-reacts-to-movies-and-tv-shows-about-illusions.html

Brown, D. (2019c). Derren Brown: The magician's secrets. BBC World Service: Outlook. https://www.bbc.co.uk/programmes/w3csyhj9

Brown, D. (2019d). *The Adam Buxton podcast.* Ep.110: Derren Brown. https://www.adam-buxton.co.uk/podcasts/17

Brown, D. (2020a). *The path to less stress? Strategic pessimism.* | Derren Brown | Big Think. https://www.youtube.com/watch?v=wKfUK1Gd6YM

Brown, D. (2020b). Derren Brown's new book offers advice on overcoming anxiety. *Sky News.* https://www.youtube.com/watch?v=lKqwl4hb-ew

Brown, D. (2020c, August 16). *20 Years of Mind Control.* Channel 4.

Brown, D. (2021a). *A book of secrets: Finding solace in a stubborn world.* London: Penguin.

Brown, D. (2021b, September 11). *Showman.* Empire Theatre.

Campbell, J. (1949). *The hero with a thousand faces.* Pantheon.

Evans, A. (2017). *The myth gap: What happens when evidence and arguments aren't enough.* Eden Project Books.

Flood, C. (2002). *Political myth.* Routledge.

Kelsey, D. (2015). *Media, myth and terrorism: A discourse-mythological analysis of the 'Blitz Spirit' in British newspaper responses to the July 7th bombings.* Palgrave.

Kelsey, D. (2017). *Media and affective mythologies: Discourse, archetypes and ideology in contemporary politics.* Palgrave.

Kelsey, D. (2018). Affective mythology and 'the notorious' Conor McGregor: Monomyth, mysticism, and mixed martial arts. *Martial Arts Studies, 5,* 15–35.

Kelsey, D. (2020). Psycho-discursive constructions of narrative in archetypal storytelling: A discourse-mythological approach. *Critical Discourse Studies.* https://doi.org/10.1080/17405904.2020.1802766

Larger Us. (2018). *A larger us.* https://larger.us/ideas/?report

Lule, J. (2001). *Daily news, eternal stories: The mythological role of journalism.* Guilford.

Acknowledgements

Special thanks go to my beautiful and supportive wife, Monica, and my funny, loving daughter, Daisy. They are what matters most and I am grateful for the love we share together. Monica has had to listen to me talk about this book a lot, and her ability to pretend she is still interested when I am waffling is admirable. Monica does not need to read or write about Stoicism to live well. She does it naturally—with care, compassion, faith, selflessness and a sense of duty to others. Her natural kindness blows my mind. What an incredible role model for Daisy to have as her mam.

Thank you to my therapist, Sam Cox, who has seen this project grow throughout the time we have worked together. Sam's help and compassion has been life-changing and I will always be grateful for the support she has provided during challenging times. Monica and Sam keep me in check and make sure I look after myself. They make a formidable force for accountability when I slip up. But they're always kind—honest. Thank you.

Thank you to all of my family and friends for their love and support, especially my parents. They have made so many things possible for me in life. As I explain later in this book, I am truly grateful to my parents for giving me the freedom to flourish and never pushing me in one direction.

Fortune has dealt me a decent card when it comes to family and friends. Special thanks go to Kieran Wood for his unconditional love and ability to be Stoic without even realising. We have been on a tremendous journey together and I am truly grateful for the connection we have.

A huge thank you to those who have provided input and advice during this project, especially Graeme McConnell, Aaron Tucker, Lucy Bennett, Ben Lamb, Leanne Pearce, Chris Hart, Chris Stovell, Tom Hewitt, Richard Clay, Jonny Ward, Emily Sweetman and Hannah Clark.

Thank you to all my colleagues at Newcastle University—especially "Team MCH". Thank you to my mentors—of whom there are many, and they know who they are. Special thanks to Rhiannon Mason. Legend.

Thank you to Alex Evans for his input in this project and thanks to the Larger Us team for all their hard work. Alex has been extremely generous with his time and we have had some inspiring conversations together.

Thank you to the lads at Barley Mow WMC—especially the Barley No Coats. We had a tough time losing Brian, but we stuck together and he would be proud to see us supporting each other and looking out for Heather.

Thank you to everyone in our local parish for their love and support. We have a thriving community at St. Joseph's. Thank you to the Exodus 90 fraternity for allowing me to attend your group in a research capacity, and thank you for paying such an enthusiastic interest in this project.

Thank you to the Whitten, McKenna and Woodhead gangs for all the love, booze and laughs.

Guildford, Cardiff, London and Newcastle host numerous circles of friends from important stages of my life. And there are plenty of wonderful people in other places all over the world who have supported me in ways that I will be eternally grateful for. Anyone who deserves a thank you will know who they are. Thank you.

And, of course, there's one person who I never forget to mention: Rob Stanley. As always, thank you Rob. None of this could have happened without you getting me started.

Thank you for reading this book. Please be kind and look after each other. We're not here for long, so let's make the most of it and do our best—for ourselves, each other and the future.

Contents

1	**Introduction: Narrative Building Machines**	1
	Mythmaking and Popular Culture	2
	Private Hallucinations	3
	A Conjuror's Story	4
	A Serendipitous Discovery	6
	Collective States of Mind	7
	The Analytical Approach of This Book	9
	The Structure of This Book	10
	Stories for a Better Future	12
	Bibliography	18
2	**The Archetypal Magician**	21
	Transformational Spaces	22
	The Stage Magician	23
	The Enlightened Magician	25
	The Shadow Magician	28
	Trust and Authenticity	29
	Stories, Memories and Experiences	30
	Our Chattering Selves	32
	Scepticism of Our Stories	34
	Bibliography	39

3 Street Philosophy and the Stoics — 41
Philosophy for Flourishing — 42
The Dichotomy of Control — 44
Purpose, Responsibility and Society — 46
Actions over Outcomes — 48
Learning and Growing — 50
Life Skills and Lessons — 51
Fate and Fortune — 52
Stillness, Egos and Obstacles — 53
Habitual Humans — 54
Perceptions and Stories — 55
Inner and Outer Worlds — 56
Emotions and Reactions — 58
Domesticate Your Emotions — 59
Taking Back Control — 61
The Unlived Lives of Our Parents — 62
Freedom to Flourish — 64
That Fraudster Feeling — 65
Hindsight and Reflection — 66
Bibliography — 70

4 Self-Help and Popular Culture — 73
An Antidote to the Self-Help Industry — 74
Strategic Pessimism — 75
The Verb of Happiness — 77
Our Protestant Past — 79
The Law of Attraction — 80
Blame and Failure — 81
Kicking and Screaming — 82
Self-Help and Celebrity — 83
The Conor McGregor Story — 84
Narrative, Ego and Persona — 86
The Outer World of Fame and Fortune — 87
Paradoxical Mindsets — 89
Trials and Tribulations — 90
Bibliography — 92

5 Angels and Demons — 95
- We Want Heroes, Not Gods — 96
- Welcome to the Dark Side — 98
- Social Compliance — 99
- Handing over Authorship — 99
- Conforming in Cahoots — 100
- Can We Push Back? — 101
- Hero Mentality — 102
- Hero's Journey — 103
- If the World Ended Tomorrow — 104
- Negative Visualisation — 106
- Taking Responsibility — 108
- Compassion, Empathy and Leadership — 109
- Gratitude and Selflessness — 110
- More Than Just a Dream — 111
- Steven's Homecoming — 112
- *The Wizard of Oz* — 114
- Transcendence and Individuation — 116
- Jung, Socrates and the Stoics — 117
- Compassion, Love and Empathy — 118
- Bibliography — 120

6 Beyond Them-And-Us — 123
- The Rise of Tribalism — 124
- In These Divided Times — 125
- The Politics of Fear — 126
- Place and Belonging — 128
- The Overview Effect — 130
- Connection and Empathy — 131
- Expanding Phil's Oikeiōsis — 132
- A Hero's Calling — 134
- Dialogue Between Sides — 136
- Fate and Perspective — 138
- Beyond Madness and Badness — 139
- The Human Problem — 141

	Ethical Cosmopolitanism	142
	The Quest for Complexity	144
	Bibliography	147
7	**Reflections and Transformations**	149
	Collective Reflections	150
	Getting to Know Our Shadows	152
	Introspection and Transformation	153
	One Team, Many Stories	155
	The Changing World of Work	157
	A Secular Void?	158
	Filling the Secular Void	159
	Transformative Philosophy	160
	Communal Connections	162
	Transformative Mythologies	163
	Towards a Modern Monomyth	164
	The Collective Journey	165
	Stories to Save the World	167
	Collective Weaving Machines	168
	Bibliography	171

Postface: Collective Growing — 173

Bibliography — 179

Index — 189

About the Author

Darren Kelsey is Reader in Media and Collective Psychology at Newcastle University's School of Arts and Cultures. Darren's teaching, research and previous publications have focused on storytelling, mythology and psychology in media, politics and popular culture. Darren currently lives in County Durham with his wife and daughter.

1

Introduction: Narrative Building Machines

Humans are narrative building machines. We are constantly telling stories to understand who we are and what is happening around us as we make our way through life. From individuals to families, communities, institutions, nations and civilisations, we conjure up stories that form our identities and are used to create our sense of place and purpose in the world. Our stories determine who we are, how we live, what we think and how we feel—as people and societies. Stories bring out the best and worst in human nature. Our stories can be enlightening and transformational, but they have their dark side and they can be destructive.

Historian and philosopher, Yuval Harari, describes what distinguishes humans from chimpanzees: a mysterious glue that enables millions of us to cooperate effectively and organise entire civilisations through the stories we tell. As Harari puts it: "You can never convince a chimpanzee to give you a banana by promising him that after he dies, he will get limitless bananas in chimpanzee Heaven. Only Sapiens can believe such stories".[1] Humans are creatures of story.[2]

Stories are more than just spoken or written words. As Will Storr explains in *The Science of Storytelling*, stories are fusions of our biology and culture, which enable us to create meaning: while our biology gives us the ability and inclination to tell stories, our culture narrows down, selects and distorts the bandwidth of information available to us, establishing the moral codes of our stories and the rules that we are expected to adhere to.[3] These deeper stories—that have been retold for centuries to help us understand our place in the world, how to live as a species and how to follow the rules of our culture—are also known as myths.

Mythmaking and Popular Culture

In his documentary, *21st Century Mythologies*, art historian, Richard Clay explains why French philosopher, Roland Barthes was so critical of seemingly insignificant texts in 1950s popular culture: because we often fail to stop and question the meanings of those stories that we are most familiar with.[4] Clay shows why Barthes' principle is as crucial now as it was then. The signs and symbols that our culture bombards us with require us to be more critically aware of those stories that often go unquestioned in our busy lives.

As Clay points out, whether these are the stories of capitalist money-making machines, political leaders, publicists and propagandists, or our internal life narratives and identities, we cannot take our stories for granted. We need to understand the purposes that stories serve and how they shape the inner and outer worlds of our lives.

Different stories about the same events can provide contrasting accounts of what happened because narrative allows us to decide what we include or exclude in a story and how we represent things that have happened. The *what* and *how* of our narrative building tendencies need to be constantly kept in check, whether we are reflecting on our personal or societal stories—our lives and the lives of others are continually framed through the narrative building machinery that makes us human.

Societies need storytellers, orators, narrators and performers who can share their skills, wisdom, intuitive tendencies, healthy scepticism and visionary talents for the benefit of others. It is easy to overlook or dismiss the intellectual and transcendental potentials of popular culture. But as this study shows, there are performers who offer some clarity amongst the noise and confusion, helping us to learn more about the popular myths of our times—drawing attention to our deepest flaws and greatest potentials.

Popular culture is the space in which we scream out for the stories we need as often as we roll our eyes at the banality of entertainment that feels so familiar and predictable. The stories we seek in popular culture might appear to be monotonous at times, but in some of these stories we can often find deeper meanings to make sense of the complex reality we face in life. As Will Storr argues, our culture is more than a surface-level phenomenon; it is an integral part of our neural machinery through which our brains construct our hallucinations of reality.[5]

Private Hallucinations

Likewise, Derren Brown reminds us that we all live in private hallucinations, which influence us more than we often stop to appreciate: "Things are rarely as they seem, nothing stands in isolation, our very self is changed by what surrounds it. We all live in our private hallucinations".[6] The work of magicians and illusionists provides neat analogies for how we move through life telling stories, trying to process and understand the chaos around us.

Like magic, stories work in mysterious ways: they can dupe us and fool us, but they can also inspire us and open our minds to new possibilities. They can bring about change or they can paralyse us with fear. Either way, they are essential to our being and influence how we live.

This is more than a fun book about a magician. This study shows us what we can do about those stories that cause us harm and mislead us as we float along in the private hallucinations of our minds and daily lives. To do this, we sometimes need to examine stories in places where we might not think to look. And sometimes we need some help in the process.

As we shall see, archetypal magicians can offer more than fancy tricks, a sleight of hand or the spectacular shenanigans of a Hollywood blockbuster movie. They're about wisdom, guiding us through the journey of our daily lives, and being a step ahead in the narrative.

The philosopher and scientist, Daniel Dennett describes human consciousness as a type of stage magic. Consciousness, he argues, is just a bunch of tricks—an illusion formed through our highly evolved brains.[7] For Dennett, our evolutionary traits such as self-protection, self-control and self-definition are fundamental tactics of our humanness that we pursue through our stories.

Like other animals that build dams or spin webs, we tell stories because they provide our sense of self and enable our preservation. But most of the time, when we tell ourselves stories about who we are, we do not consciously select the narrative building blocks we use or think about how we use them. As Dennett puts it: "Our tales are spun but for the most part we don't spin them; they spin us. Our human consciousness, and our narrative selfhood, is their product, not their source".[8]

Our stories and neural machinery are often forming illusions of reality more than we take the time to appreciate. It is much easier, and somewhat comforting, to tell ourselves that our perceptions are correct—we see reality for what it is and tell ourselves that everybody else has missed the trick. But, in reality, it is never this simple.

Our stories can be tricky, but we need them, and we need to master the magic of stories in order for them to enlighten us and transform us. To help us with this daunting task, let's turn our attention to the focal point of this study in search of some wisdom and guidance on our journey.

A Conjuror's Story

Derren Brown began his career doing table magic in restaurants around Bristol, England before his first television show, *Mind Control* in 2000. Stage performances and television shows followed for over two decades as Brown became a familiar household name in British popular culture. More recently, Brown has written a book on philosophy and self-help and has become a regular guest on podcasts and talk shows where he's discussed his fascination with the mind, how we behave as people and societies and what it means to be human.

In his appearance on the BBC's Desert Island Discs, Lauren Laverne introduced Brown via specific reference to his focus on belief and stories:

"If there is a common thread in this varied portfolio, it might be an enduring fascination with the nature of belief—the stories we tell ourselves about what is true".[9] This book is about that common thread in Brown's work. I show how this thread resonated with me, why I think it is important to society and what we can learn from it.

Laverne asked Brown if magic can be meaningful. He agreed that it can but it took him about 15 years of doing stage shows to realise this because performing magic is full of childish urges to impress people—a point to which I shall return later.

Brown realised that rather than performing tricks for applause, more meaningful magic can be used as a good analogy for how we face the world:

> We have this infinite data source coming at us, there's an infinite number of things we could think about and pay attention to, but we choose what to pay attention to, and we edit and delete and so on, and we start to make up a story of what's going on, and we mistake that story for the truth. And that's exactly what a magician is doing … it isn't that the hand is quicker than the eye, it's just you only paid attention to certain things because you only thought that certain things were important.[10]

Brown says that magic teaches us some useful lessons in this sense. He explains that there's so much more going on than we are able to take in when we try to absorb and understand this infinite data source that we are bombarded with on a daily basis. This infinite data source that is chopped up and edited into a story is similar to the process of writing this book.

This is my story about Brown, which is critically and reflectively analysed using methodological and philosophical toolkits that I have developed and applied throughout my research respectively.[11] This story might not be to everyone's liking, but it focuses on rigorous examples of an archetypal magician playing a narrative and societal role that has recurred throughout the world for centuries, and is as relevant to society today as it has been in the past.

A Serendipitous Discovery

Back in 2018, I had not seen any of Brown's shows for many years. It was only by chance, during the early stages of receiving Cognitive Behavioural Therapy (CBT), that I came across Brown talking about happiness, psychology and ancient philosophy.

Before Brown appeared on *Making Sense with Sam Harris*,[12] he was the most requested guest by listeners of the podcast. Around the same time as his conversation with Harris, Brown also appeared on *The Joe Rogan Experience*.[13] The connections Brown drew between CBT and Stoicism, and the way in which he talked about the human mind, developed a sense of intrigue that took me further into the world of Stoicism and led to this book. Due to my early and somewhat mixed experiences with CBT, this immediately led me to reading and learning more about its philosophical grounding and connection to the Stoics.

When Albert Ellis invented CBT in the 1950s, he drew on Stoic philosophy when he designed the ABC model of emotions.[14] This model encourages us not to ignore our emotions but to control them by managing our perceptions of events in life. In an interview with philosopher Jules Evans, Ellis explained how he had been influenced by a saying from the Stoic philosopher, Epictetus: "Men are disturbed not by things, but by their opinions about them".[15] In the spirit of Socrates and Epictetus, Ellis believed that we can manage our emotions if we understand how our unconscious beliefs deeply affect our responses to events in life.

Aron Beck, another founding figure of CBT, was also influenced by the Stoics—particularly this idea that people are affected by the meaning of events rather than events themselves. As Evans discovered from his conversations with Ellis and Beck: "These two pioneers … took the ideas and techniques of ancient Greek philosophy, and put them right at the heart of Western psychotherapy".[16]

Through this method that Ellis and Beck developed, we can transform how we understand ourselves and the world around us in order to remove some of the emotional disturbances that we create through our perceptions. Rather than investing our emotions in those external factors that are beyond our control, CBT encourages us to focus on what is within our control and make pragmatic sense of how we should respond.

As Brown explained to Joe Rogan, these same grounding principles resonated with him when he read the Stoics.[17] Likewise, CBT started to make sense to me and the effectiveness of my therapy increased once I had read Brown's book and the Stoics. As a privileged person with a life that is relatively absent of significant disturbance beyond my own thoughts and stories, I began to understand that despite my worries, things were fine. This reassurance was a message that I continually noticed in Brown's work as he tried to connect with audiences and offer insights to better understand how we think and behave as humans.

I understand that CBT has its limitations and criticisms, which are addressed later in the book. We must not fall into the trap of believing that only the individual is responsible for their own wellbeing—it is our collective responsibility to foster social and institutional environments that are conducive to human flourishing and less reliant on therapy. Nonetheless, for many people CBT is valuable and has proved to be effective.

I became intrigued by Brown's persona and ethos as a performer and the way that he reflected on his work as an illusionist. Brown seemed less concerned with showing off his tricks and more concerned with the meaning-making processes that resonate with his audiences. I was particularly struck by Brown's interest in those unconscious behaviours and beliefs that shape our thoughts and actions in life and his interest in Carl Jung—who has featured prominently in my research.[18]

As impressive as he was as a performer, it was this attention to our habitual tendencies and unquestioned patterns of behaviour that intrigued me more than anything else. It seemed apparent that Brown was using his skillsets to teach us valuable lessons about who we are as people and the importance of storytelling in our personal and collective lives.

Collective States of Mind

During this time, there were three recurring themes that resonated with me and became a primary focus in the project behind this book: firstly, how stories in our personal lives shape our perceptions of people and events, and subsequently impact upon our personal wellbeing; secondly, the role that our unconscious minds play in our personal and collective stories and how we commonly underestimate the significance of the unconscious in our narrative building machinery; and thirdly, the notion that human flourishing is dependent on the state of our collective psychology, which requires attention to both the inner conditions of our minds and the outer environment of the world around us.

Our future depends upon our collective psychology. Alex Evans and the Larger Us team identify three key psychological factors that we need to address in order to make collective transitions in the way that we think and live: from fight or flight to self-awareness; from powerlessness to agency; from disconnection to belonging. In discussing these transitions, the report considers whose job it might be to grow our capacities for a healthier collective psychology that nurtures the conditions of our inner and outer worlds, while also harnessing a healthy balance and interaction between the two.[19]

We need stories that bind us together with a shared sense of common interest beyond the individual. We need stories that enhance our sense of self-awareness, agency and belonging. We need to pay closer attention to those communal stories we tell as a culture, which speak to our inner world as individuals and in relation to the outer world as a collective.

But where should we look to do this? Larger Us suggests we should be looking everywhere in our culture. Given all aspects of society can be examined in relation to collective psychology, the report argues that every media platform and cultural space in which we share stories, values and content warrants critical examination that fosters better storytelling for ourselves and society.

But when we examine these cultural spaces we also need to identify what our stories are *not* telling us. Our personal and collective psychology is often shaping and shaped by those social tensions that edit our stories to suppress those awkward characteristics, traits and tendencies that we would prefer not to think or talk about.[20]

This can be a problem because those unconscious aspects of the psyche that we deny in our personal (and collective) lives often operate in what the psychologist Carl Jung identified as our shadows. As Jung once said:

Unfortunately there can be no doubt that man is, on the whole, less good than he imagines himself or wants to be. Everyone carries a shadow, and the less it is embodied in the individual's conscious life, the blacker and denser it is. If an inferiority is conscious, one always has a chance to correct it. … But if it is repressed and isolated from consciousness, it never gets corrected.[21]

So we need some introspection to help consciously integrate a deeper understanding of who we are as people and societies.

We can retell personal and societal stories. Through conversation, education and cultural introspection, we can get to know more about our collective stories and integrate those traits we are less proud of as a society—learning lessons from our past and allowing those lessons to shape our future.

We can apply reason in our conscious examination of beliefs and values. We can change our beliefs as individuals and societies. We can create new habits of thought and behaviour based on those changing beliefs. In doing so, we can use philosophy to live more virtuous lives that enable human flourishing.

The Analytical Approach of This Book

The approach I adopted in preparing this book synergised a selection of research methods designed to analyse storytelling, collective psychology and personal experiences whilst applying ideas from ancient philosophy and other relevant literature, which I draw on throughout each chapter.[22]

My personal stories and insights are not self-indulgent—they should reflect common experiences and contexts that are relevant to people's personal and professional lives, who Brown tries to speak to throughout his work.[23] Whilst I do not discuss the development of my methodological framework in detail here, those readers who are interested can find a summary of my approach to this project in the notes at the end of this chapter.

I want this book to take you on a journey through the same material I consumed in the story I outlined in the Preface. This explains why I have written this book from a personal perspective: a self-reflective analysis that enabled me as a researcher to show what we can take from performative figures in popular culture; drawing helpful connections with important concepts relating to our psychology and mental wellbeing; showing how philosophy can be applied in daily life as it was on the streets of ancient Athens. Most of all, I want to show you how storytelling is so vital to everything that we do, and philosophy can help us tell better stories to improve our collective psychology.

When I draw on personal examples, I am not suggesting that any reader should be interested in my personal life. Quite the opposite. As philosopher Alain de Botton points out, writers will often share their personal flaws and foibles because they are familiar enough traits for readers to relate to—creating a valuable connection between author and reader.[24]

The fact that my widely unknown life (as a parent, husband, friend, colleague, etc.) is no more intriguing than anyone else's helps me to show that the concepts, philosophies and principles I cover are applicable in all our daily lives. It is my experience as a researcher in storytelling and collective psychology that I hope can make the stories and case studies in this work meaningful to readers.

As Brown explains, we tell ourselves harmless or inconsequential stories every day, just to plan out our schedule for the day or understand our interactions with other people. These are completely necessary stories. Without them, our lives would be a confusing, meaningless mess. Brown himself describes these stories as "neat narratives" that help us to arrange and assemble the complex reality we face into a "satisfying and tidy parcel".[25]

I have tried to build a neat narrative that assembles the data that I have consumed, selected and edited from Brown's work into a tidy, and hopefully satisfying, parcel.

The Structure of This Book

In Chap. 2, I discuss the magician archetype and how it applies to Brown's performative persona and ethos through examples from a range of interviews and his stage show, *Miracle*.[26] Archetypes are recurring behavioural patterns that feature in our personalities and are often expressed through characters in stories.[27] The magician archetype is a potential behavioural pattern that sits deep within us all but is more prominent in some personalities than others.[28] It plays out in many forms and applies to the multiple aspects of Brown's work across each chapter. As we see, Brown plays this role in the way that he communicates with both the participants (individuals) in his shows and his wider audiences (collectives).

In Chap. 3, Brown takes us back to the ancient Greeks to show us how the wisdom of Stoic philosophy is more applicable to modern life than we might expect. As Brown shows, Stoicism offers us the kind of self-help that enables us to cope with adversity and sit more comfortably with those elements of fate that are beyond our control. He shows us how the Stoics encourage us to keep our stories in check, and how we might tell better stories that are more conducive to living a more considered life.

Chapter 4 considers Brown's criticisms of the self-help industry as he sheds light on the remnants of our Protestant past and the unhelpful messages that we often receive in self-help literature. I provide a case study of the mixed martial artist, Conor McGregor to show how Brown's concerns play out in popular culture. Here, I consider the messy tensions that our minds get entangled with, in response to that infinite data source we are faced with. We often struggle to negotiate and understand the intricate nuances of our own minds and complexes, and there's much more going on beneath the surface than we're usually aware of.

Chapters 5 and 6 show how Brown's television shows teach us about our darkest and greatest potentials as humans. These shows involved a turning point in Brown's career and a developmental trait in his performative persona as the archetypal magician. Here we see Brown guiding his participants through life lessons and heroic struggles—confronting their shadows and individuating for the benefit of themselves and the collective.

Chapter 5 focuses on Channel 4 television shows called *The Heist, The Push* and *Apocalypse* to reflect these different shadow potentials; showing how our cultural environments and life experiences both trigger and suppress different behaviours and characteristics in our psyche. Chapter 6 focuses solely on *Sacrifice*, a Netflix special in which Brown creates a hero through a dramatic spectacle that resonates with current times, and teaches us collective lessons about storytelling, othering, tribalism and polarisation.

Shows like *Apocalypse* and *Sacrifice* reflect the ethics of Stoic oikeiōsis—developing an interpersonal sense of what belongs to us and how we behave towards others. As discussed in Chap. 3, the Stoics defined oikeiōsis as a characteristic that develops at different stages of life: as infants we learn to understand that body parts belong to us and we develop self-awareness; as we grow up, we start to think about how we relate to other people in our families, social groups and wider society.

The Stoics believed we should foster our social oikeiōsis as widely as possible in order to pursue justice through a sense of moral and social responsibility to all of humanity.[29] Through social oikeiōsis we act in accordance to virtue—feeling that sense of common empathy that connects us with something beyond ourselves.[30]

In Chap. 7, I consider how we might continue to pursue this collective ethos through our stories. I return to some of my personal and professional reflections on Brown's work before discussing the broader social transformations that we can consider in relation to storytelling and collective psychology. I then show how Brown's work supports an approach that oscillates between the interests of individuals and collectives and attends to the inner and outer crises that we face personally and socially. I finish by addressing the growing conversations about transformational philosophies and mythologies that might help us to improve our collective psychology for the benefit of future societies and the planet.

Stories for a Better Future

Social psychologist, Jonathan Haidt says that people who dedicate their lives to studying something often develop a belief that the object of their inquiry is the key to understanding everything.[31] After many years of researching, writing and teaching about storytelling, I have reached this point. This book is all about stories and understanding why they are so significant in our personal and collective lives.

Stories are what make us human, binding us together, pulling us apart, helping and hindering our experiences as a species distinguished by our narrative building machinery.

Whether we are individuals working through our problems, or societies looking to create a better world, we can tell better stories for a better future. And we can look to the wisdom of an archetypal magician for some help along the way.[32]

Notes

1. Harari, 2014.
2. In *The Storytelling Animal*, Jonathan Gottschall (2012) shows how neuroscience, psychology and evolutionary biology have helped us understand more about our storytelling instincts that have evolved to ensure our survival. Gottschall describes storytelling as "the grease and glue of society" that serves the "ancient function of binding society by reinforcing a set of common values and strengthening the ties of common culture". As he explains, stories still enculturate our youth and help us define ourselves and others, and they teach us the rules and social codes of our culture.
3. Storr, 2019.
4. Clay, 2020.
5. Storr, 2019: 79.
6. In February 2020, Brown made this point when he posted two examples of optical illusions on Instagram: https://www.instagram.com/p/B8_FQ9XnCO9/?utm_source=ig_web_copy_link
7. Dennett, 2017.
8. Dennett, 1992:148.
9. Brown, 2019a.
10. Ibid.
11. Kelsey, 2015, 2017, 2018, 2020. Notes 22 and 23 provide further attention to these approaches.
12. Brown, 2018e.
13. Brown, 2018a.
14. Jules Evans (2013:4) explains how Albert Ellis was inspired by the Stoics: "Albert Ellis told me … that he had been particularly impressed by a saying of the Stoic philosopher Epictetus: 'Men are disturbed not by things, but their opinions about them.' This sentence inspired Ellis's 'ABC' model of the emotions, which is at the heart of CBT: we experience an event (A), then interpret it (B), and then feel an emotional

response in line with our interpretation (C). Ellis, following the Stoics, suggested that we can change our emotions by changing our thoughts or opinions about events".
15. Ibid.: 4.
16. Ibid.: 4.
17. Brown, 2018a.
18. Jung, 1938, 1959; Kelsey, 2017, 2020.
19. "Adaptation" was a term used by psychologist Carl Jung to describe the balancing of internal and external factors. For Jung, the failure to adapt could cause neurosis through unhealthy conflicts and imbalances between the personal and collective demands of inner and outer worlds in their personal and cultural contexts. As Samuels et al. explain (1986), excessive concentration on meeting the requirements of one mode of adaptation (seeking to meet the demands of only the inner or outer world rather than a balance between the two) could also cause neurosis. This concept is significant to how we think about collective psychology as much as our personal wellbeing.
20. As Brown (2021a: 40–41) points out in *A Book of Secrets*: "While we choose to 'own' certain … qualities, we also forget that it is precisely what lurks unseen that truly owns *us*. Thus as we deny ambiguity in our natures, those parts of us with which we refuse to engage have a habit of wreaking revenge. From what … Jung called our Shadow side, they demand attention and reintegration. (It's worth mentioning that some of Jung's notions can seem a little fruity from today's perspective but the structure of his thought remains enormously valuable.)"
21. Jung, 1938: 131.
22. These insights are combined with the discourse-mythological analysis that I conducted during this research project. DMA is a qualitative methodological framework designed to analyse psychodiscursive constructions of narratives and personae in archetypal storytelling. DMA initially adopted the tools of Critical Discourse Analysis (CDA) to analyse the semiotic construction of mythologies in the British press (Kelsey, 2015). Here, Kelsey (2015) analysed the myth of the Blitz spirit (UK) in historical and contemporary contexts to show how the myth from 1940 was reused to serve numerous (often oppositional) ideological purposes in 2005. More recently, the analytical scope of DMA was expanded to consider the archetypal conventions of mythological storytelling in politics, celebrity personae and popular culture (Kelsey, 2017, 2018, 2020).

Throughout the development of this approach in my research, I have argued that the *what* and *how* of narrative warrants the concerns of researchers in the social sciences who scrutinise the language, representation, communication and storytelling to understand the contexts in which narratives are constructed and what they reflect about society. Discourse, semiotic and psychoanalytical theory have been synergised through the development of DMA in my research (for a rigorous explanation of what psychodiscursive analysis entails, and how the discourse-mythological framework has been developed in previous work, see Kelsey, 2020). DMA enabled me to examine Brown's performative persona and provide a discursive analysis of his work and the social contexts that it relates to—helping me to understand the role of Brown as an archetypal magician in popular culture. The selection of Brown as a case study was informed by the personal rationale and context explained in the Preface.

23. DMA has always been an expansive and innovative framework that has synergised new toolkits and theories throughout its development. In this project, given the self-reflective context informing this research, I introduced autoethnography to expand the analytical scope of DMA. I adopted autoethnography as a framework for self-reflection and applied experiential analysis throughout my preparation of this book (for eclectic and interdisciplinary examples of how these approaches can be used, see: Bochner, 1997; Ellis, Adams and Bochner, 2011; Bochner & Ellis, 1992; Couser, 1997; Denzin, 1989; Evers, 2006; Sikka, 2021). As Ellis, Adams and Bochner (2011) point out: "Autoethnography is an approach to research and writing that seeks to describe and systematically analyze personal experience in order to understand cultural experience. This approach challenges canonical ways of doing research and representing others and treats research as a political, socially-just and socially-conscious act. A researcher uses tenets of autobiography and ethnography to do and write autoethnography. Thus, as a method, autoethnography is both process and product". In the project behind this book, autoethnography enabled me to reflect on my personal experiences in relation to the philosophical ideas Brown offers from Stoicism, the Socratic methods behind that philosophy and the relevance of Brown's work and my personal experiences in relation to collective psychology. My reflections combine personal, professional and research-based insights to understand the importance of storytelling in relation to individual and collec-

tive wellbeing. These insights have adopted and applied the tools of discourse-mythological analysis (Kelsey, 2017, 2020) to the work and persona of Derren Brown, in combination with autoethnographic insights of my own story that stem from the context outlined in the Preface. As Ellis, Adams and Bochner (2011) explain: "Most often, autobiographers write about 'epiphanies'—remembered moments perceived to have significantly impacted the trajectory of a person's life (Bochner & Ellis, 1992; Couser, 1997; Denzin, 1989), times of existential crises that forced a person to attend to and analyze lived experience (Zaner, 2004), and events after which life does not seem quite the same. While epiphanies are self-claimed phenomena in which one person may consider an experience transformative while another may not, these epiphanies reveal ways a person could negotiate 'intense situations' and 'effects that linger—recollections, memories, images, feelings—long after a crucial incident is supposedly finished' (Bochner, 1984: 595)".
24. De Botton, 2013.
25. Brown, 2016a: 18.
26. Brown, 2018d. Examples from *Miracle* recur throughout various chapters in this book.
27. Carl Jung's work provides a useful starting point when we begin to think about the depth and significance of archetypes as narrative building blocks that operate in our unconscious minds. It was here that Jung proposed the concept of a collective unconscious—a set of shared psychic structures within all human minds that are fundamental to all psychological development: "My thesis then, is as follows: in addition to our immediate consciousness, which is of a thoroughly personal nature and which we believe to be the only empirical psyche (even if we tack on the personal unconscious as an appendix), there exists a second psychic system of a collective, universal, and impersonal nature which is identical in all individuals. This collective unconscious does not develop individually but is inherited. It consists of pre-existent forms, the archetypes, which can only become conscious secondarily and which give definite form to certain psychic contents" (Jung, 1959: 43).
28. As I have explained in previous work on archetypal storytelling (Kelsey, 2020: 7–8), when we try to understand more about what archetypes are and how they appear, we should not become preoccupied in debates about biological determinism versus social constructivism. To argue whether archetypes are purely products of neurological and complemen-

tary structures or only cultural constructs that are exclusive to their social and historical environments is too simplistic. Firstly, these positions are often wrongly presented as oppositional when they should be seen as complementary and mutually influential—archetypes are products of both biology and culture. Secondly, it is the *how* of communication that I have been primarily concerned with in DMA. So, how do archetypes operate as narrative building blocks in mythological storytelling and personas, and why do they warrant critical attention? These are the questions motivating the approach offered in DMA. It is also important to confront some common misconceptions of Jung's work: Jung did not overlook the significance of culture and personal experience in the development of one's own psychology, characteristics and personality. He recognised the importance of culture in personal and collective contexts that were significant to individual and group psyches. But Jung also proposed that deep beneath one's personal unconscious—which is shaped by their own experiences and significantly influenced by the society in which they live—exists a shared psychic structure that is universal across all individuals. Our brains are all the same. Hence, our behavioural patterns continually reproduce archetypal forms that occur in the stories we tell as people and societies. These narrative building blocks enable us to tell stories about our lives and the lives of others—they are at the core of our perceptions of who we are and form our perceptions of other people.

29. Hierocles, 2015; Gloyn, 2017, 2018.
30. I raise this point here because oikeiōsis has a recurring relevance throughout this book. Readers will recognise its relevance in a number of points and examples where it is not necessarily mentioned as a concept.
31. Haidt, 2012, xii.
32. For other insights on the social, cultural, historical and psychological roles of magic, see the following: Goto-Jones, 2016; Thorndike, 1905; Kuhn, G., Olson, J. and Raz, A., 2016; Kuhn, Amlani and Rensink, 2008; Lamont and Wiseman, 2005; Leddington, 2016; Abram and Sheldrake, 2015; Moro, 2017; Willis, 2017; Johannsen and Otto, 2021.

Bibliography

Abram, D., & Sheldrake, R. (2015, August 6). *What is magic? A dialogue with David Abram*. At Hollyhock Leadership Learning Centre. https://www.sheldrake.org/audios/what-is-magic-a-dialogue-with-david-abram

Bochner, A. (1997). It's about time: Narrative and the divided self. *Qualitative Inquiry, 3*(4), 418–438.

Bochner, A., & Ellis, C. (1992). Personal narrative as a social approach to interpersonal communication. *Communication Theory, 2*(2), 165–172.

Brown, D. (2016a). *Happy: Why more or less everything is absolutely fine*. Penguin.

Brown, D. (2018a). Joe Rogan & Derren Brown – The idea of happiness. *The Joe Rogan experience #1198*. https://www.youtube.com/watch?v=E3DigsvZCXo

Brown, D. (2018d). *Miracle*. Netflix.

Brown, D. (2018e). #143 Keys to the mind: A conversation with Derren Brown. *Making sense with Sam Harris*. https://samharris.org/podcasts/143-keys-mind/

Brown, D. (2019a, May 31). Desert Island Discs. *BBC Radio 4*. https://www.bbc.co.uk/programmes/m0005dyb

Brown, D. (2021a). *A book of secrets: Finding solace in a stubborn world*. London: Penguin.

Clay, R. (2020). 21st-century mythologies with Richard Clay. *BBC Four*. https://www.bbc.co.uk/iplayer/episode/m000p9t7/21stcentury-mythologies-with-richard-clay

Couser, G. T. (1997). *Recovering bodies: Illness, disability, and life writing*. University of Wisconsin Press.

De Botton, A. (2013). *Religion for atheists*. Penguin.

Dennett, D. (1992). *Consciousness explained*. Penguin.

Dennett, D. (2017). The illusion of consciousness. *TED Talk*. https://www.youtube.com/watch?v=fjbWr3ODbAo

Denzin, N. (1989). *Interpretive biography*. Sage.

Ellis, C., Adams, T., & Bochner, A. (2011). Autoethnography: An overview. *FQS Journal, 12*, 1. https://www.qualitative-research.net/index.php/fqs/article/view/1589/3095

Evans, J. (2013). *Philosophy for life: And other dangerous situations*. Rider.

Evers, C. (2006). How to surf. *Journal of Sport & Social Issues, 30*, 229–243.

Gloyn, L. (2017). *The ethics of the family in Seneca*. University Press.

Gloyn, L. (2018). Stoicism and the family by Liz Gloyn. *Modern Stoicism.* https://modernstoicism.com/stoicism-and-the-family-by-liz-gloyn/

Goto-Jones, C. (2016). *Conjuring Asia: Magic, orientalism and the making of the modern world.* University Press.

Gottschall, J. (2012). *The storytelling animal: How stories make us human.* Mariner.

Haidt, J. (2012). *The righteous mind: Why good people are divided by politics and religion.* Penguin.

Harari, Y. N. (2014). *Power and imagination.* http://www.ynharari.com/topic/power-and-imagination/

Hierocles. (2015). *Ethical fragments.* Penguin.

Johannsen, D., & Otto, B. (2021). *Fictional practice: Magic, narration, and the power of imagination.* Brill.

Jung, C. G. (1938). Psychology and religion. In *Psychology and religion: West and east, collected works of C.G. Jung* (Vol. 11). Routledge.

Jung, C. G. (1959). *The archetypes and the collective unconscious.* Routledge and Kegan.

Kelsey, D. (2015). *Media, myth and terrorism: A discourse-mythological analysis of the 'Blitz Spirit' in British newspaper responses to the July 7th bombings.* Palgrave.

Kelsey, D. (2017). *Media and affective mythologies: Discourse, archetypes and ideology in contemporary politics.* Palgrave.

Kelsey, D. (2018). Affective mythology and 'the notorious' Conor McGregor: Monomyth, mysticism, and mixed martial arts. *Martial Arts Studies, 5,* 15–35.

Kelsey, D. (2020). Psycho-discursive constructions of narrative in archetypal storytelling: A discourse-mythological approach. *Critical Discourse Studies.* https://doi.org/10.1080/17405904.2020.1802766

Kuhn, G., Amlani, A., & Rensink, R. (2008). Towards a science of magic. *Trends in Cognitive Sciences, 12*(9), 349–354.

Kuhn, G., Olson, J., & Raz, A. (Eds.). (2016). The psychology of magic and the magic of psychology. *Frontiers in Psychology.* https://doi.org/10.3389/fpsyg.2016.01358

Lamont, P., & Wiseman, R. (2005). *Magic in theory: An introduction to the theoretical and psychological elements of conjuring.* University Press.

Leddington, J. (2016). The experience of magic. *The Journal of Aesthetics and Art Criticism, 74*(3), 253–264.

Moro, P. A. (2017). Witchcraft, sorcery, and magic. *In The International Encyclopedia of Anthropology.* https://doi.org/10.1002/9781118924396.wbiea1915

Samuels, A., Shorter, B., & Plaut, F. (1986). *A critical dictionary of Jungian analysis*. Routledge.

Sikka, T. (2021). The Neoliberalization of sleep: A discursive and materialist analysis of sleep technologies. *Journal of the Swiss Anthropological Association, 26*, 105–121.

Storr, W. (2019). *The science of storytelling: Why stories make us human and how to tell them better*. Abrams.

Thorndike, L. (1905). *The place of magic in the intellectual history of Europe*. University Press.

Willis, D. (2017). Magic and witchcraft. In A. Kinney & T. Hopper (Eds.), *A new companion to renaissance Drama*. https://doi.org/10.1002/9781118824016.ch13

2

The Archetypal Magician

Carl Jung described the magician archetype as an embodiment of "knowledge, reflection, insight, wisdom, cleverness, and intuition on the one hand, and on the other, moral qualities such as goodwill and readiness to help, which make his 'spiritual' character sufficiently plain".[1] Sometimes we see this archetype in the literal figure of a fictional or non-fictional magician, but it takes on many forms that reflect this deeper human trait that we collectively share and recognise, often unconsciously, when we see, feel or experience its essential qualities.[2]

Magicians create initiations for people and societies to guide them on journeys into new territory for growth and transformation. The old wise man, or a mentor figure, commonly appears in fairy tales to fulfil this role. These figures often provide a spiritual meaning or moral guidance to a confused or struggling hero in a desperate situation.[3]

We can look to films and fictional texts for clear examples of this: Gandalf in *The Lord of the Rings*; Doc Brown in *Back to the Future*; Mr. Miyagi in *The Karate Kid*. In its shadow form, we might look to Darth Vader in *Star Wars* or Moriarty in *Sherlock Holmes*—master manipulators who use their skills and knowledge to control others for power, destruction or personal gain as opposed to the collective good.[4]

Of course, when we analyse celebrity personas we should avoid the mistake of reducing their complex personalities into simplistic archetypal categories. That is not my intention here. Like any personality, there will be numerous archetypal complexities to Brown's character within and beyond his public persona, and my job here is not to psychoanalyse someone I have never met.

Rather, by identifying a significant archetypal trait in Brown's persona and ethos as a performer, we can appreciate the contribution his work makes to society—from the perspectives of both his admirers and his critics. The transformational experiences created by magicians typically enable both introspection of the inner self and a stronger sense of connection to the outer world. Familiarising ourselves with the narrative and social roles of the magician archetype in this chapter will help us to make sense of Brown's work throughout the book.[5]

Transformational Spaces

Susanna Barlow describes the mystery, alchemy and transformational qualities that the magician tends to hold through their innate relationship with new potentials and possibilities. They can think, weave and create sacred spaces through their vision and intuition. In secular societies, these sacred spaces are not necessarily religious. Rather, the magician creates spaces in the material world that enable people and societies to spiritually regenerate or transcend without any religious connotations or belief in a particular God.[6] They bring a sense of meaning and transcendence that is not necessarily religious to an otherwise chaotic or nihilistic world—finding a sense of purpose in the common good beyond the sole interests of the individual.

Jungian analysts, Robert Moore and Douglas Gillette, argue that in modern life our material connection with the magician is strong because of the technological innovations and expansions we have made to create new possibilities in modern life. However, our spiritual connection is where we have lost touch with other elements of the magician archetype—we lose our sense of spiritual grounding or deeper meaning of what it means to be human when we are too focused on the material world and what we deem to be "rational".[7] Here, we tend to drift away from those deeper questions about our humanness and the interconnected experiences of life that can point us to transcendental experiences of consciousness. These lines of inquiry are not inevitably religious or mystical, but Western culture especially has a tendency to reject them on the grounds of being irrational forms of spirituality.[8]

As Brown has often pointed out, myths and rituals play an important role in our psyche—they might not offer factual truths but they are a psychological necessity for us.[9] Hence, it is typical for the magician to share their interest in psychotherapy and mythology among their numerous fields of material and spiritual expertise. The magician typically embodies this variety of skillsets, characteristics and specialisms that are expressed through a dynamic persona.

As we shall see in Brown's work, a typical trait in his persona is the magician's tendency to share their intellect for collective interests by connecting the inner world of the mind with the outer world of society.

When we see this archetype play out on stage, for example, it is the meaning-making and storytelling function of the magician that Brown deems to be a significant performative trait.

The Stage Magician

Like a typical stage magician, Brown uses illusions to create otherworldly atmospheres that play around with audience perceptions in ways that open their minds to new possibilities. As Brown states in his description of stage magic, the trick of the magician is about jumbling up a story to create a sense of meaning that resonates with the audience:

> When I perform my day job as a kind of magician, I work with people's capacity to fool themselves with stories. A good magic trick forces the spectator to tell a story that arrives at an impossible conclusion, and the clearer the story is, the better. Normally, everything you need to solve the puzzle happens right in front of you but you are made to care only about the parts that the magician wants you to. When you join up *those* dots, so misleadingly and proactively arranged, you are left with a baffling mystery. A good

magician might make the trick *mean* more, by elevating it beyond the mere disappearance or transposition of some props. If it can be made to feel somehow more relevant to *you*, rather than a mere display of skill, then the story is likely to have more import and the trick more impact.[10]

For Brown, it is *what* the illusionist does with this otherworldly atmosphere that is almost as important as the trick itself. As we shall see, it is, arguably, this principle that has enabled Brown to transcend the world of stage performance and operate in other cultural and transformational spaces beyond traditional stage magic.

In an interview for *Vulture* magazine, Brown reflects on a series of clips from movies and TV shows about illusionists and provides a series of metaphorical analogies to explain the resonance of particular tricks on stage in their technical, social and historical contexts.[11] Here we see Brown contextualising the role of the stage magician as one requiring more than a self-satisfied persona to show off how clever they are. He focuses on the connection that magicians need to establish with their audience and what happens if that connection is absent.

For example, a clip from *L'illusionist* shows a magician performing a trick to an almost empty theatre.[12] A child near the front row asks a woman next to him how the trick is done and the woman tells him to shush. Brown praises the clip for portraying the "sadness of magic" and the challenge performers face in getting audiences to care about it. He states: "The best magicians … make the performance about something else other than 'look how clever I am, look at what I can do', which is the mistake this magician is making [and] is the reason why his audience is so small and why the kid is only interested in how the trick is done".

In contrast, a scene from another film, *The Illusionist* shows a magician balancing a military officer's sword on the stage as if it were standing upright like Excalibur's sword in the stone.[13] As the officer comes forward to take the sword, he cannot lift it and the audience laughs at his expense. Brown comments: "Here we have a magician who is making a human connection … [which] is all about power: the guy with the medals and that sense of pomposity and everything has been burst by this very quiet character and this trick". Brown's following point is important: "Even if we think it's just a big magnet under the floor or whatever it kind of doesn't matter, there's just something very human going on there, which is great".

Brown praises Ed Norton's character as the illusionist in this film due to his quiet persona through which he stands back and lets this connection with the audience play out: the meaning resonates through the connection between the trick and the audience. In other words, there is a meaning to the trick beyond the ego of the magician.[14]

Likewise, Brown states the metaphorical significance of a clip from *Houdini* where Houdini calmly escapes from a strait jacket.[15] Other men around him are attempting the same trick and failing while frantically rolling around on the stage in frustration. Commenting upon the seemingly calm and effortless manner in which Houdini escapes the jacket compared those desperate men rolling around next to him, Brown points to the social context of Houdini's popularity: he was popular around the time of the Great Depression and the idea of escaping from shackles resonated at a time when people felt constrained.

Through his own work, Brown uses the meaning-making mechanisms of his performances to speak to audiences about the times in which they live and offers them lessons that they might benefit from. Brown uses his stage presence to put these lessons and morals into theatrical form. Rather than bamboozling us, he draws attention to behavioural habits, psychological traits and narrative building tendencies that we might perhaps otherwise remain oblivious to. For those participants and audiences who find meaning and resonance in Brown's work, he fulfils the enlightening role that the magician archetype often fulfils.

The Enlightened Magician

Susanna Barlow describes the enlightened magician's instinct for understanding the laws of the universe, providing them with the ability to help people by positively altering their perceptions of reality. These qualities provide solutions to societal problems by seeing the bigger picture while appreciating the significance of minutiae. The minutiae of Brown's work might be meticulously constructed for stage performances or carefully designed to create a dramatic spectacle on screen, but it often reflects simple meanings and messages, which relate to the bigger picture. This bigger picture appears through narratives and meanings that resonate with audiences.

These narratives and dramatic spectacles are all about transformation. Barlow's description of the enlightened magician refers to a natural ability to create opportunities for change and transformation. This is a significant aspect of the magician's performative persona because it's often the case that the enlightened magician has experienced their own initiation or been through a painful developmental process in their past through which they have transformed from shadow to light.

As one example of this, Brown has discussed his sexuality as an influential factor in his persona and public performances. In an interview with Emily Webb, she asked him if the attention seeking persona he had in his twenties was somehow a way of deflecting from his sexuality. Brown agreed: "Definitely. … If you're closeted, if you feel essentially quite shameful about what's going on inside, you get very good at deflecting measures on the outside. You create dazzling surfaces that distract people, and magic's very good at that".[16]

Brown sees his work in mentalism and hypnosis as examples of this. He explains how much easier it is to create a persona where nobody is likely to start asking you about sex. But when Brown did come out about his sexuality he realised that nobody really cared—it wasn't a big deal in his life or to those around him. That said, Brown is grateful for fact that he didn't come out earlier because the tension he carried was something that drove and shaped his career—he suspects that he might not be where he is now if he had come out earlier.

Due to their own transformational experiences, the enlightened magician often becomes an agent for the transformation of other people in the community. As we shall see, the compassionate and considered manner that Brown encourages us to embrace throughout his work reflects those qualities where the enlightened magician makes others feel at ease and recognises the value in everyone. The transformational spaces that the enlightened magician creates are less about them showing off their mysterious trickery and more about the potential of the individual who undergoes seemingly impossible acts or personal transformations.

The enlightened magician has a tendency to monitor their ego. This is important since it not only reflects those values that Brown discussed earlier (in relation to stage performance) but, as we shall see, it chimes with the philosophical grounding that he offers in *Happy*. Brown reflects the acts of conscious self-reflection while communicating his motivations to his audience—a quality that Barlow uses to distinguish the enlightened magician from the shadow magician. The enlightened magician chooses to act consciously, carrying and communicating a clear sense of purpose and principle in their actions.

As Lauren Laverne points out, Brown "has a side-line in uncovering tricksters who manipulate other people's credulity for their own ends—debunking the methods of psychics, mediums, faith-healers, new-age gurus and ghost hunters".[17] This is a typical trait of the magician: with a tendency to expose those who exploit the trust of others, they are less likely to be fooled and duped by shadow-magic—those masks and manipulations of frauds and charlatans.

In *Miracle*, for example, Brown exposes the fallacy of faith healing as a cruel scam that instils false hope through a belief in the physical healing power of God—an example of shadow-magic in action, and being taken to task by the enlightened magician for the benefit of those prospective victims.[18] After performing a series of tricks replicating the performances of faith healers, Brown states:

> The miracle here is not the healing power of the lord or magic tricks or floating people in the air. The miracle is the fact that a lifetime of chronic pain can just disappear in an instant when we tell ourselves a different story. The moment that you entertain the notion that healing might be moving through the room those symptoms can just go. And that is so much more beautiful and resonant to me because it isn't about the power of God, it's about the power of us, as human beings, so it's real. That's a miracle.[19]

When this magician's work resonates with audiences, it takes an element of trust and connection with the magician's wisdom for us to align ourselves with the lessons they offer us. Of course, this does not always happen, and Brown certainly isn't trusted by everyone. That's not because the magician archetype fails to resonate at all, it just takes on a different form that stimulates a different reaction.

In these cases, audiences perceive Brown to be a shadow magician. They feel that *he* is the fraudster, and his work is dishonest, egotistical and sanctimonious—showing off and manipulating at the expense of others.

The Shadow Magician

The shadow magician is often seen as a know-it-all with a sense of superior intellect who is trying to get one over everyone else. So they might carry the same skillsets as the enlightened magician, but how they use their knowledge in social and ethical contexts will differ.

Hence, the persona of any performer like Brown is not entirely under their control—it is dependent on audience perceptions of their actions and motivations and whether they trust what they see. We all adopt what we believe are appropriate personae in personal, professional and social environments, but as we all know from experience, we cannot control how others perceive us and we are not always understood in the ways that we intend or anticipate.

When someone is perceived to be playing the role of shadow magician they are deemed to be in it for themselves and the nurturing of their egotistical interests rather than the common good. A shadow magician will tend to take advantage of their skillsets and subjects by exploiting the control they can have over other people's actions, and bamboozle them with the alternative realities and otherworldly atmospheres that they are able to create.

The shadow magician will be manipulative and not reveal any of their secrets or motivations for the benefit of others involved in an experience. Since their ego is the primary source of interest and preservation, they will manipulate and misdirect other people's perceptions of them to conceal the intentions and motivations in what they do.

There was a time when Brown was incidentally drawn into this shadow territory. After he predicted the National Lottery numbers on live television, for example, there was a follow-up show the next week in which Brown was set to provide an explanation for how he pulled the trick off.

Brown had intended to provide one suspect explanation followed by a twist that would reveal the truth behind the trick. But regulatory bodies restricted what could be shown and Brown left his audience hanging in a way that he wasn't happy with either:

> The level of scrutiny from Camelot, the BBC and the government meant we couldn't finish it the way we wanted, which was to have a fishy explanation about the wisdom of crowds followed by a massive twist. … We weren't allowed to do the twist so we ended up with the fishy explanation on its own, which is not how I like to treat people.[20]

Audience perceptions of the shadow magician are evident in other criticisms that Brown has faced. When *Sacrifice* was released on Netflix, an article in the *Guardian* said: "Brown, once about entertainment and fun, has now restyled himself as an all-powerful, egocentric sage. And he's lost his magic in the process".[21] The *Guardian* article does not doubt that Brown is a "clever man" and has always been known for being "fun" and "entertaining". But it goes on to suggest that *Sacrifice* reflects a "God complex" in Brown who has become a "sanctimonious knobhead".

This reflects a social tension in the archetypal role of the magician—audience perceptions can quickly slip from trust and faith in a performer to suspicion, criticism or judgement. For example, the same *Guardian* article said: "Brown is keen to assure us that 'everything you see is 100% real', like a secondhand car salesman who says that the mileage on that motor definitely hasn't been tampered with, although the jeopardy is never his". Trust and authenticity are significant factors for Brown.

Trust and Authenticity

A criticism that Brown often faces, particularly in relation to his TV shows, is the accusation that his work is fake or hoaxed. Brown said he has never used stooges or actors because he deems it to be "artistically repugnant, lazy and just unnecessary".[22] Nonetheless, these accusations will always recur regardless because we have a deeper awareness (and suspicion) in our culture of that shadow form that magicians often take.

After *Apocalypse* first aired on television, the show's main participant (Steven Brosnan) was accused of being an actor. The actor concerned turned out to be Karl Greenwood. Greenwood does look very similar to Brosnan, and Brosnan himself had tried getting acting work in the past, hence his profile appeared on a casting site, which added to the speculation. Brown eventually got the pair together in the same room at the same time to be interviewed and verify their identities.[23]

Despite Brown's efforts, there are still vocal critics who believe that his work is not authentic and his shows in general are just hoaxes. There are ample videos on YouTube and various articles online claiming to "debunk" or "expose" Brown as a fraud. This is a familiar problem, especially for the stage magician: regardless of the performer's ethos and motivations, the shadow elements cannot always be avoided in terms of audience perception.

My point here is not to endlessly prove or disprove the validity of Brown's shows. The point is that some welcome Brown's enlightened persona and take meaning from his work, while others condemn him as a charlatan from the world of shadow-magic. We know that not all audiences interpret celebrity personas and performances in the same way. This criticism Brown receives is somewhat inevitable: it comes with the territory of being a stage performer, and an illusionist in particular.

Regardless of the criticisms they typically face, magicians are always learning, and in their enlightened form they will jump at the opportunity to share that knowledge with others. In *Happy*, for example, Brown discusses psychological research that has shown how our stories are often shaped by memories and perceptions that misrepresent our experiences.

The material I cover below sets us up nicely for the journey ahead, as we look more closely at Brown's focus on the significance of stories in our lives.

Stories, Memories and Experiences

Brown discusses research by the psychologist and economist, Daniel Kahneman. In Kahneman's research he distinguished the *experiencing self* from the *remembering self* to show why our stories are often poorly authored and mnemonically flawed in terms of our perceptions and experiences.[24] In Kahneman's experiment, participants put their hands in uncomfortably cold water for a full minute. Seven minutes later they were invited to repeat the exercise with the other hand. This time, the water for the full minute was the same temperature but this was followed by an extra 30 seconds with the water temperature raised by one degree (and a slight reduction of pain).

When participants were invited to repeat one of the exercises again, 80% of them chose the second option. Note here that the first version was only 60 seconds of discomfort, compared to 90 seconds of discomfort in the second (with a reduction of pain for the final 30 seconds).

Kahneman says this preference is due to the differences between "decision utility" and "experienced utility", which demonstrate that we do not make decisions based solely on our experiences. Instead, according to Kahneman, we make decisions based on the stories we tell ourselves about our experiences, which are inaccurate and poorly edited accounts. Because the second session contained an extra 30 seconds that were less painful at the end, participants were left with a different story to reflect on the experience.

As Brown points out, we build our stories like novelists, and we are always looking for a good ending.[25] The ending here seemingly overrides the broader experience that contained more pain for a longer period. But by emerging from the experience of the second session with an element of relief (albeit minimal), we will typically tell a story about how the experience improved. As Brown explains: "Our capacity for storytelling allows us to misremember the extent of pain or pleasure we felt during an experience. We then make our decisions based on that misinformation".[26]

When reflecting on Kahneman's research, Brown is particularly concerned with the remembering self and provides a number of examples to support this position. For example, he asks, "would you go on holiday knowing that all memory of it would be wiped from your brain (and camera) the moment it was over? Probably not. Mere pampering to the experiencing self is not enough; we want memories too".[27] As Brown acknowledges, "we rely on our remembering self when we consider those stories we have internalised about ourselves; we join the dots in such a way that gives us our sense of identity. It is the remembering self that is a large part of what makes us human: a product of our highly evolved brains".[28]

When we try to fix our broken stories (perhaps through CBT or other forms of therapy) we are trying to harness the remembering self without misrepresenting or reducing those experiences into stories that do us harm. For this reason, Brown believes we should manage the immediate urges of the experiencing self in the moment for the benefit of those memories we later create for the remembering self. For example, Brown explains how choosing to go to a theme park for an afternoon with friends might seem more appealing than caring for a sick relative, yet the "fun option" here only serves the experiencing self. We know that the remembering self will likely provide a story that we are more comfortable with afterwards if we attend to the relative.

The remembering self, therefore, plays a significant role in determining whether we live a more considered life that is conducive to tranquillity or one that is detrimental to our wellbeing because we are not mindful of our decision-making and its impact upon our inner dialogue. This is why Kahneman warns us about the potential "tyranny of the remembering self". Brown makes the point that we do not need to treat the remembering self as an oppressive function on this basis, but we should accept its influence and engage with it in order to manage it the best we can.

Of course, it is not that these "selves" are *literally* separate entities that exist within us. Rather, they reflect two complementary dynamics of processing within our brains, which fulfil different aspects of experiential and mnemonic cognition. Hence, we need to be more attentive in our efforts to manage the chitter chatter of our inner voice(s).

Our Chattering Selves

We should not overlook the significance of the experiencing self either. Neuroscientist and philosopher, Sam Harris highlights the experiencing self for its potential to be both prohibitive and conducive to our wellbeing.[29] If we are not present and self-aware in a moment it can control us through negative emotions and behaviours that we fail to regulate.

Equally, it can be used to harness mind skills, such as meditation, to be present in a moment without our remembering self being allowed to unhelpfully ponder the past or future.

The experiencing self may reflect our more bestial tendencies, but our immediate experiences are crucial components that act as narrative microcosms for the remembering self to weave into a story. Without the experiencing self, the remembering self becomes the quilt maker with no needle, no thread, no materials, no colour and no patchwork.

In other words, we should not be too concerned about *which* self is most important or problematic and we must not be a slave to either of them. These chattering selves are not oppositional: they are entwined and combinatory elements of consciousness and human experience. Oscillation and equilibrium are important here when we think about these cognitive dynamics. The remembering and experiencing selves are constantly influencing, complementing and contradicting each other. While the remembering self has its potential for tyranny, the experiencing self also needs curbing or resisting in pursuit of a more considered decision-making that will allow the remembering self to tell a more helpful story.

As Brown shows us throughout his work, when we synergise modern psychological research with ancient philosophy, we can learn more about the mind and apply those philosophies for life with a better understanding of why we need them. In the case of Kahneman's research, Brown believes our understanding of this internal dynamic can help us appreciate the nature of happiness and identify those habitual behaviours that hinder our wellbeing.

A couple of years after reading *Happy*, I was listening to William Irvine's keynote lecture at the annual Stoicism conference, Stoicon.[30] Irvine is a professor of philosophy at Write State University where he currently teaches about Stoicism. Like Brown, Irvine made the connection between Kahneman's research and Stoicism; making the point that in order to live tranquil lives that are conducive to positive wellbeing, we need to be aware of the mnemonic and experiential dynamics of our brains and how they impact upon the way that we live. To do this, we need to be more sceptical of our stories.

Scepticism of Our Stories

In an interview about *Happy*, Brown explained why he went back to the Stoics for some ancient wisdom that could help us today by enabling us to take control of our stories about who we are. Brown reiterates this connection between magic and storytelling—reflecting an ethos that transcends the world of magic, philosophy and popular culture:

> What a magician does is sell you a story. So, you think the story went from point A to point B to C and then that's some amazing impossible thing. Normally all the information you need to work out the trick is right there in front of you but you're subtly nudged into editing that story to tell yourself 'the impossible event has happened'. And that's what we do in life all the time.[31]

As Brown points out, the Stoics argued that it's not events in the world that cause us harm, but rather the stories we tell ourselves about those events. He explains how our anger or frustration is often not really about the thing itself because if we ask ourselves whether we face a real problem in that moment, we find that seldom we do. It is often just the story we tell ourselves in relation to the issue at hand that flares our emotions. As Brown states: "We entertain how things are going to be in the future. Or we replay stuff that's happened in the past. Taking control of those stories that we tell ourselves and not just succumbing to them is a very useful thing and it does, absolutely, tie in with magic".[32]

In many cases, not only are the stories we tell ourselves focused on things beyond our control, but they are inaccurate products of our poor internal authorship. In other words, these stories are often manipulations, fabrications and misinformation, projected from the unconscious depths of our inner world, rather than anything "out there" per se. As Brown states during his stage show, *Miracle*:

> It is not just the future that we fixate upon, it's also the past. We tend to dwell on our pasts and think they somehow define who we are. But our pasts are just stories that we tell ourselves in the present. ... When we say, 'I'm this sort of person because this happened to me' or 'I am a lucky

person or an unlucky person'. Whatever it is they are just stories and we can be more sceptical of those stories if it helps us.[33]

I urge readers to keep an open mind as we proceed through the following chapters of this book. Be aware of the stories you tell about yourself and other people in your life. Take some time to reflect on this principle and ask yourself how often you are disturbed by stories based on past and future fabrications rather than real problems in the present moment itself.

As Brown said earlier, things are not always as they seem. People are not always who you might think they are. Your stories about yourself might not be as accurate or inevitable as you once thought they were. There might be better stories we can tell for better lives and a better world. We can be enlightened. And we can enlighten others. We can grow as individuals and flourish as collectives.

However, I am fully aware that this is easier said than done. One reason for this is because we often become fixated and emotionally invested in aspects of life that are beyond our control. This habitual thinking might have engrained itself in our unconscious complexes for many decades in our lives before we try to fix it. It can often feel impossible to tell a better story when we are so bound to what we deem to be the "truth" of our inner dialogue. This problem has hampered human happiness for many centuries, and some of the best advice we've had on how to overcome it occurred around 2000 years ago on the streets of ancient Athens.

Notes

1. Jung, 2014: 406.
2. As writer and memoirist Susanna Barlow points out, the archetypal magician tends to wear many hats as they share their wisdom and goodwill through a variety of skillsets. Brown is most commonly known for his stage and television performances, which have varied from magic tricks and psychological illusions to theatrical stunts, dramatic spectacles and hypnosis. He has written books about magic, published a book about happiness and ancient philosophy, and often sells portraits and

photography that he produces as a hobby. As Barlow points out, these many hats and talents are typical traits of the magician archetype.
3. Bassil-Morozow, 2018: 25.
4. In much of the literature on archetypes, the magician has historically been associated with men. However, this is a cultural tendency that has been critically and necessarily refined in more recent literature. The likes of Helena Bassil-Morozow (2018), Rikki Tannen (2007) and Maya Zuckerman (2016) have shown how archetypes do not need to be gendered as they have been in the past. Likewise, Scott Jeffrey acknowledges that despite the likes of Moore and Gillette (1990) exploring the magician archetype in relation to masculine psychology, we should not approach this as an archetype exclusive to men. Women can (and do) access and express this archetypal thought pattern and its associated behaviour. To suggest otherwise is to make an ideological proposition that is beyond the scope and position of my discussion here.
5. This book provides the fields of Persona Studies and Celebrity Studies (among other disciplines) with a rigorous application of discourse-mythological analysis (DMA), combined with autoethnography, to conduct a psychological and philosophically oriented study of a performative persona in popular culture. Rather than challenging other studies on the role of celebrity and persona (Marshall et al., 2015, 2019; Giles, 2020; Marshall, 2016; Marshall, 2014; Usher, 2021; Deflem, 2016), this book expands the scope of this field—providing eclectic insights that will benefit the growing body of literature associated with celebrity and persona research. These fields are renowned for their interdisciplinary frameworks of analysis, and this book will be of particular interest to researchers who adopt discursive, psychological and philosophical toolkits to understand the role(s) of celebrity persona in society (for examples of other studies more specifically focused on archetypal forms of celebrity persona, see: Kelsey, 2017, 2018; Steenberg, 2019; Polaschek, 2018; Nartey, 2021). From personal and cultural perspectives, this book considers how a celebrity persona can function as an affective, socially interventionist and intellectually positive influence in the communicative landscape of popular culture—while demonstrating how and why this case is relevant to collective psychology. Especially given my focus on the magician archetype, this book shows how psycho-discursive analyses of storytelling and celebrity personas can benefit from autoethnographic insights on the archetypal resonance of popular

figures—showing how they provide critical commentary, observations and advice on cultural phenomena that impact upon our collective psychology.
6. When I discuss transcendence throughout this book I am not offering a religious definition of the term. Transcendental experiences can be understood from secular perspectives—moving beyond the interests of the individual to invest in something beyond the self (see Maslow, 1971; Messerly, 2013; Kaufman, 2020). As Maslow stated: "Transcendence refers to the very highest and most inclusive or holistic levels of human consciousness, behaving and relating, as ends rather than means, to oneself, to significant others, to human beings in general, to other species, to nature, and to the cosmos" (Maslow, 1971: 269).
7. Moore and Gillette, 1990.
8. Brown recently touched upon this point in *A Book of Secrets* (2021a: 40–41): "We have cultural Shadows too. Since the Enlightenment of the seventeenth and eighteenth centuries we have written ourselves into a powerful narrative of progress, of understanding, and of the pioneering human intellect. And we have proudly redacted from the human story any value that might be found in myth, spirit, even superstition and the unquestioned authority of religion. This turning away has brought an extraordinary age of accelerating technology and a richer understanding of our place in the cosmos. But when we bury these age-old aspects of ourselves, we lose track of our needs. Myths, like fairy stories and the rich narratives of religion, are powerful by virtue of their psychological resonance. They seem to have developed in part to support the human experience as we seek existential signposts to guide our way. For example, folklore surrounding death and what happens thereafter may be factually untrue, but it can nonetheless remain psychologically legitimate. It has doubtless aided many in their final days to believe that the soul endures beyond bodily health".
9. See, for example, Brown 2018a.
10. Brown, 2016a: 18.
11. Brown, 2019b.
12. *L'illusionist*, 2010.
13. *The Illusionist*, 2006.
14. "According to Jung, the ego represents the conscious mind as it comprises the thoughts, memories, and emotions a person is aware of. The ego is largely responsible for feelings of identity and continuity"

(McLeod, 2018). So, while the ego needs to be kept in check through conscious introspection, it also provides an important component in the psyche to enable self-preservation, survival, personal identity and an awareness of our experiences.
15. *Houdini*, 1953.
16. Brown, 2019c.
17. Brown, 2019a.
18. In his television show, *Miracles for Sale*, Brown exposes the shadow-magic of the faith healing industry. He opens with the following line: "You are about to see a world where greed and deceit raise their ugly heads, where lives have been needlessly lost, and where hope, the most precious gift of all, is peddled at a price. This is the wickedness in the world of faith healing". After showing how these stunts can be set up to dupe audiences, Brown states towards the end of the show: "But this particular fraud shows no sign of slowing down. People fooled by it can be left in a spiralling depression when they see God won't heal them or refuse medication which they believe would show a lack of faith to accept. And they're making many healers absurdly rich in the meantime".
19. Brown, 2018d.
20. Nissim, 2011.
21. Sturges, 2018.
22. Brown, 2012b.
23. Brown, 2012c.
24. Kahneman, 2012.
25. Brown, 2016a: 81.
26. Ibid.: 78.
27. Ibid.: 78.
28. Ibid.: 79.
29. Harris, 2019.
30. Irvine, 2020.
31. Brown, 2016b.
32. Ibid.
33. Brown, 2018d.

Bibliography

Bassil-Morozow, H. (2018). *Jungian theory for storytellers: A toolkit*. Routledge.
Brown, D. (2012b). *Apocalypse Q&A*. https://derrenbrown.co.uk/apocalypse-qa/
Brown, D. (2012c). *Steven and Karl*. https://www.youtube.com/watch?v=AqAqhaa0DhE
Brown, D. (2016a). *Happy: Why more or less everything is absolutely fine*. Penguin.
Brown, D. (2016b). New Derren Brown "Happy" book interview. *BBC Breakfast*. https://www.youtube.com/watch?v=ay7IyqQLjtg
Brown, D. (2018a). Joe Rogan & Derren Brown – The idea of happiness. *The Joe Rogan experience #1198*. https://www.youtube.com/watch?v=E3DigsvZCXo
Brown, D. (2018d). *Miracle*. Netflix.
Brown, D. (2019a, May 31). Desert Island Discs. *BBC Radio 4*. https://www.bbc.co.uk/programmes/m0005dyb
Brown, D. (2019b). An illusionist reacts to movies and TV shows about illusions. *Vulture*. https://www.vulture.com/2019/08/derren-brown-reacts-to-movies-and-tv-shows-about-illusions.html
Brown, D. (2019c). Derren Brown: The magician's secrets. BBC World Service: Outlook. https://www.bbc.co.uk/programmes/w3csyhj9
Brown, D. (2021a). *Book of secrets*. Penguin.
Deflem, M. (2016). *Lady Gaga and the sociology of fame: The rise of a pop star in an age of celebrity*. Palgrave.
Giles, D. (2020). A typology of persona as suggested by Jungian theory and the evolving persona studies literature. *Persona Studies, 6*(1), 15–29.
Harris, S. (2019). #150 – The map of misunderstanding. *Making sense with Sam Harris*. https://samharris.org/podcasts/150-map-misunderstanding/
Houdini. (1953). George Marshall. Paramount Pictures.
Illusionist, The. (2006). Neil Burger. Yari Film Group / Freestyle.
Irvine, W. (2020). *Stoicon 2020. William B. Irvine*. https://www.youtube.com/watch?v=QfdvrY731yc
Jung, C. (2014). *The collected works of C.G. Jung*. University Press.
Kahneman, D. (2012). *Thinking, fast and slow*. Penguin.
Kaufman, B. (2020). *Transcend: The new science of self-actualization*. Penguin.
Kelsey, D. (2017). *Media and affective mythologies: Discourse, archetypes and ideology in contemporary politics*. Palgrave.
Kelsey, D. (2018). Affective mythology and 'the notorious' Conor McGregor: Monomyth, mysticism, and mixed martial arts. *Martial Arts Studies, 5*, 15–35.

L'illusionist. (2010). Sylvain Chomet. Warner Bros.

Marshall, D. (2014). *Celebrity and power: Fame in contemporary culture.* University Press.

Marshall, D. (2016). *The celebrity Persona pandemic.* University Press.

Marshall, D., Moore, C., & Barber, K. (2015). *Celebrity Studies, 6*(3), 1–18. https://doi.org/10.1080/19392397.2015.1062649

Marshall, D., Moore, C., & Barber, K. (2019). *Persona Studies: An introduction.* Wiley.

Maslow, A. (1971). *The farther reaches of human nature.* Penguin.

McLeod, S. (2018). Carl Jung. *Simply Psychology.* https://www.simplypsychology.org/carl-jung.html.

Messerly, J. (2013). *The meaning of life: Religious, philosophical, transhumanist, and scientific perspectives.* Darwin & Hume Publishers.

Moore, R., & Gillette, D. (1990). *Magician warrior king lover: Rediscovering the archetypes of the mature masculine.* HarperOne.

Nartey, M. (2021). Yvonne Nelson and the heroic myth of Yaa Asantewaa: A discourse-mythological case study of a Ghanaian celebrity. *Critical Studies in Media Communication, 38*(3), 255–268. https://doi.org/10.1080/15295036.2021.1907429

Nissim, M. (2011, June 2). Derren Brown: 'Lottery twist was banned'. *Digital Spy.* https://www.digitalspy.com/showbiz/a322800/derren-brown-lottery-twist-was-banned/

Polaschek, B. (2018). The dissonant personas of a female celebrity: Amy and the public self of Amy Winehouse. *Celebrity Studies, 9*(1), 17–33. https://doi.org/10.1080/19392397.2017.1321490

Steenberg, L. (2019). Bruce lee as gladiator: Celebrity, vernacular stoicism and cinema. *Journal of Global Media and China, 3*, 4. https://journals.sagepub.com/doi/full/10.1177/2059436419874625

Sturges, F. (2018, October 13). Derren Brown: Sacrifice – Have the illusionist's party tricks lost their shine?. *The Guardian.* https://www.theguardian.com/tv-and-radio/2018/oct/13/derren-brown-sacrifice

Tannen, R. (2007). *The female trickster the mask that reveals: Post-Jungian and postmodern psychological perspectives on women in contemporary culture.* Routledge.

Usher, B. (2021). *Journalism and celebrity.* Routledge.

Zuckerman, M. (2016). Transformative media: From the hero's journey to our collective journey. *Kosmos Journal.* Online at: https://www.kosmosjournal.org/article/transformative-media-from-the-heros-journey-to-our-collective-journey/. Last accessed 8 Apr 2020.

3

Street Philosophy and the Stoics

The Stoa Poikile was where it all began. Around 300 BC, Zeno of Citium stood on a famous painted porch of an ancient Athenian marketplace to teach the philosophy of Stoicism, which took its name from that location—the Stoa Poikile. Stoicism was a philosophy for life that could help manage emotions and respond to adversity with virtue and reason—learning to cope and even thrive in challenging times.[1]

Our use of the term "stoic" in the English language has become somewhat detached from the philosophy itself, and we should avoid any misconceptions here.[2] As Donald Robertson explains in *How to Think Like a Roman Emperor*, "Lowercase stoicism is just a personality trait: it's mental toughness or the ability to endure pain and adversity without complaining. Uppercase Stoicism is a whole school of Greek philosophy".[3]

The Stoics were not about stiff upper lips or concealing emotions. They were more concerned with managing their emotions and conducting themselves in accordance with to reason and virtue. As ethicist and psychoanalyst, Nancy Sherman points out: "Despite the popular view of Stoicism as a philosophy that would strip us of most emotions, the ancient Stoics argue that the very best of us show rational exuberance and desire, and a cautious wariness, lest we be too easily led astray or deceived".[4]

© The Author(s), under exclusive license to Springer Nature Switzerland AG 2022
D. Kelsey, *Storytelling and Collective Psychology*,
https://doi.org/10.1007/978-3-030-93660-0_3

The Stoics were concerned with their civic duties, kindness to others and pursuing justice in the world. But they did so with temperance (moderation), according to what was realistically possible without causing themselves unnecessary disturbance. They pursued *eudaimonia* (happiness or flourishing) and sought to appreciate the tranquillity of those present moments that are absent of disturbance regardless of past or prospective events.

As Marcus Aurelius wrote in *Meditations*: "All you need are these: certainty of judgement in the present moment; action for the common good in the present moment; and an attitude of gratitude in the present moment for anything that comes your way".[5] Stoicism was a practical philosophy designed for anyone in daily life.

Brown makes the point that philosophy in modern life has become "highly academic, concerning itself more with matters of language, logic and metaphysics, rather than with the business of living well".[6] While he agrees that there is a place for this level of academic inquiry, he is right to suggest that this cannot be the exclusive role or purpose of philosophy.

The likes of Alain de Botton and Jules Evans have sought to take public philosophy back to its humanitarian roots—teaching us the practical values of philosophy in daily life through accessible and applicable means.[7] Brown shares this sentiment, and it is the spirit of this humanitarian ethos in street philosophy that I offer from my perspective in this book.

Philosophy for Flourishing

Brown explains how Socrates—prior to the Stoics—was the first philosopher to depart from metaphysical conversations that had little relevance to people living through the daily challenges of ancient life. Socrates brought philosophy to the people, which could be taught on the streets and applied by anyone seeking to live a more robust life with less disturbance.

In Brown's discussion of the Socratic tradition behind Stoic philosophy, he refers to Jules Evans who clearly outlines the four steps that can help us live more flourishing lives:

1. Humans can know themselves. We can use our reason to examine our conscious beliefs and values.
2. Humans can change themselves. We can use our reason to change our beliefs. This will change our emotions, because our emotions follow our beliefs.
3. Humans can consciously create new habits of thinking, feeling and acting.
4. If we follow philosophy as a way of life, we can live more flourishing lives.[8]

I am interested in how Brown's work speaks to all four steps of this Socratic tradition. As Evans points out, ancient philosophy can teach us "self-help of the very best kind, that doesn't focus narrowly on the individual, but instead broadens our minds and connects us to society, science, culture and the cosmos".[9]

As we see in Brown's stage magic, his writing and the dramatic spectacles in his TV shows in later chapters, those Socratic principles are evident in the ethos of his work and his attention to storytelling.[10]

Brown suggests that self-enquiry is as necessary now as it was back when Zeno stood beneath the Stoa, and philosophy for living daily life can be found in those classical texts that were taught on the streets of the Athenian marketplace. By rediscovering the spirit of street philosophy and the Stoics, Brown makes the case for us to consider the wisdom of the ancient Greeks as a means for enabling human flourishing.

This meant living according to four Stoic virtues: justice, wisdom, courage and temperance. We want to pursue justice for the common interests of our society. So we need wisdom and courage to do so: we must be willing to learn and we must have the courage to do what is right. But we must do so with the temperance (or moderation) required to inform our judgements and apply those virtues in response to any circumstances that arise.

For the Stoics, virtue was the highest good, the "summum bonum", which they believed should influence our choices and actions in daily life. As Ryan Holiday points out, this was not a holy or religious concept, but rather one that was defined by moral and civic excellence in daily life: "It's sense of pure rightness that emerges from our souls and is made real through the actions we take".[11]

But the Stoics argued that we can only pursue those four virtues if we distinguish between what is within and beyond our control. We must moderate our emotions accordingly, regardless of what fate might throw at us, and we must take back control of our thoughts, emotions, stories and actions. This control of our thoughts and actions was fundamental to Stoic philosophy and resonated with Brown when he read the likes of Marcus Aurelius, Epictetus and Seneca.

The Dichotomy of Control

In his interview with *The Daily Stoic*, Brown explained how the dichotomy of control provided a helpful premise that he kept returning to when he was writing *Happy*, stating: "I was so impressed again and again by the wisdom of not trying to control those things you cannot; by the mantra of 'It's fine' in the face of how things are working out beyond the limited remit of your thoughts and actions".[12]

Brown makes the point that if you allow this principle to embed into your psyche, then you have a good foundation for avoiding the undue stress and anxiety that often compromises our wellbeing. He doesn't pretend this is easy and he acknowledges that it can feel like an unnatural response to begin with, but over time we can start to feel the benefits of this considered response to the circumstances we find ourselves in.

As another *Daily Stoic* article explains, the Stoics used the dichotomy of control to advocate for complete sovereignty over our thoughts, emotions and actions:

> The main practice of Stoicism is remembering what is within our control and what is not. What this means is that the things that are frustrating to us are not frustrating in and of themselves. They are just things and it is we who get frustrated. The Stoics knew that the minute they let something outside their control affect their peace of mind, they lost. They lost because they gave up their most important power which is sovereignty over their emotions.[13]

Let's consider a couple of examples where Stoic philosophers contemplated this dichotomy of control. Writing in *The Art of Living*, Epictetus said:

> Happiness and freedom begin with a clear understanding of one principle: Some things are within our control, and some things are not. It is only after you have faced up to this fundamental rule and learned to distinguish between what you can and can't control that inner tranquillity and outer effectiveness become possible.[14]

In *Discourses*, Epictetus also identifies this principle as the chief task in life in order to establish clarity and determine what actions are required from within the self:

> The chief task in life is simply this: to identify and separate matters so that I can say clearly to myself which are externals not under my control, and which have to do with the choices I actually control. Where then do I look for good and evil? Not to uncontrollable externals, but within myself to the choices that are my own.[15]

Likewise, in *Letters from a Stoic*, Seneca shared this sentiment:

> Floods will rob us of one thing, fire of another. These are conditions of our existence which we cannot change. What we can do is adopt a noble spirit, such a spirit as befits a good person, so that we may bear up bravely under all that fortune sends us and bring our wills into tune with nature's.[16]

This seems like a simple principle to follow, but applying it on a daily basis is a tougher task than one might expect. In my case, applying this principle took a couple of years of perseverance before it really set in for me. Even now, I still have days when I find my thoughts running away with themselves into territory that fractures contentment and encourages disturbance. This is usually because I am worried or worked up about matters beyond my control and I have to bring my thoughts back into line with this principle.

It is not that my worries aren't legitimate. Through the combination of a global pandemic and Brexit, for example, I have been understandably worried about the future of universities, how we would respond to changing circumstances, the wellbeing of my colleagues and students, the financial impact on Higher Education and even the long-term security of my job. Like most people, in my personal life I often worry about the health and wellbeing of relatives and friends. Since becoming a father, I have become increasingly concerned about the stability of the world that my daughter is growing up in—politically, socially, economically, ethically and environmentally.

The point here is not that I should stop caring about legitimate concerns. But I must avoid investing my time and energy in a spiralling narrative of hypothetical outcomes that cause me unnecessary angst on matters beyond my control. The latter only prohibits me from managing thoughts, emotions and actions while compromising the energy and focus I can apply to influence what is within my control.

In other words, I need to apply some toolkits that protect my mind from becoming all-consumed by those concerns. By only focusing my thoughts and actions on those things within my control, I can then respond—socially, professionally and domestically—to those challenges in ways that are beneficial to my interests and those around me.

Purpose, Responsibility and Society

As Brown points out, the Stoics were "movers and shakers" and, unlike the Epicurean philosophers around at the same time, were actively engaged in public and political life—often using their power and status to influence society.[17] For the Stoics, a duty to actively pursue the common good through whatever actions were within their control was crucial to living in accordance to those four virtues of courage, justice, wisdom and temperance.

On this point, Brown addresses another stand-out question that often arises in response to Stoicism, and particularly the dichotomy of control: what about social injustice? Do we just sit back and accept that the world is unfair and dismiss social injustice as a matter of fate and circumstance and just carry on as normal? No, absolutely not. The Stoics believed we must pursue justice and we may use our courage and wisdom to do so, but we can apply temperance here to ensure our thoughts and actions remain focused on what is within our control.

It is important to note that the Stoics did not advocate laziness, apathy or a lack of ambition. Returning to my earlier point, the Stoics argued that a social oikeiōsis was crucial to pursuing justice—not just to protect those we deem closest to us in our families or tribes but to pursue the interests of humanity as a whole. Liz Gloyn, a researcher in Latin language and literature, uses an analogy from Hierocles to make sense of this concept:

> To explain this process, the Stoic Hierocles used an image of concentric circles. He wrote that the smallest circle is the one that includes the individual and the individual alone; the second circle, which surrounds the first, contains immediate blood relatives; the third circle contains more distant relations, like grandparents, uncles and aunts; the fourth circle contains any remaining relatives. The circles continue, gradually expanding to include neighbours, then members of the same tribe, then inhabitants of the same city, until finally the circles encompass the whole human race.[18]

As Gloyn explains, the process of oikeiōsis accounts for the way that an aspiring Stoic starts to incorporate the interests of those in each circle into that containing the self, until the interests of all of humanity belong to them. The perfection of this technique was to the Stoic Sage—a figure that the Stoics argued we should aspire to regardless of our inevitable flaws and failings, since it is our pursuit of virtue that defines our actions.

Brown distinguishes between our justified investment in actions to tackle injustice and our over-investment of concern in the outcomes that arise as a result. In an interview with the *Big Think*, Brown explained how the decision and commitment to take action against social injustice is within our control.[19] We can decide on what actions we will take and how much time and effort we will invest in any given cause. Beyond our control are the outcomes: the direction of an entire political movement, governmental responses to political protests or other events that determine the influence we have on social change.

Of course, anger and sadness might initially help us to identify injustice and motivate us to continue taking those actions that are within our control. But we avoid becoming all consumed by those emotions—a point I shall return to later. How we respond thereafter, and how we allow those circumstances to make us feel, requires us to remember that only our actions are within our control.

Actions over Outcomes

The Stoics used the analogy of an archer to illustrate the importance of focusing on actions over outcomes: the archer should be entirely invested in *preparing* to fire the arrow—through the best technique and aim they are capable of until the arrow leaves their bow. What then happens to the arrow once it is in the air is beyond their control. The archer is only focused on their actions, not the outcome. The point here is not that the outcome lacks importance. Rather, to increase the chances of the desired outcome, the focus must be invested in the process that is under the archer's control.

Brown refers to another popular analogy in a game of tennis where, instead of "trying to win", we invest our efforts in trying to play the very best we can.[20] This way, we do not invest in the outcome of the tennis match, which is beyond our control. Instead, we focus on playing the very best we can, which means our energy is only invested in what we can control—rather than being emotionally distracted by frustration and anger if we start to lose.

This principle can easily be misunderstood. The Stoics were not suggesting that winning is irrelevant or that we should not appreciate victory or success when it happens. They were, quite rightly, pointing to the fact that our overt focus on winning (especially against what might be a superior opponent) detracts from our focus on maximising our performance, which we can control. Less focus on the outcome and more focus on our actions actually increase the likelihood of winning.

Either way, win or lose, we should remain focused on whether we performed the best we could and what we might do to improve our performance. For the Stoics, excess pride in victory is not only self-indulgent and egotistical, which they warned us against, but egotism also blinds us to the faults in our performance. Without improvement, these faults might prove costly in future against a better opponent.

Brown provides another example of an actor going for an audition. The concern here needn't be on "getting the part".[21] Rather, it should be on the actor maximising the quality and authenticity of their performance according to their capabilities. The decision of the panel judging the performance is beyond the actor's control. As long as the performer has provided the best account of themselves as possible then they can be content with the outcome that fate presents them with.

I have provided a few examples here because when they are applied with discipline they can be liberating and ease the unnecessary disturbances we cause for ourselves throughout the daily challenges of life. It can be difficult to resist the interventions of ego or anxiety, but we can persevere and utilise these tools by remaining focused on our thoughts and actions over outcomes.

I look back at the gruelling process of trying to get a job in academia after I had finished my PhD and the countless rejections I faced before a successful interview. My morale was rock bottom, I was becoming increasingly self-conscious, anxious and doubtful that I would ever get the job opportunity I had spent so long working towards. The process might have been slightly less stressful, ego-crushing and demoralising if I had the same toolkits to hand then as I do now.

That's not to suggest it would have been easy. But my entire outlook at the time was anything but considered; I lacked calmness, I was tense, resentful at times, awkward to be around, and my emotions were invested in so many elements beyond my control. That said, we should be content in learning from these lessons in life. It is easy for me to look back now, in the comfort and privilege of current circumstances, and be critical of myself. But in reality it was a difficult situation to be in and one that I would learn and grow from, rather than regret. And age is a significant point here, which is worth considering in critique of the Stoics.

Learning and Growing

When Kay Burley interviewed Brown about Stoicism and tackling anxiety, she pointed out that these principles are easier to apply as you get older, but aren't so easy when you're young and keen to get on in life.[22] Burley raised a good point.

If someone could have given me a crystal ball when I was 20 or 25 years old, showing me where I would be at 35, it is easy to think I might have relaxed a bit. But it is important to understand that our experiences shape us. As long as we reflect upon them and understand what they mean to our development then they become part of who we are and how we navigate the path ahead. *This* is what enables us to grow—the hypothetical crystal ball would only be detrimental to our development.

Nonetheless, it is the possibility of failure—prospective unemployment, the fear of ending up alone or the anxiety that your hard work may never deliver those desired outcomes—that is often an overwhelming factor when we are young. When we are young it is hard to understand that some failures are what will help us succeed because failures provide essential life lessons.

Brown also agreed with Burley's point and explained how these Stoic principles are typically more applicable to the second half in life when we tend to invest in something beyond ourselves. Brown explained that when we are wrapped up in the ambitions of early life and establishing our place in the world, it is much more difficult to apply these principles.

During those early years it feels like so much of our fate is determined by those few exams, a single decision or that one interview. That's not to suggest the Stoics can't offer us sound advice when we are young, but we should not underestimate how impenetrable one's mindset can be at this time. This is especially the case when, during those early years, we are bombarded with so many warnings, admonitions and seemingly contradictory advice about our future prospects.

At all stages of life, we can learn valuable lessons through our mistakes, flaws, failures, successes and personal growth. If we advocate philosophies for life, especially in our advice to young people, our intention should be to encourage reflection and growth through experience. As mentors we can kindly steer our mentees with reassurance and encouragement rather than unfairly pressurising them or trying to preload them with dogmatic virtue.

Life Skills and Lessons

Around the same time that I was working on this chapter, I heard a couple of interviews with Trevor Wittman—coach of the UFC fighter, Justin Gaethje. In the build up to Gaethje's world title fight against Khabib Nurmagomedov, Wittman was discussing his preparations for the fight and his ethos as a coach; offering life skills and lessons for his fighters to take from the sport. Wittman wants his fighters to grow as people rather than reducing a fighter's story and character down to mere victories or defeats.

In one interview, Wittman said: "It is not about winning or losing to me. It really isn't. I'm a coach and I coach to perform. ... I want to coach people for life and for experiences and one thing about fighting is I've seen it change people's lives". Wittman described how seeing his fighters adapt to chaos through the sport of mixed martial arts gives him the reassurance that they will develop the ability to adapt to adversity in their daily lives.[23]

Wittman was not openly referring to Stoic philosophy, but he showed how this ethos is applied by professionals in those higher pressure scenarios. Ryan Holiday makes the point that we should not only learn from those who wrote as Stoic philosophers—we should observe Stoic traits in those who might not identify as Stoics but whose actions embody Stoic virtues.[24]

When asked about the prospective outcome of Gaethje's fight with Khabib, Wittman said: "The outcome? I don't look into that. I look at going out there and making sure I am on point. ... I am not here to hope he does well. I am focused on me performing and that's all I can control". All Wittman's fighters can do is perform according to their training, regardless of the outcome. For Wittman, adapting to adversity is a greater life skill than winning a fight.[25] As Wittman points out, fights are similar to life because events rarely unfold in accordance with the plans that you make. You have to be prepared to make adjustments and adapt because fate couldn't care less about your plans.

Fate and Fortune

In his interview with Kay Burley, Brown discussed the importance of accepting fate and fortune—something the ancient ancestors were much better at than we are now. Brown feels we have lost touch with our ability to accept fate in modern times, and rediscovering it would help us to cope in difficult circumstances. We would be more comfortable rolling with whatever happenings occur by recognising that some negative events in life are both inevitable and beyond our control.

We can let certain emotions come and go, and accept them as part of what life is all about. Brown uses sadness as an example of an emotion that we might almost allow to sit more comfortably within us, more like a sense of melancholy, rather than resisting, denying or becoming overwhelmed by it. Brown also explained that by the time he had finished writing *Happy*, he had grown to appreciate the importance of anxiety as an emotion.

Rather than avoiding anxiety or attempting to remove it from our lives, we can use it to understand the circumstances we find ourselves in. Brown made the point that we might be stuck in a job or profession that is making us unhappy but we only know that we need a change because anxiety has prompted us to do so. So as long as we reflect on the causes of anxiety with reason and manage our thoughts and actions accordingly, anxiety can actually play an important role in our lives.

However, these considered reflections and responses require robustness. The Stoic reading marathon I went on after *Happy* brought my attention to the work of Ryan Holiday. Holiday's work offers some key principles in how to live more robustly in accordance to those stoic virtues of justice, wisdom, courage and temperance: we need to find stillness and learn to hold a calm head; we need to resist the selfish and corrupting urges of our ego; and we can learn to approach obstacles and adversities as opportunities to grow.

Stillness, Egos and Obstacles

In *Stillness is the Key*, Holiday states: "We must cultivate mental stillness to succeed in life and to successfully navigate the many crises it throws our way".[26] Holiday argues that stillness brings us to the present and if we can find that stillness without worrying about the past or future then we can make better judgements about the circumstances we face in the here and now. We cannot find stillness if we are frantically trying to control things beyond our control.

Neither can we find this stillness if we are blindly pursuing endless goals that are purely driven by the quick fix desires of our egos, which are never satisfied. In *The Ego is the Enemy*, Holiday states:

> When we remove ego, we're left with what is real. What replaces ego is humility, yes—but rock-hard humility and confidence. Whereas ego is artificial, this type of confidence can hold weight. Ego is stolen. Confidence is earned. Ego is self-anointed, its swagger is artifice. One is girding yourself, the other gaslighting. It's the difference between potent and poisonous.[27]

By putting our egos to one side and remaining calm and considered in our actions, we can adapt to adversity. If we accept that things will go wrong, and the world does not revolve around our needs and desires, we can, according to Holiday, turn adversity into advantage.

In *The Obstacle is the Way*, Holiday recalls what the Stoics told us about our perceptions and our internal stories that define how we know what happens to us, rather than external events in the world. With the wrong perspective, he says, we add self-doubt as an additional element to the obstacle itself: "[W]ith the wrong perspective, we become consumed and overwhelmed with something actually quite small. So why subject ourselves to that? The right perspective has a strange way of cutting obstacles—and adversity—down to size".[28]

In the spirit of Brown's earlier point, we need to rediscover our respect for fate so that we can sit more comfortably with life's circumstances, be more accepting of challenges that arise, and be more robust in the face of adversity. As Holiday points out, many problems we face come from our judgements about them because we have a habit of thinking that there was a way things were *supposed* to be—in accordance with those desires that make demands for things beyond our control.[29]

The Stoics offered three mantras that we can continually refer to in order to be more accepting of factors beyond our control, remaining in the moment and maintaining gratitude for what *really* matters. The Stoics didn't just encourage us to accept or tolerate fate, but to actually love our fate and view difficult situations as moments to embrace and seize upon as opportunities. Those three mantras are Amor fati (love fate), Memento mori (the inevitability of death) and Carpe diem (seize the moment). If we remember our mortality and remind ourselves that every moment is precious because life could end sooner than we think, then we can appreciate what we have in the here and now, beyond the trivia that we have typically allowed ourselves to be angered by for thousands of years.

Habitual Humans

As Holiday states: "On the outside, life today couldn't be more different from life one hundred years ago, let alone two thousand years ago. … But internally, humans have pretty much stayed the same. We lose our patience over petty things, care too much what other people think, and struggle to deal with change".[30] But these behavioural traits aren't inevitable. They're habits that we can change—through those Socratic methods that encourage us to know ourselves, change our beliefs, manage our emotions, create new habits and realise our potential to flourish. We can seize the moment for what it is, embrace fate, remember we are mortal, turn adversity into opportunity and be grateful for what we have, regardless of the outcome.

Stoicism is not a magic trick that can vanish away all our worries and problems. Rather, it offers intuitive reminders that can help us to live with more tranquillity and gratitude in the present moment. Stoicism can help in response to most situations that life throws at us on a daily basis—a robustness that the ancient Greeks called *ataraxia*. When we achieve ataraxia we experience tranquillity—an acceptance of fate and gratitude for life.

Stoicism offers not a dogma, but a grounding, which gives us more realistic expectations in life by accepting that an element of misfortune and suffering will come our way from time to time. These circumstances won't necessarily be our fault, but how we perceive them is down to us. We need to manage our perceptions because our perceptions form our stories.

Perceptions and Stories

As Brown states: "It is not events out there that cause our problems but rather our reactions to them: the stories we tell ourselves". Given we have to tell stories to make sense of what is happening around us, they become the connective component in the perceptions that form our inner dialogue. Our perceptions often instigate a self-perpetuating cycle of stress, anxiety, frustration and anger that are reinforced through those stories about who we are and what the world is like. Epictetus and Marcus Aurelius offer us some insight here respectively:

> "Men are disturbed not by things, but their opinions about them"[31]

> "The happiness of your life depends upon the quality of your thoughts: therefore, guard accordingly, and take care that you entertain no notions unsuitable to virtue and reasonable nature."[32]

Brown explains how we can often see that our inner dialogue dictates our stories because if we stop to think about how someone else we know would react to the same situation, their response might be entirely different. To quote Marcus Aurelius: "The same experience befalls another, and he is unruffled and remains unharmed; either because he is unaware that it has happened or because he exhibits greatness of soul".[33]

So, our feelings and emotions are constantly entangled with the narrative building processes through which we try to interpret the infinite data source available to us. However, it is due to the sheer vastness of this data source that we struggle to manage our perceptions and distinguish what is within or beyond our control. Another technique the Stoics applied here was to differentiate between our inner and outer worlds.

Inner and Outer Worlds

As Brown says, "the Stoics have some powerful advice about how to appreciate and maintain a distinction between the outer and inner worlds, and therefore how to reduce anxiety".[34] He deems it helpful for us to recognise this because when we realise that it is not necessary or inevitable for us to react unhappily to events in the way we often do, we can start to rethink our relationship with the outer world.

When we do this, Brown explains, "we can apply the same understanding more deeply to our *inner* world and the story we tell ourselves every day about who we are".[35] As Brown says, it is in our power and interest to control how we feel about what happens to us:

> Out There and In Here are two very different kingdoms, and other people are not accountable for how we feel. No one, however ridiculously they behave, has the right or the direct means to affect your self-control or dignity. No one need annoy us so much that we in turn become a source of annoyance to others.[36]

Whether it's the actions of other people or natural events in the world, they require a reasoned response that is less disturbing to our inner world. Our inner world is the one place where we have ownership of what goes on and we can choose how we want to feel about what happens in life and those stories we choose to tell. Brown offers another analogy from Marcus Aurelius here:

> In one passage, Marcus tells himself to see those things that infuriate him as no more than the equivalent of sawdust and wood clippings on the floor of a carpenter's workshop. These things that obstruct us are the inevitable by-product of nature, and it would be mad to become enraged about them. This is typical of the Stoics' aligning of themselves with fate (that is, whatever the world throws at them), but it also should inform our first impressions and stop us from interpreting events in such a way that makes us feel worse.[37]

When I am getting irritated or unnecessarily wound up by people or circumstances around me, I think back to this analogy of the wood clippings on the workshop floor. These "irritations" are inevitable by-products of life—it makes no sense to get angry with the incidental nature of fate, even if those circumstances are caused by actions, attitudes and agendas we disagree with. Some of those things might be genuinely irritating. But the point here is that they are inevitable by-products of life and human nature.

Through our ability to reason and control our inner world, we can consciously remove the disturbance that we allow these things to impose upon our inner peace. Of course, there are reasonable responses we can take to challenge wrong-doing or unacceptable behaviours that we are confronted by, but we should do so with temperance and reason.

We should remember that it is much easier to tell a story about the ridiculous behaviour of someone else than to recognise our own flaws. Carl Jung reminds us that our flaws are quick to sneak off into the shadow whilst we project them onto others instead. In response to this tendency we have as humans, Marcus Aurelius reminded himself: "Be tolerant with others and strict with yourself".[38]

Whether it's our flaws as individuals, injustice in our communities or reprehensible behaviour in the social groups that we identify with, we should seek to address the flaws and failings that we are part of before we judge the moral inferiority of our foes. As Holiday explains, Stoicism is not about fostering a sense of moral superiority. He suggests when we look around and see bad behaviour or hear abhorrent opinions we should use these observations to try and understand how they have been misled so that we avoid the same mistakes—since we all have the potential for moral failure. We should aim to do better ourselves without judging others.[39]

Once again, this is easier said than done. When Carl Jung talked about the shadow, he warned us that introspection and integration of the unconscious is anything but comfortable work. Confronting our flaws and undesirable traits is something our ego wants to stop us from doing. Sometimes we are not even delving as deep as the unconscious mind to confront those less admirable aspects of our character; on the surface of our consciousness lie other egotistical tendencies that we are aware of but we conceal, and we are just as prone to projecting those conscious faults onto others to save ourselves from introspective critique.

Our irritations, emotions and reactions are often as much about us as anyone else. As we try to manage our perceptions, we try to manage those emotions that fuel our reactions to events and the stories that we tell about the world.

Emotions and Reactions

Brown suggests that rather than seeing our judgements and perceptions as the *sole cause* of our negative feelings, it would be more helpful to view them as one constituent part.[40] He uses the example of almost being hit by a car, where your reaction to the situation and danger in that moment allows you to stop or step out the way. This reaction is not because of any judgement you have made, but because evolutionary mechanisms of senses and self-preservation have kicked in automatically before you have any chance to make a judgement about the situation. This is helpful.

It is only afterwards that you have time to decide whose fault it was and whether you allow that event and near miss to bother you for the rest of the day—particularly if you decide it was the driver's fault and the abuse he shouted from his window was unkind and unjustified. Remember, there's every chance your memory of the incident is misinforming the story you tell. And you never know what the perspective of the person driving was, as they sit at home telling someone a very different story, which they are equally convinced is accurate, and where *you* are the villain.

As Seneca said, the initial flush of emotion following a near-accident is fine, but to remain enraged or disturbed many hours later is an investment of emotion in something that has been and gone.[41] After all, our ability to reason after an event is as much a product of our evolution as the flush of emotion when an event occurs.

That said, it is important to understand our emotions, especially if they continually recur sometime after an event has passed. We can allow our emotions to sit and allow them to help us understand *why* something is disturbing us—whether that's an event that has passed or one that might happen in the future.

This is why CBT was so helpful for me because it allowed me to take a step back, look at what emotions I was feeling, how they were affecting my reactions and how they were affected by my stories. Only then could I rationalise what was happening. It was often the case that evolutionary traits—such as fight or flight instincts—were being stimulated in circumstances where they didn't need to be. It was my story that needed editing in order to stop my inner dialogue catastrophising and anticipating things that hadn't happened.

To reiterate the difference between Stoic philosophy and what it means to be stoic in the English language: we should not be concealing, suppressing or denying emotions in order to adopt a stoic persona or "stiff upper lip"; rather we should process, control and understand our emotions so that they are just one constituent part of our feelings, perceptions and stories.[42]

In other words, emotions should not *control* us exclusively at the cost of reason and reflection, but we can comfortably confront whatever emotions arise.

Domesticate Your Emotions

Ryan Holiday makes the point that through Stoicism we are not discouraged from expressing our emotions, nor should we allow cultural stereotypes to regulate them on our behalf. Rather we should domesticate our emotions:

> No one said you can't ever cry. Forget 'manliness'. If you need to take a moment, by all means, go ahead. Real strength lies in the control or, as Nassim Taleb put it, the *domestication* of one's emotions, not in pretending they don't exist. So go ahead, feel it. Just don't lie to yourself by conflating emoting about a problem and dealing with it. Because they are as different as sleeping and waking. You can always remind yourself: *I am in control, not my emotions. I see what's really going on here. I'm not going to get excited or upset.*[43]

If we deny our emotions the recognition that they warrant, they are more likely to compromise our reason and judgement.[44]

Donald Robertson addressed this point when explaining the difference between stoicism and Stoicism. When people try to use lower-case stoicism as a coping strategy for concealing or denying emotions, he calls it "pseudo-stoicism" because even the attempt at having a stiff upper lip simply fails to distinguish between the initial flush of emotion that we feel and those other cognitive aspects thereafter. This results in people unhealthily trying to "shove all of their emotions down, forcing them out of their minds". Not only does this misinterpret Stoicism, but it is a significant problem in the shadow dynamics of the psyche that Jung was concerned with.

As Holiday explains, life's challenges make us emotional, but if we keep our emotions in check, if we can stay calm and steady whatever happens, regardless of the external events that arise, we achieve what the Stoics called apatheia: a state of calmness through the removal of irrational or extreme emotions. Likewise, Nancy Sherman welcomes the presence of certain emotions that are a necessary part of the human experience: "We cherish our friends and nurture warm and welcoming attitudes toward them. This is what it is to be righteous. Put bluntly, even sages have emotional skin in the game".[45]

That said, the Stoics still accepted that we could appreciate and integrate "good passions", which they called "eupatheia".[46] Through reason and virtue, the Stoics believed we could distinguish good passions from destructive desires and disturbing emotions. They listed them under three categories, which Donald Robertson recalls as follows:

1. A profound sense of *joy* or gladness and peace of mind, which come from living with wisdom and virtue.
2. A healthy feeling of *aversion* to vice, like a sense of conscience, honour, dignity or integrity.
3. The *desire to help* both ourselves and others, through friendship, kindness and goodwill.[47]

It is through reason that we can rise above our baser instincts and take back control of our emotions so that they align with those key virtues for a more considered life. The considered life enables us to identify, understand and control our emotions and desires and, in doing so, we can avoid those common misconceptions of Stoicism: rather than shutting down or denying emotions, we can understand them and control them; rather than suppressing desires, we can refine them and guide them towards more dignified actions; rather than withdrawing from society and lacking empathy, we can reach out with compassion and fulfil our duty to others. In other words, we must use our sense of reason to retain, or sometimes regain, our sovereignty.

Taking Back Control

Brown addresses this principle by drawing attention back to that control of our inner world. We do not need to blame ourselves or deny that our anxieties, frustrations or other emotions exist. But we must domesticate them. When we take back control of these emotions and reactions we ease a bit of pressure on ourselves:

> We can take responsibility for how we feel by realising that ultimately it is our after-the-event, ongoing *reactions* to what happens around us that are the cause of our problems. The point of this is *not* to blame ourselves. It is to begin to dissolve unwanted frustrations and anxieties in our lives. Once we stop blaming the world for our problems we can achieve some control. Whether we see our judgement as a cause or a constituent part of our emotional pain, the same conclusion remains for us as for Marcus Aurelius. "Cast out the judgement, you are saved. What hinders you?"[48]

However, despite being a practicing Stoic himself, Massimo Pigliucci makes the point that the Stoics were overly optimistic about the extent to which humans can control their own thoughts.[49]

As he explains, modern research in psychology and cognitive science shows that our judgements and perceptions are constantly influenced by cognitive bias and delusions. And as we saw earlier, Daniel Kahneman's research shows us how flawed our memories, perceptions and stories about very recent experiences can be.

Long after the Stoics, psychoanalysts became increasingly interested in our unconscious minds and how our psyche is shaped by our culture and upbringing. When we pay closer attention to the role of the unconscious mind in our personal and collective lives, we realise that we do not have quite so much control as the Stoics believed.

As Brown points out, our perceptions of ourselves and our surroundings are shaped from a very young age, when we internalise messages from our caregivers and begin to build narratives about who we are.

The Unlived Lives of Our Parents

Brown has often referred to the following quote from Carl Jung: "The greatest burden a child must bear is the unlived lives of its parents".[50] Now before I get myself in trouble, let me be clear: the point here is not to blame mum and dad. Rather, it is to think about the environments we are/aren't exposed to while growing up, which subsequently shape our perceptions and experiences of the world.

By understanding these influences, we can better understand ourselves and adjust our perceptions accordingly. The point here is not to dwell on the past or to weaponise ourselves with a victim narrative that casts blame on our upbringing. Rather, it is to confront our unconscious narratives from the past and where they are unhelpful we reconstruct them for a better future.

We learn the rules and codes of conduct around what is deemed acceptable (or not) in the cultural environments that we live in. As Brown explains, this "burden" Jung spoke of was not exclusively negative per se: "We can carry around the psychological legacy of our parents for our whole lives, whether good or bad. Where they have unfulfilled wishes and regrets, these are commonly passed to us as a template for storytelling".[51]

Brown tells the story of an actor (Andy Nyman), a mother and a daughter. The mother asks Nyman if he would have his photo taken with the daughter. Nyman agrees. The daughter is visibly nervous and Nyman can feel her trembling as they pose for the shot. After the mother takes the photo Nyman sees that the girl wasn't smiling and he asks her if she wants to take it again. The mother said, "Oh she always looks terrible in pictures." Nyman was shocked and jumped to the daughter's defence, only for the daughter to respond: "Oh, it's okay, it's true."

Brown describes the story as a snapshot of a life, "one of wretched self-esteem for the girl, and its apparent maternal origins". Rather than encouraging and nurturing her daughter in the way we might expect her to, the mother seemed to help perpetuate the daughter's lack of self-belief. As Brown states: "The damning word in the mother's remark is 'always', because 'always' tells us there is a pattern, a story at work. And stories affect us deeply".[52]

When it comes to stories about ourselves, Brown states that we are "master editors, tirelessly working to communicate to others and ourselves a meaningful tale". Like this case of the mother and daughter, we learn stories about ourselves, which become ingrained as "truths" in our psyche, like a window onto who we are through unconscious self-reflection. We form perceptions of ourselves through stories about our past and draw conclusions about how that past defines us now and in the future.[53]

It is important to remember that these stories are not only shaped by our parents. Like our parents, we are exposed to stories from an early age in friendship circles, schools, media and other institutions that contribute to the formation of narratives that we build over time, which influence our internal dialogue, character and conduct—personally and culturally, individually and collectively. These stories are the cumulative products of multiple ideologies and cultural complexes of the outer world, which our inner worlds are entangled with on a daily basis.

As with all these narratives, we often fail to question the stories we tell about ourselves because they become an unconscious editorial package of our identity. Therefore, the moral and ethical state of the society in which we live, and the kind of stories that society tells us about who we are, should be attended to as essential building blocks of our collective psychology. As damaging as some stories might be, we can also create narrative legacies that enable human flourishing.

Freedom to Flourish

As Brown points out, the psychological legacy that we carry over from our parents is not all bad or wrong or prohibitive. It can also enable flourishing. In a conversation with Adam Buxton, Brown talked about a letter he wrote to his parents when he was at university studying law.[54] In his letter he thanked his parents for never being pushy or making him feel pressured on what to study or what career he should pursue.

Brown was surrounded by fellow students who were under immense pressure to make it to the top of the class and get their career-defining opportunity to become a successful lawyer. Brown didn't carry this pressure, and he didn't go into law when he graduated either. He was free to learn for the love of learning and choose his own way in life, according to whatever he enjoyed doing. Brown was grateful for this freedom to flourish.

I can relate here. In my case, I was the first person in my family to go to university. My parents were proud but never pushy. They were very open about the fact I was pursuing an educational journey that they were not familiar with. They trusted me to pursue whatever I felt was best for me. They were pleased that I had opportunities that weren't available to them.

In this respect, the unlived life of my parents was anything but a burden, but rather a liberating gift that enabled life-changing opportunities for exploration and growth. They trusted my judgement and ambitions without any negative discouragement or pushy over-encouragement. When I graduated, I was never pressured to "get a proper job" as I moved on to postgraduate studies and research. Through their desire to see me pursue opportunities that *weren't* available to them, I was allowed to flourish.

However, my inner dialogue still caused me problems. Crippling imposter syndrome (among other compulsive thought patterns that I would eventually fix with therapy) made university difficult and my self-doubt had only increased in my first year when I realised how far behind I was in the classroom compared to my peers.[55]

I asked myself how I had fluked this opportunity and when it would all come to an end? I had not done particularly well in my GCSEs. I had attended a failing secondary school from which very few people went on to university. I was feeling like a fish out of water academically. Surely, there had been some kind of mistake?

But this wasn't the case. Despite falling short of the entry grades required, someone at Cardiff University had given me a chance, and I was extremely grateful. But these circumstances formed a very convincing narrative that I carried throughout (and beyond) my time as a student.

That Fraudster Feeling

I was completely unaware that this nagging source of anxiety was just a story—imposter syndrome fused with other complexes I was carrying—my poorly edited inner dialogue, telling me I shouldn't be at university. From my undergraduate studies through to my PhD, my career and fatherhood, no matter how hard I worked, how much I learnt or however much I achieved, my story was authored by a voice that said I was living a life I was not entitled to.

Somewhat paradoxically, the better my life got, the more anxious I became. I could deal with a real challenge or a real problem. But the ever-increasing worry of losing everything I had, because my story told me I did not deserve those things, was a hypothetical catastrophe that became crippling. This imposter mindset that was driving my work ethic was a psychological burden that I could not carry around forever—especially with a career, a team to lead as a manager, and a family to take care of. Without therapy, I could not confront or untangle these narratives to form a healthier inner dialogue for my mental wellbeing.

I had no knowledge of Stoicism until much later in life and I would not seek the help of a therapist until I was 35 years old. If someone handed me a copy of *Happy* or *Meditations* in my earlier years, I would have thrown it in the bin—"a load of old nonsense", I would have said. I was convinced by my story.

That said, my fear, insecurity, anxiety and gratitude meant I never took opportunities for granted. Even the drive and determination that got me through my studies and the early stages of my career were a product of that imposter voice in my head. There's no self-pity here, this was part of my journey.

Rather than seeing this psychological journey as a harrowing or negative experience, it is one that I have chosen to reflect on constructively. It was a process through which I flourished. We shouldn't view these dynamics of the human psyche with anguish, resentment, shame or disapproval. We should learn to grow from them and support each other in developing our collective ability to manage our minds.

Given these characteristics are shared traits of the human psyche, it is more important that we appreciate how culture and circumstance can significantly harness these habitual patterns of thinking and behaving—for better or worse. More awareness of these factors in our personal and collective psychology can help develop cultural environments that are more conducive to human flourishing.

Hindsight and Reflection

In hindsight, when reflecting on my educational and psychological journey, the words of Marcus Aurelius resonate: "Our actions may be impeded, but there can be no impeding our intentions or our dispositions. Because we can accommodate and adapt. The mind adapts and converts to its own purposes the obstacle to our acting. The impeding to action advances action. What stands in the way, becomes the way".[56]

Rather than seeing life's challenges as difficulties to avoid, feelings to deny or hardships to resign to, Marcus Aurelius saw them as opportunities that we use to grow and flourish through endurance, patience and resilience. For Marcus Aurelius, hardships become opportunities to learn more about ourselves through action—by applying those Stoic virtues of wisdom, justice, courage and temperance.

As individuals and collectives, some experiences we have are unpleasant but there are often lessons to learn and opportunities to develop. What we should avoid is the presumption that our thoughts and actions will always provide the outcome we desire. We must be ready to reflect and learn—to pursue justice for ourselves and society.

As we shall see in Chap. 4, our culture feeds us many messages that do not sit well with this philosophical grounding offered by the Stoics. The cultures in which we live play games with our minds. Our minds operate as a blend of conscious and unconscious tensions that accommodate a number of mixed messages that we are bombarded with in daily life. These messages encourage us to think in particular ways that are not always conducive to human flourishing.

Many ideas about human consciousness and the universe have survived over time—some of them we need to hang on to or be reminded of, while others we would be better off without. The latter have created a problem that Brown is concerned with. There is an industry telling us we can be happy while often selling us a story that might not be as conducive to happiness as we are told. In fact, it might even be making us unhappy. Brown has made it his business to critically intervene and object to some of the messages we are sold by the self-help industry.

Notes

1. Zeno was a wealthy dye merchant who lost his fortune when he was shipwrecked off the coast of Greece. Zeno made his way to Athens where he approached a bookseller and began to read Xenephon's *Memorabilia*. Impressed by Xenephon's account of Socrates, Zeno began to study philosophy under one of the Cynics, called Crates of Thebes. Zeno spent a decade studying various schools of philosophy under a number of teachers before beginning his own teaching in the Athenian marketplace. While there are similarities between the Cynics and Stoics, Zeno incorporated the wisdom of multiple teachers to establish a distinct school of philosophy that was more politically engaged and driven by virtue and social duty. By acting in accordance to virtue and accepting that some social norms were beyond their control, the Stoics would not advocate the social disruptiveness endorsed by their Cynic predecessors. Hence, Stoicism became the preferred school of philosophy that was apt for coping with adversity through virtuous behaviour.

2. As Brad Inwood (2018: 84) points out: "There is a stereotype of Stoicism familiar to everyone, the claim that Stoicism involves being relentlessly rational, but without a trace of emotion—Mr Spock from Star Trek, only more so. That this isn't the right view of Stoicism is now generally understood, and specialists will even point out that the passions (pathē) from which the Stoic wise person is said to be free are not what we mean by emotions but a more narrowly defined group of states of mind that are by definition pathological. The wise person may well be perfectly rational, but that doesn't deprive him or her of all affective or emotional experience".
3. Robertson, 2019: 43.
4. Sherman, 2021: 80.
5. *Meditations*, 9.6 (this particular translation can be found in Holiday and Hanselman, 2016:12).
6. Brown, 2016a: 86.
7. In de Botton's case, he established The School of Life to help people lead more resilient and fulfilled lives for the benefit of individuals and broader society. For more information on the globally established *School of Life*, visit: https://www.theschooloflife.com
8. Brown, 2016a: 88; Evans, 2013: 21.
9. Evans, 2013: X.
10. For a more rigorous exploration of the Socratic method, including detailed examples of how it influenced Stoicism, see: Farnsworth, 2021. For a manual on practicing Stoicism in everyday life, see also: Farnsworth, 2018.
11. Holiday, 2019: 98–99.
12. Brown, 2017.
13. Daily Stoic, 2020a.
14. Epictetus, 2007.
15. Epictetus, 2012.
16. Seneca, 2004.
17. Brown, 2016b.
18. Gloyn, 2018.
19. Brown, 2020a.
20. Brown, 2016a: 177.
21. Ibid.: 177.
22. Brown, 2020b.
23. Wittman, 2020a.
24. Holiday, 2020a.

25. Wittman, 2020b.
26. Holiday, 2019: 21.
27. Holiday, 2016: 8. It is important to note that Holiday is not discussing the ego in reference to Jung or other psychoanalytical theory. Rather, he is referring to a specific form of ego, and a more common point of reference in popular culture, which points to the destructive and selfish traits of negative "egotistical" behaviour.
28. Holiday, 2014: 37.
29. Ibid.: 33.
30. Holiday, 2020c.
31. Epictetus, 2012: 3.
32. Aurelius, Collier, Dacier, Gataker, 1726: 155.
33. Aurelius, 1998: 40.
34. Brown, 2016a: 22.
35. Ibid.: 22.
36. Ibid.: 22.
37. Brown, 2016a: 165.
38. Ibid.: 165.
39. Holiday.
40. Brown, 2016a: 165.
41. Quoted by Robertson (2020) in relation to cognition and emotion.
42. On this point, Graver (2007) provides an extensive inquiry into Stoicism and emotion.
43. Holiday, 2014: 30.
44. Robertson (2020).
45. Sherman, 2021: 80.
46. Robertson, 2019: 42.
47. Ibid.: 42.
48. Brown, 2016a: 167.
49. Pigliucci, 2017: 11.
50. Brown, 2016a: 75.
51. Brown, 2016a: 19.
52. Ibid.: 19.
53. Ibid.: 18.
54. Brown, 2019d.
55. Thank you to Matt Bailey for his generous guidance and support during my first year at university.
56. Aurelius, 2002: 60.

Bibliography

Aurelius, M. (1998). *Meditations*. University Press.
Aurelius, M. (2002). *Meditations*. Penguin.
Aurelius, M. Collier, J., Dacier, A., & Gataker, T. (1726). The emperor Marcus Antoninus: His conversation with himself.
Brown, D. (2016a). *Happy: Why more or less everything is absolutely fine*. Penguin.
Brown, D. (2016b). New Derren Brown "Happy" book interview. *BBC Breakfast*. https://www.youtube.com/watch?v=ay7IyqQLjtg
Brown, D. (2017). *Renowned illusionist Derren Brown on stoicism and why more or less everything is absolutely fine*. https://dailystoic.com/derren-brown/
Brown, D. (2019d). *The Adam Buxton podcast*. Ep.110: Derren Brown. https://www.adam-buxton.co.uk/podcasts/17
Brown, D. (2020a). *The path to less stress? Strategic pessimism. | Derren Brown | Big Think*. https://www.youtube.com/watch?v=wKfUK1Gd6YM
Brown, D. (2020b). Derren Brown's new book offers advice on overcoming anxiety. *Sky News*. https://www.youtube.com/watch?v=lKqwl4hb-ew
Epictetus. (2007). *Art of living: The classical manual on virtue, happiness, and effectiveness*. HarperCollins.
Epictetus. (2012). *Discourses and selected writings*. Penguin.
Evans, J. (2013). *Philosophy for life: And other dangerous situations*. Rider.
Farnsworth, W. (2018). *The practicing Stoic: A philosophical user's manual*. Godine.
Farnsworth, W. (2021). *The socratic method: A practitioner's handbook*. Godine.
Gloyn, L. (2018). Stoicism and the family by Liz Gloyn. *Modern Stoicism*. https://modernstoicism.com/stoicism-and-the-family-by-liz-gloyn/
Graver, M. (2007). *Stoicism and emotion*. University Press.
Holiday, R. (2014). *The obstacle is the way: The ancient art of turning adversity into advantage*. Profile.
Holiday, R. (2016). *The ego is the enemy: The fight to master our greatest opponent*. Profile.
Holiday, R. (2019). *Stillness is the key: An ancient strategy for modern life*. Profile.
Holiday, R. (2020a). Daily Stoic Sundays: 10 of the most Stoic moments in history. *The Daily Stoic Podcast*. https://dailystoic.com/daily-stoic-sundays-10-of-the-most-stoic-moments-in-history/
Holiday, R. (2020c). *7 benefits of adopting a Stoic practice in 2020*. https://dailystoic.com/benefits-stoicism/
Holiday, R., & Hanselman, S. (2016). *The daily Stoic: 366 meditations on wisdom, perseverance, and the art of living*. Penguin.

Inwood, B. (2018). *Stoicism: A very brief introduction*. University Press.
Pigliucci, M. (2017). *How to be a Stoic: Ancient wisdom for modern living*. Rider Books.
Robertson, D. (2019). *How to think like a Roman emperor*. St Martin's.
Robertson, D. (2020). *The difference between stoicism and Stoicism*. https://medium.com/stoicism-philosophy-as-a-way-of-life/the-difference-between-stoicism-and-stoicism-907ee9e35dc5
Seneca. (2004). *Letters from a Stoic*. Penguin.
Sherman, N. (2021). *Stoic wisdom: Ancient lessons for modern resilience*. University Press.
Wittman, T. (2020a). *Justin Gaethje's coach Trevor Wittman reacts to Khabib weighing in and previews UFC 254 card*. https://www.youtube.com/watch?v=Hzaev5R6uBM
Wittman, T. (2020b). *UFC 254: Trevor Wittman pre-fight interview*. https://www.youtube.com/watch?v=B3V2Wz9LY68

4

Self-Help and Popular Culture

Brown has described *Happy* as an anti-self-help book. The self-help industry bombards us with books and messages about how to live happier lives. But it isn't always helpful advice. Celebrity endorsements of self-help methods and mythologies in popular culture create communicative tensions in our collective psyche, feeding messages of hope and optimism that are often, somewhat ironically, detrimental to our happiness. As a result, we now have a growing body of anti-self-help literature telling us to ditch the positive thinking, cut the endless fixation on goal-setting and live more resiliently in the face of life's inevitable adversity.[1]

Celebrities who tell mystical stories about secret laws in the universe and the magnetic power of positive thinking often tap into the psyches of hopeful self-help consumers who painfully fall for the confirmation bias of celebrity success stories.[2] Those advocates and followers of Rhonda Byrne's *The Secret*, for example, rarely stop to ask where the unsuccessful people are—those who tried to "think positive" but didn't try hard enough and failed to attract fortune, fame and success.

This positive thinking model of self-help has been critiqued as an unhelpful hangover from our Protestant past, which the author and political activist, Barbara Ehrenreich, argues has had a particularly detrimental impact on American society.[3] We shall return to this point later in this chapter. For now, let's consider Brown's response to the problems with positive thinking, which often occur in messages endorsed by the self-help industry. When pseudoscientific claims—that are often apparent in the "magical thinking" of some self-help texts—dupe and mislead their victims, we see the darker side of the magician archetype functioning through the form of shadow-magic.

When enlightened, a magician typically uses their performative skills, intellectual knowledge, intuitive tendencies, healthy scepticism and visionary talents to the benefit of others. As Moore and Gillette would put it, this is the magician's bullshit detector in practice. In this case, Brown attempts to shed light on the shadows of illusive self-help dupes, dreams, false promises and pseudoscience.

An Antidote to the Self-Help Industry

As we saw in the previous chapter, Brown makes a convincing case for Stoicism as a philosophy for life, and his work here steered us towards other authors who provide valuable insights on the Stoics. Brown adopted this approach as an anti-dote to the messages often sold to us by the self-help industry. Reflecting on why he wrote *Happy*, he states:

> I had internalized the thinking of the Stoics and built on and fleshed out my own undeveloped thoughts on the matter of what happiness might mean. I felt they offered a much more helpful message than the nonsense of 'believe in yourself and set goals' and so on, which leads to so much feeling of failure and confusion. I wanted to offer a therapeutic message that I felt was of far deeper worth than the panicked and ill-thought through messages we are fed today by that self-help world.[4]

While Brown accepts that an element of short-term goal-setting in life can be helpful and pragmatic, he is concerned that we are encouraged to set goals too often in life—especially in our long-term pursuit of happiness. Instead, he suggests we should be more critically reflective about what goals we pursue, how and why we pursue them, and the sense of purpose and meaning that those goals provide us with.

Brown believes that the positive thinking model of happiness that is often sold to us by the self-help industry pulls us into a trap of pursuing the allusive dream of happiness "out there" in the world. Instead, with the help of the Stoics, Brown encourages us to endorse an element of strategic pessimism in our lives.

Strategic Pessimism

Neurologist and psychoanalyst, Sigmund Freud did not set out to make his patients permanently happy. Rather, he wanted his patients to sit more comfortably with unhappiness as an inevitable part of life.[5] Similarly, Jung did not view neurosis an exclusively negative form that should be eliminated from the psyche.[6] Rather, he viewed anxiety disorders as opportunities for change and growth by learning from what they mean and why they happen.[7]

With reference to Freud and Jung throughout his work, Brown offers a "strategic pessimism" that is cautious of any pursuit for unnatural happiness; fostering a sense of tranquillity (ataraxia) in which we can cope with, rather than completely avoid, disturbance in our lives. Writing for the *Daily Stoic*, Brown states the importance of understanding "natural unhappiness" through an element of pessimism:

> When Freud created psychoanalysis, he had no intention of making people happy: it was to restore 'natural unhappiness'. Life, he felt, warrants some pessimism. Nowadays we look to be unnaturally happy and we worry that we've failed if we're not. The Greeks lived and breathed all this because they of course understood tragedy. Today, we pretend that fortune doesn't exist or wield any power, and thus we end up with a very inflated attitude towards our desires and how the world should accommodate them.[8]

This principle is evident both in Brown's criticism of the self-help industry and the alternative philosophy that he turns to instead. One of those philosophers—who was not a Stoic but does feature in Brown's work due to his strategically pessimistic outlook—was Arthur Schopenhauer. Commonly known as a philosopher of pessimism, Schopenhauer proposed that in a world of inevitable suffering and adversity, humans could exercise their intellect and ability to reason in order to rise above our baser instincts and the pertinacious nature of what he called "the Will"—a primal, driving force behind everything that exists in the universe.[9]

Similarly, as Donald Robertson points out, the Stoics described our ability to reason as our "ruling faculty". Like a king holding court, our reason enables us to identify what elements of our human nature are best for our wellbeing and responsibilities. It is natural to hold certain desires and urges, but our reason—our inner king that gives us sovereignty to decide how we order our desires and urges—enables us to rise above the baser instincts and pursue wiser pathways for ourselves and others.[10]

Brown feels we can take valuable lessons from Schopenhauer to establish a mindset that is conducive to living a more considered and tranquil life: by not pursuing egotistically driven desires or concerning ourselves with the trivial opinions of others, we can turn our attention to self-enquiry where we can engage more deeply with our inner story about who we are and how we live.

This can help us to develop a more tranquil mindset through which we find pleasure in a sense of kindness to ourselves and to others. For Brown, we can follow this principle to accept that life is more complex, adverse and ambiguous than we are often inclined to acknowledge—we needn't be too hard on ourselves or think too highly of ourselves either.

Brown makes the case that if we take some of Schopenhauer's advice as prudent pessimism, we can realistically appraise our strengths and weaknesses with "neither self-aggrandisement nor abnegation, and reflect upon our inevitable failings with kindness and good humour". This is where Brown believes we can find that sense of ataraxia that the Stoics sought.

On this basis, in contrast to the advice we are often sold by the self-help industry, Brown sees happiness as something that we do. Happiness is not so much an object we obtain through the pursuit of external desires—it's not a noun; it's a verb.

The Verb of Happiness

For Brown, happiness is about *how* we live, not *what* we can get. Our actions can provide us with a sense of meaning and purpose, while our appreciation of the present moment can enable us to enjoy an absence of disturbance that the Stoics advocated through more robust authorship of our inner dialogue. When we recognise that happiness is a verb, we can appreciate that it is not the illusive object on the horizon; it is not a perfect point of life that we finally reach. It is not the existential Holy Grail that we are often told to pursue through endless goals, dreams and visions. We can be happy *now*.[11]

Throughout his work, Brown has argued that partly due to our consumer mindset, our sense of entitlement in modern life often leads us down a blind alley through our misconceptions of what happiness really is and where it can be found:

> All the things we think will supply [Happiness]—the goals we set, or the wanting to be a millionaire, or to retire—don't. They rarely end up supplying the goods when we get there. Rather than seeing it as a thing, we should see it more as the absence of disturbances or anxieties. The pre-Christian ideal which pervaded philosophy is that people used to see happiness as tranquillity, as calmness that remains when disturbances are avoided.[12]

Brown's concern here is that the self-help industry's common focus on positive thinking and goal-setting often sets us up for failure and disappointment in ourselves.

This is not to suggest we shouldn't have goals and ambitions, but we should avoid the belief that those goals contain happiness like an object that we try to obtain. Goals are somewhat inevitable since we aim for objectives and desired outcomes to guide our short-term and long-term plans in life. If we enrol on a degree programme, for example, our goal is to graduate with the best grade we can. If we go into a new career, then we often aim to progress through promotions and rewards for our hard work.

But Brown is not advocating laziness, apathy or indifference. Rather, he is concerned with *how* and *why* we pursue our goals, and *what* we believe those achievements will do for us. He often uses his own work as an example of what makes him happy throughout the creative process. Whether a show or book or painting sells well or is highly rated is not the prime focus for Brown—these are outcomes rather than actions and the latter is where the pleasure lies.

In many cultures, professions, institutions, families and other social environments, an unwavering sense of self-belief and a relentless focus on goal-setting is often viewed by those around us (and even praised and encouraged) as admirable determination. But Brown urges some caution here and warns that this work ethic can only take us so far.

He believes we should enjoy our stories rather than focusing on their endings. In the opening narration of *Miracle*, he states the importance of appreciating the present moment:

> Now. This moment, right now. Is all there ever is. Any book on happiness is likely to tell you to set clear goals on what you want to achieve and then work towards achieving them. The problem is; it doesn't really work. You might become a millionaire by the time you're forty but then you realize you haven't been able to sustain a happy relationship. Or when it doesn't work out you feel lost and you blame yourself. When we live for our goals we forget to live now.[13]

Brown provides the example of philosopher Allan Watts who made the point that when you listen to a piece of music you don't just skip to the end because that's where it all comes together. Likewise, as he explains, we don't read the last chapter of a book so that we can skip straight to the climax. But our narrative building tendency leads us back to that focus on endings. We study for our exams, perhaps so we can go to university, in order to get a job, and then work our way up in our career—continually unable to enjoy one ending before we find the next narrative stage is drawn up before us.

As Brown points out, those happy endings we are constantly working towards never really arrive as the rainbow continually leaps back to the horizon, always beyond our reach. Suddenly, we are in our fifties and asking ourselves what we have been working towards for all those years. Brown urges us to remember that our lives should be more like music; whatever the ending might be, we can dance along in the here and now. But the problem, he argues, is that we are constantly lured in by a lingering work ethic from our Protestant past.

Our Protestant Past

Brown argues that the self-help industry's continual promotion of positive thinking and goal-setting reflects the historical and philosophical shifts that occurred through the rise of Christianity. With the Calvinist movement as one example, particularly in American culture, Brown argues that this work ethic remains influential in the self-help industry and how we often think as a society.[14]

As he explains, the opposite of Stoicism is positive thinking and blind optimism: the idea that by believing in yourself and setting goals, you can bring the world into line with your aims. In reality, the latter is not the case. While this approach might keep us focused and determined for occasional short-term goals, it is ultimately setting us up for disappointment and a feeling of personal failure—since it seeks to influence elements of fate that are beyond our control. As Brown points out, this "idea of 'Believe in yourself! Set your goals! Keep believing in yourself!' is still based on a lingering ghost of the Protestant past".[15]

To provide a further example of this, author and political activist, Barbara Ehrenreich critically examines this problem that Brown points to in the hangover of our Protestant past.[16] Ehrenreich traces this model of positive thinking back to the ideological doctrine of Christian Science and the New Thought Movement—with a particular focus on the Calvinist movement in America. She shows how this ideological doctrine of positive thinking has continued to morph through modern-day movements and gurus, from prosperity-gospel preachers to corporate motivational speakers.

It is not that the likes of Brown and Ehrenreich are promoting doom and gloom messages here. But they do address the problems with a particular model of positive thinking that does not realistically face the realities of life—neither providing us with the personal robustness to face adversity nor instilling the collective will to acknowledge wider injustices that lie beyond the blame or responsibility of individuals.

As Ehrenreich rightly points out, positive thinking is not the same as existential courage. Courage is not blind faith, hope or optimism, but rather a virtuous commitment to worthy causes—a duty to ourselves and others who need us—through the pursuit for wisdom and justice in the world.[17]

Another concern with the self-help industry's lingering ghosts of our past is the pseudoscientific doctrine that has morphed through those movements over time: a dogma that tells its believers that our thoughts and visualisations can control external forces in the universe. The Law of Attraction is an idea that has become increasingly prevalent in popular culture, often via celebrity endorsement. I shall focus on this phenomenon for the rest of this chapter in order to show how messy our minds get and how our culture constantly bombards us with that infinite data source of noise and confusing advice on how to live well.

The Law of Attraction

Rhonda Byrne's *The Secret* is one example of Brown and Ehrenreich's concerns here. *The Secret* goes as far as suggesting that positive visualisation and the Law of Attraction will magnetise good fortune through "mind frequencies" that send out positive signals to the universe.[18] Much like the faith healers that he has exposed throughout his career, Brown calls out the pseudoscience of a confidence trick that is played on audiences. This is a common trait of the archetypal magician in its enlightened form: unlike the magician's shadow, it expresses the tendency to detect and expose a confidence trick rather than duping and misleading the audience.

The Law of Attraction first appeared in a late nineteenth-century book written by the Russian occultist, Helena Blavatsky.[19] Blavatsky was describing what she deemed to be a special power that exists between elements of spirit and external entities in the universe, which the human mind could connect with. Just a few years later, the humourist author,

Prentice Mulford wrote about the Law of Attraction as a key principle for the New Thought movement in his essay, titled, "The Law of Success".[20] Mulford was a respected figure in the field and a number of New Thought authors followed with their endorsement, which continued to gain significant attention throughout the twentieth century when a number of popular books were written about it.[21]

Drawing on the Law of Attraction, *The Secret* claims that through "positive visualisation" we can attract what we desire. According to this principle, if we do not think positively enough—or worse still, if we think negatively or lack self-belief—then we will fail to attract those positive outcomes. In other words, our fate, wealth and fortune are dependent on the power of our positive thoughts and how strongly we visualise ourselves obtaining what we desire.

As Brown points out, those who insist that *The Secret* works by providing examples from their own lives are exercising the most selective confirmation bias they can possibly apply. By cherry-picking those instances where they claim to have received what they desired through positive visualisation, they ignore all the other instances where the Law of Attraction failed them. Alternatively, any time the Law of Attraction doesn't work, the individual can just be blamed for not visualising positively enough, adding further weight to one's baggage of self-doubt and disappointment.

Brown makes the point that Byrne's endorsement of this mystical pseudoscience reflects a source of great anxiety in our culture: the temptation to try to control those things that are beyond our control.

Blame and Failure

This tendency is detrimental to happiness because it stimulates feelings of disconnect and hopelessness when we cry out for more influence over our destiny than fate allows. Like many critics of positive thinking in self-help literature, Brown argues that it consequently leads to a destructive cycle of self-blame and condemnation when things don't go to plan: "Byrne's system would be bad enough if it simply reneged on its promises, but, like the promise of the [faith] healers, it is particularly foul for placing the blame for its inevitable failure on its poor victims."[22]

This self-blame and disillusionment creates the psychological burdens that feed our fears and anxieties of powerlessness and isolation in society. These socially disconnecting traits among disempowered and disillusioned individuals are detrimental to our collective psychology. As discussed earlier, we need to increase feelings of connection, inclusion, inner control and empowerment rather than mystifying these elements through the mythologising of mysterious external energies and forces in the universe.

The misleading guidance of these self-help narratives often encourage the antithesis of what Brown is proposing through lessons offered in ancient philosophy. As Brown points out, it is our human tendency and desire to control things beyond our control that magicians, scam artists, faith healers and other charlatans have exploited for centuries. Its advocates who knowingly offer pseudoscientific claims are prime examples of the archetypal shadow magician at work; trust, power and "knowledge" are abused to dupe people for other financial and egotistical gains. Likewise, those enlightened magicians of our culture have their own tendency to expose those charlatans and fraudsters that prey on our vulnerabilities.

Kicking and Screaming

When we are duped by The Law of Attraction it exploits our inner child as we scream out to the world in the hope it will meet our needs. Brown alludes to this role of the inner child to show how *The Secret* affects us through a form of denialism that *insists* we can control fate to cater for our needs and desires. As Brown points out, this is not a healthy way for us to behave (or hope) as adults. Neither is this conducive to understanding the genuine autonomy that we do have over our actions and the grounding that can connect us with a sense of legitimate sovereignty in ourselves.

When our inner child screams out like this, we compromise our sovereignty. As the entrepreneur and futurist writer, Jordan Hall points out, during infancy our sovereignty is minuscule; our survival is entirely dependent on other people helping us so that we can develop our own sovereignty. Hall reminds us how important it is for us to grow and protect our sovereignty in order to maximise our autonomy and agency when we need to take responsibility for the future of our personal lives, communities, society and the planet.

When we desperately continue to think positively in the hope that mystical forces in the universe will hear and respond to our needs, our sovereignty is minimalised and our infancy is brought back to the forefront where those feelings of disempowerment and vulnerability are reignited. When the inner and outer crises that we face seem overwhelming, we are more likely to slip into a mindset that makes unrealistic demands on the world around us. We then become resentful when the world fails to deliver on those needs despite the fact that we believe we are kicking hard enough and screaming loud enough to be heard.

But despite its flawed mysticism, *The Secret* is a popular text has reflects a common narrative in self-help literature and has received significant celebrity endorsement. The alluring glamour and glitz of celebrity success stories accommodate a narrative appeal to the envious voyeurism of our egos.

Self-Help and Celebrity

The Law of Attraction has been endorsed by numerous celebrities, including Oprah Winfrey, Arnold Schwarzenegger and Jim Carrey. However, even these figures have said that this belief in positive thinking needs to be accompanied with actions—we cannot just sit and wait for wealth and good fortune while thinking positively and visualising what we want in the hope that our "brain frequencies" will call out and magnetise what we want.

Nonetheless, the mysticism creeps in, and the belief that we can control our fate (beyond action) is what this narrative alludes to. It suggests there is more at play than actions and fate because positive thinking is rewarded when the *outer world* responds to the energy that you create from the thoughts of your *inner world*.

A case in point here is UFC fighter, Conor McGregor, who endorsed the Law of Attraction and positive visualisation early on in his career. McGregor is a former UFC double world champion from Ireland who was renowned for his flamboyant press conferences, fighting flare and mystic persona when he regularly predicted the outcomes of his earlier fights. During his rise to global fame, he talked about the Law of Attraction as if its mystical qualities offered him a powerful source of external energy that he tapped into through positive visualisation.

I have been fascinated by McGregor's public persona for some time and have written about his mythos in previous research on this topic.[23] After winning his first world title, McGregor transcended the sport of mixed martial arts to become a global superstar. But much has happened in his life since then. The Law of Attraction worked as a powerful narrative tool in his public persona, but McGregor's story reflects some of the downsides and problems that Brown alludes to. Let's consider McGregor as a short case study to explore this phenomenon and the tensions between these different mindsets that Brown has discussed so far.

The Conor McGregor Story

In my previous research I wrote about the role of *The Secret* in the mythos and persona of McGregor. I was interested in McGregor's public appearances, his popularity in Ireland and how his story resonated with fans and audiences within and beyond the UFC. I was particularly intrigued by the *metaphorical* role that The Law of Attraction played as a narrative tool, motivational concept and mystical spectacle in McGregor's mythos—despite its flaws and misconceptions. At the same time, I had not entertained any possibility that it was scientifically rational, pragmatically plausible or persuasive.

McGregor endorsed the Law of Attraction after his sister recommended *The Secret* and talked about using positive visualisation to picture himself becoming a rich and successful world champion. He once said:

> I have always had visions of better. I've always visualised better, and in times of struggle. Driving around in a banger of a car that I had to push

4 Self-Help and Popular Culture   85

start, I would still be [visualising] riding a soft-top Bentley around beautiful California in my head. And low and behold, now I am driving a beautiful soft-top Bentley around California. I always visualise good things. I always visualise victory, success, abundance. I visualised it all and it's all happening.[24]

Here's another example of McGregor responding to a question in a press conference after he had accurately predicted the outcome of a fight he had just won for his first UFC world title:

If you can see it here [in your head] and you have the courage enough to speak it, it will happen. I see these shots, I see these sequences, and I don't shy away from them. A lot of times people believe in certain things but they keep it to themselves, they don't put it out there. If you truly believe in it and you become vocal with it, you are creating that Law of Attraction and it will become reality.[25]

McGregor has also talked about the time when he was stuck in a traffic jam and was going to be late for a flight so he visualised the traffic clearing—miraculously, the traffic cleared and he made his flight. Likewise, he would visualise a parking space being available next to a store he'd be visiting—sometimes it worked, sometimes it didn't.

Of course, it never literally "worked". His thoughts had no control over parking spaces or traffic jams. Only some crude confirmation bias can suggest otherwise. Nonetheless, McGregor has described these instances as him "practising" positive visualisation as a way of focusing his mind on his plan of action—perhaps suggesting that he values it as a meditation for concentrating on the task at hand, rather than a literal belief in mysterious forces and frequencies connected between our minds and the universe. But we have a tendency to add these mystical narrative layers to our stories that can, in reality, only be explained by our actions (within our control) combined with fate (beyond our control).[26]

Our egos construct a world in which we can take the credit for everything when positive thinking chimes with positive outcomes. But as Brown points out, the Law of Attraction only provides a helpful story while things are going well. It was fine for McGregor when he was accurately predicting the outcomes of his fights and calling himself "Mystic Mac". It was genuinely impressive when he delivered on the performances and victories that he visualised and vocalised—the *metaphor* worked splendidly as a narrative spectacle. When things were going well, this was a powerful narrative for his public persona, fame and ego. But this story was not sustainable.

Narrative, Ego and Persona

McGregor's ego and persona appeared to be as damaged as his career when things went wrong. After winning the UFC Lightweight title in 2016 and becoming the UFC's first ever double champion in two weight classes at the same time, McGregor did not appear in the Octagon again until 2018, when he lost to Khabib Nurmagomedov. During his time away from the octagon, McGregor had also been defeated in a boxing match with Floyd Mayweather. Arrests, court appearances, assault charges, vandalism and other accusations followed as common news stories about McGregor who appeared to have gone off the rails.

Prior to his comeback fight, due to an ongoing feud with his prospective opponent, McGregor had attacked a UFC bus with Nurmagomedov on board—throwing a dolly through the bus window, injuring other fighters who shared no involvement in the conflict with his rival. With McGregor's narrative and legacy fractured, his popularity waivered significantly. His usual pre-fight bravado had lost the entertaining quick-whit and rhetorical flare that fans had come to know and love. The controversies and incidents he became embroiled in were nasty and distasteful. This was not the showmanship that his fans were used to and it seemed his fractured ego was running the show. By McGregor's own admission, it felt like a "knife to the heart" when he heard that the Irish fans were beginning to lose faith in him.

It was not until 2020 that McGregor reappeared with a seemingly refined mindset. Rather than the usual trash talking, mental warfare, bravado and intimidation tactics that audiences were used to hearing before his fights, McGregor had been apologetic in public following the controversies of recent years. He significantly toned down his act and pre-fight spectacle. He carried a humble and more reserved persona with a respectful attitude towards his opponent during the build up to his UFC comeback fight against Donald Cowboy Cerrone. McGregor was talking openly about the life coaching he had received from Tony Robbins, and began to share a different philosophical outlook than he had previously vocalised. He reflected on some of his negative behaviour, his neglect towards his inner self and his preoccupation with external factors, material objects and the opinions of others.

The Outer World of Fame and Fortune

Reflecting on the chaos of recent events at the time, McGregor talked openly about how he'd become emotionally invested in factors beyond his control—allowing the outer world to disrupt his inner peace and dialogue. This was by no means an open endorsement of Stoicism, but it did reflect a psychological shift that placed an emphasis on those principles that resonate in a more Stoic mindset. In an interview with journalist Ariel Halwani, he said:

> Nothing external can defeat the internal. The only thing that can take someone down or break you down is internal. Nothing external is strong enough. It is just about making sure your internal dialogue and your internal belief in yourself is strong enough. ... Nothing can infiltrate my internal thoughts, no external.[27]

In the same interview he recalled how early on in his career he would laugh off the negativity of other people's stories and opinions about him, but as time went on, he gradually got drawn in, emotionally invested and preoccupied with other people's perceptions and opinions. He eventually snapped and allowed those external factors to control his emotions. McGregor's self-reflective ethos at the time suggested he had returned to his inner self to seek that robustness and tranquillity, which we find if we force our egos to let go of those things beyond our control.

What was interesting here was the way in which McGregor's statement still reflected the unwavering self-belief that Brown is wary of. But it was expressed through McGregor's distinction between the inner and outer worlds that were discussed earlier. It reflected the importance of not reacting or investing emotions in things beyond our control. Whether McGregor maintains this refined mindset or not is another matter.[28] But his turbulent persona throughout the journey of his career—with his explicit attention to the psychology of sport and fighting—has reflected the drifting and shifting mindsets that we often move in and out of over time, as we try to make sense of everything that life throws at us.

Our minds get entangled in multiple narratives, habits and persuasions that can often accommodate mixed traits of different philosophical influences. That's not to suggest we always consciously learn these philosophies in a pedagogical or scholarly manner. But these ideas float around in our culture, and our minds reflect those different behavioural and cognitive patterns of thinking that appear through various philosophies and messages among the infinite data source that Brown speaks of.

For many of us, most of the time our minds are not clear-cut endorsements of one particular philosophy. Nor do they operate through static psychological complexes. The likes of Marcus Aurelius and Seneca did not live faultlessly Stoic lives that were never hindered by anxiety, anger or a temporary lapse of composure and discipline. As William Irvine points out in *A Guide to the Good Life*:

> When we measure our progress as Stoics, we might find that it is slower than we had hoped or expected. The Stoics, though, would be the first to admit that people can't perfect their Stoicism overnight. Indeed, even if we practice Stoicism all our life, we are unlikely to perfect it; there will always be room for improvement.[29]

Irvine refers to Seneca as an example of someone practicing Stoicism without the expectation of becoming a sage; rather, Seneca saw his personal progress as an adequate way of reducing his daily vices while acknowledging his own mistakes.

The Stoics were real people with real flaws. We should acknowledge those flaws and failings too. Prior to Seneca's admirable final stand against Nero, a stand that would ultimately cost him his life, he spent many years in complicity with Nero's wrongdoing. Marcus Aurelius had failings as a parent. As Ryan Holiday points out: "To study the past is not just to pick what you like and be inspired by it. The pursuit of wisdom demands that we look at the failures too".[30]

Philosophies for life provide an ideal way of living that we aspire to. Those virtues from 2000 years ago float in and out of our times and the messages we are fed through popular culture. Some people have the discipline to live according to a particular philosophy in a conscious and committed manner, but for most of us this is seldom the case, and none of us is perfect regardless of our aspirations.

In terms of celebrity self-help narratives, audiences are often the ones who decide what story they want to tell about the motivational traits of figures like McGregor.

Paradoxical Mindsets

Even when McGregor endorsed *The Secret*, various videos on YouTube made the case that McGregor reflected a Stoic mindset.[31] These would feature McGregor talking about the importance of gratitude, making a point of not concerning himself with factors beyond his control, valuing voluntary discomfort, managing his perceptions and emotions and sharing his sense of inner sovereignty. "Improvise, adapt and overcome" was a common mantra that McGregor would refer to in his preparation and training before fights.

Despite McGregor's talk of money and cars, desiring material objects, and his belief in the Law of Attraction, he has been equally vocal about the importance of appreciating what you have in the present moment and not taking things for granted—family, friends, teammates, success and circumstance. In June 2015, before he had won either of his world titles, he tweeted: "Be grateful with everything you have and you will be successful in everything you do."

Other videos on YouTube set out to show that the Law of Attraction worked for McGregor, holding him up as an example of the power of positive visualisation. There are paradoxical messages running through these different perceptions of McGregor's story. This is partly because audiences select those traits that fit into their mythos around celebrity figures and the psychology behind motivational success stories—celebrities are framed through narratives that reflect all kinds of ideological, mystical and philosophical persuasions.

At the same time, people themselves (myself included) are walking and talking contradictions—we shift between various mindsets and perceptions all the time, especially when we are not consciously applying philosophies for life. Despite the innate messiness and contradictions of our minds, we continually build tidy narratives about our lives and the lives of others.

McGregor's persona reflects many layers of contradiction and complexity that run through the human psyche. These are tensions that we all share and experience in different ways. The drama of celebrity culture might lead us to believe that the extremities of heroism and vilification are "out there" for us to be entertained by during the banality of our daily lives. But in reality, our potential for greatness and self-destruction in our own lives should not be overlooked.

It is easier to see the drama out there in the world of fame and fortune, but we all face trials and tribulations in our struggles as humans.

Trials and Tribulations

The extremities of human potential in their greatest and darkest forms are not only evident in the trials and tribulations of someone like McGregor. We are not fascinated by the drama of celebrity stardom because it is different to our world—on a deeper level, it *reflects* our world. In the most dramatic form, it projects characteristics of the psyche that are often banished to the shadows of the unconscious mind—our greatest and darkest potentials. In the next two chapters, I will focus on those unconscious shadow forms that Brown draws our attention to through the dramatic spectacles he constructs in his shows.

So far, we have seen Brown sharing his knowledge for the collective benefit, and we have seen him shed light on the shadow-magic of self-help literature. These next chapters will reflect another significant dynamic in Brown's archetypal role as the magician: guiding individuals through transformational journeys, facing trials and tribulations that teach us more about who we are and what we are capable of.

Notes

1. Brown, 2016a; Manson, 2016, Brinkmann, 2017; Ehrenreich.
2. Kelsey, 2018.
3. Ehrenreich, 2010.
4. Brown, 2017.
5. Freud, 2017.
6. Jung, C.G. (2019) 'Carl Jung and The Value of Anxiety Disorders'. *Academy of Ideas*. https://www.youtube.com/watch?v=WBAFPbypyn4
7. This is a position that Brown has developed further in his more recent work (see Brown, 2021).
8. Brown, 2017.
9. Schopenhauer, 1969.
10. Robertson, 2019: 40.
11. More recently, in *A Book of Secrets* (2021), Brown has applied this principle to the Self as a verb rather than a noun. Rather than identifying the Self as a fixed thing, he suggests it is more fluid since it is something that we *do* and act out differently through those varying and evolving personae that we adopt in different places and spaces. Our sense of Self also changes over time; it is not a static thing.
12. Brown, 2016b.
13. Brown, 2018.
14. Brown, 2016a, 2020.
15. Brown, 2020.
16. Ehrenreich, 2010.
17. Ibid. See also Holiday, 2021a.
18. *The Secret* was released as a book (Byrne, 2006a) and a film (Byrne, 2006b), both written by Rhonda Byrne.
19. Blavatsky, 1877.
20. Mulford, 1910.
21. Hill, 1937; Peale, 1952; Hay, 1984.
22. Brown, 2016a.
23. Kelsey, 2018.
24. Ibid.: 27.

25. Ibid.: 27.
26. Sometimes we are told that external, invisible forces are at play in the universe and are somehow connected to our thoughts, which influence our fate—this is a cultural trait that occurs within and beyond a text like *The Secret*. In fact, it is more present in our "rational" lives than we might think. Clay Routledge, an experimental psychologist at North Dakota State University, asserts that our need for transcendent meaning and our fear of death drives our innate and universal tendency to believe in the supernatural. In his book, *Supernatural: Death, Meaning and the Power of the Invisible World*, Routledge provides a comprehensive account of data showing how even people who identify as atheists often reflect a belief in the supernatural. Our culture exposes us to so many messages and we conjure up so many beliefs (consciously and unconsciously) that create constant tensions in our minds as we try to understand our sense of meaning, purpose and place in the world.
27. McGregor, 2020.
28. More recently, McGregor has been defeated twice by Dustin Poirier, with their second fight resulting in a severely broken leg for McGregor followed by major surgery. His temperament has been unpredictable and he has found himself embroiled in public conflicts with both Poirier and rapper, Machine Gun Kelly. His ongoing behaviour has been erratic and attracted further criticism from UFC peers, fans and the press.
29. Irvine, 2008: 124.
30. Holiday, 2021b.
31. https://www.youtube.com/watch?v=r1zyVGooNME / https://www.youtube.com/watch?v=6tZGFa3-uN8

Bibliography

Blavatsky, H. (1877). *Isis unveiled*. Theosophical University Press.
Brinkmann, S. (2017). *Stand firm*. Polity Press.
Brown, D. (2016a). *Happy: Why more or less everything is absolutely fine*. Penguin.
Brown, D. (2016b). Derren Brown: 'Performers can be shy and despite my dramatic stunts, in reality, I truly do not like the attention'. *The Belfast Telegraph*. https://www.belfasttelegraph.co.uk/entertainment/news/derren-brown-performers-can-be-shy-and-despite-my-dramatic-stunts-in-reality-i-truly-do-not-like-the-attention-35064763.html

Brown, D. (2017). *Renowned illusionist Derren Brown on stoicism and why more or less everything is absolutely fine*.https://dailystoic.com/derren-brown/
Brown, D. (2018). *Miracle*. Netflix.
Brown, D. (2020). *The path to less stress? Strategic pessimism.* | *Derren Brown* | *Big Think*. https://www.youtube.com/watch?v=wKfUK1Gd6YM
Brown, D. (2021). *A Book of Secrets: Finding Solace in a Stubborn World*. London: Penguin.
Byrne, R. (2006a). *The secret*. Atria.
Byrne, R. (2006b). *The secret*. Prime Time Productions.
Ehrenreich, B. (2010). *Bright-sided: How positive thinking is undermining America*. Picador.
Freud, S. (2017). *Studies in hysteria*. Penguin.
Hay, L. (1984). *You can heal your life*. Hay House.
Hill, N. (1937). *Think and grow rich*. The Ralston Society.
Holiday, R. (2021a). *Courage is calling: Fortune favours the brave*. Profile.
Holiday, R. (2021b). *You have to see both*. https://dailystoic.com/you-have-to-see-both/
Irvine, W. (2008). *A guide to the good life: The ancient art of Stoic joy*. University Press.
Kelsey, D. (2018). Affective mythology and 'the notorious' Conor McGregor: Monomyth, mysticism, and mixed martial arts. *Martial Arts Studies, 5*, 15–35.
Manson, M. (2016). *The subtle art of not giving a fuck*. HarperOne.
McGregor, C. (2020). *Conor McGregor on UFC 246, Khabib, Mayweather | extended interview*. Ariel Helwani's MMA Show https://www.youtube.com/watch?v=0lzbKIwLc8k.
Mulford, P. (1910). *Your forces and how to use them*. F. J. Needham.
Peale, N. V. (1952). *The power of positive thinking*. Vermilion.
Robertson, D. (2019). *How to think like a Roman emperor*. St Martin's.
Schopenhauer, A. (1969). *The world as will and representation, Vol. 1*. Dover: New York.

5

Angels and Demons

When Carl Jung talked about "individuation" he was concerned with the psychological development of an individual who could work on themselves to confront the deeper, unconscious aspects of their mind, which often get denied or suppressed from their conscious self.[1] Jung believed that we could only understand ourselves fully if we integrated our shadow (the unconscious mind) in order to control those deeper thoughts, persuasions, behaviours and characteristics that we are less comfortable accepting into our conscious minds.[2]

If they remain unconscious, Jung argued that our shadows simmer away beneath the surface and cause us problems beyond our conscious control as we fail to confront those repressed traits of our identity, our hidden fears, experiential resentments and unwelcome desires. As we see in various examples throughout Brown's work, our culture and upbringing contribute to this repression of certain traits as we learn the rules and codes of our society and what are deemed acceptable or unacceptable traits in our psyche. This might be in accordance to our gender, family values, schooling, sexuality or other personal and cultural characteristics.

Jung argued that these shadow potentials of our character would often appear through our *projections*: our judgements and enmity towards other people and groups who we cast blame and aspersions upon instead. Through individuation, Jung believed that by integrating the shadow we could understand and control our least desirable traits, enabling empathy with others and recognition of one's own flaws instead of exercising those projections and judgements stimulated by the shadow.

Jung argued that individuation enables us to reconnect with the outer world and make a better contribution to society. It is through this transformational struggle that we typically see heroes enduring through their trials and tribulations in popular stories. Heroes are human—they are flawed and imperfect so that we can relate to them.

We Want Heroes, Not Gods

In *20 Years of Mind Control*, Brown recounted a conversation he had with Teller (from the comedy magic duo, Penn and Teller) in which Teller compared magic with bad drama.[3] He made the point that magicians are often God-like figures; they can just click their fingers and make stuff happen. The problem Teller points to here is the fact that this kind of figure isn't very interesting because what we really want in drama are heroes; characters who struggle through conflicts and end up somewhere different from where they thought they were heading.

These hero narratives, struggles and conflicts have become a distinct feature in Brown's work. His television shows put individuals through transformative experiences that are designed to encourage audiences to reflect on their characteristics, tendencies and patterns of behaviour that often go unchecked. These transformative journeys reflect a significant part of the individuation process that Jung was concerned with: the integration of our shadow.

Let's remind ourselves of what Jung said about the shadow: "The unconscious is not just evil by nature, it is also the source of the highest good: not only dark but also light, not only bestial, semihuman, and demonic but superhuman, spiritual, and, in the classical sense of the word, 'divine'."[4] Through the shadow work that is pursued in these shows, Brown encourages audiences to reflect on the different potentials of human nature, *which we are all capable of.*

The archetypal magician often appears in mythological storytelling as a mentor figure or wise old man who helps the hero find their way on their journey.[5] Fictional magicians use their powers and supernatural aid to manipulate the elements and create new possibilities for the hero. When we see this archetype play out in the real world, magicians tend to use their knowledge and intellect to inform and enlighten us—protecting the interests of society and guiding the heroes in their stories. Magicians tend to create those "sacred spaces", as discussed earlier, through which initiations and transformations can occur. We see this in Brown's meticulous preparation for his shows that create artificial but convincingly real worlds for his participants to undergo their transformative experience.

As Robert Moore and Douglas Gillette explain in *King Warrior Magic Lover*, the magician tends to understand energies and behavioural patterns of human nature on a deeper unconscious level. They know how to contain and channel the power and potential of humans and society for the common good.[6] As we shall see, this is precisely what Brown does: he is not the central figure of the drama or transformative journey, but he uses his skillsets to guide his heroes through their struggles and conflicts, which teach us personal and societal lessons as an audience.

In a number of interviews, Brown has explained that when he reached his mid-thirties he'd become less motivated by merely performing magic tricks—his attention-seeking tendencies and the need to impress others gave him a drive early on in his career that was not fulfilling him later in life. Since that turning point, Brown has described how he's become more motivated by a sense of meaning and purpose in his work—to invest in something greater than himself and to share this sense of transcendence with others.

Brown's shows point to common, connective traits in our collective psychology and try to make us think about how we behave as humans. Even when these shows explore the darker side of human nature, there are lessons to learn beyond the drama itself—it's about our learning more than his performative ego and his previous need to impress.

Welcome to the Dark Side

In 2006 Brown made *The Heist*, in which he tried to persuade four middle-management business people to commit armed robbery (with a toy gun) by stealing £100,000 from whom they believed to be a real security guard in London.[7] Starting with a group of 13 men and women, Brown hosted what the participants believed to be a motivational seminar where they would learn some of his techniques that would benefit them as professionals.

In reality, Brown used the seminar to get the group unconsciously focused on the idea of stealing by applying a number of psychological tools such as anchoring, suggestion and conditioning. From the activities during the seminar, Brown then selected the four participants who he believed would be most susceptible to committing the robbery. Brown conducted some further conditioning exercises on those selected, with the aim of triggering an unconscious mindset in a staged scenario two weeks later.

When that moment arrived, three out of the four selected did commit the robbery. Unaware that they were walking through a staged scenario on a street in London, those three held up a security guard outside the Bank of England with no direct instruction to do so. A number of staged props and triggers on the street were used to stimulate the powerful state of mind that Brown had developed in them. Brown explained that those participants who committed the crimes proved a point about human nature; how we are unconsciously influenced by our environment and good people can easily be influenced into deviant behaviour.

The participants in the show talked about how much they benefited from the experience. It helped them to grow and learn more about themselves. As Brown said, the point of the show was not to say "look at this bad person", but to get us to think about how we could find ourselves doing this kind of thing under certain circumstances. We often underestimate how easily our behaviours might slip into uncomfortable territory. This is especially the case when we consider how susceptible we are to social compliance—a premise that Brown explored in *The Push*.[8]

Social Compliance

In *The Push*, Brown uses social compliance techniques to test whether someone could be persuaded to commit murder by pushing a person off the roof of a building.[9] In the opening scene, Brown shows how social compliance works by staging a scenario where a café worker receives a phone call from an actor pretending to be a police officer. The officer tells him to walk away from the café with someone else's baby. The café worker follows the instructions and walks away with the baby because the actor pretending to be a police officer has told him that the woman with the baby is a known child abductor.

Brown shows how easy it is for someone pretending to be an authority figure to order a complete stranger to do something they would never normally do. While the example from the café is an extreme case of social compliance, authority figures who tell us what is the right thing to do appear in many areas of our lives—peers, leaders, social groups and ideologies. Brown makes the point that these authority figures and their stories that influence us can be used to maintain public order and keep the peace, but can equally be exploited to create disorder and civil unrest and persuade people to act abhorrently.

Brown acknowledges that social compliance is part of life because evolution has taught us that it is safer to be one of the crowd. But he rightly points out that given the times in which we live, we must be aware of its dangers more than ever before. Brown's description of *The Push* reflects those Stoic principles of remaining in control of our thoughts and actions—noting that social compliance is one factor that we have to contend with when we try to apply that seemingly simple advice from the Stoics: "This show is about how readily we hand over authorship of our lives every day and the dangers of losing that control".

Handing over Authorship

It takes *courage, wisdom* and *temperance* to be willing to stand out from the crowd and do the right thing—pursuing *justice* in the world. But this is hard. The situational environment that Brown creates for participants in the show demonstrates just how easily these virtues can be challenged and compromised.

The selection process for the participants in the show was based on tests to find people with high levels of social conformity—mimicking and conforming to the behaviours of others around them without any instruction or direction to do so.

The main experiment in *The Push* was designed to test the limits of social compliance and whether this human trait can be exploited to its most extreme degree—to commit an act of murder. The whole event takes place at a staged auction for a fake charity called "Push". The main participant (Chris) turns up beforehand to meet the charity director and event organiser (Tom). Chris is completely unaware that the whole set-up is fake and the people attending are part of the act.

As Brown points out, Chris was not dressed in full evening wear like the other high-profile guests he was surrounded by, and he also attended the event by himself. These subtle conditions were designed to increase the chances of conforming to instructions throughout the evening because our social compliance is higher when our sense of social status is lower and when we are surrounded by strangers. Combined with these environmental factors, other scripted events and actions were planned to gradually increase the extremity of Chris' compliance across the course of the evening. Chris gets pulled into a number of awkward situations in which, under the pressure of events unfolding, he finds himself in cahoots with the event organiser, Tom.

Conforming in Cahoots

Tom makes Chris aware that they will soon be meeting the charity's VIP guest, Bernie (another actor), who has provided the lots for the auction and will be donating £5 million to the charity. Tom makes it clear that if they don't keep Bernie happy, thousands of kids won't get the help they need from the charity. The story is important here as it provided the incentive for Chris to conform and follow Tom's lead as the authority figure. Tom's orders start small, with Chris helping Tom in the kitchen where he's asked to plate up some meat sausage rolls with vegetarian flags.

Gradually, through a number of orders and incidents, Chris ends up increasingly in cahoots with Tom.

As events unfold, Bernie becomes increasingly irritated and bad tempered about how the event has been organised. Just before the guests arrive, Bernie has what appears to be a heart attack. Tom tells Chris that Bernie is dead. But instead of calling an ambulance and jeopardising the fundraising event, Tom persuades Chris to hide the body. Later the pair try to move the body so that it looks like Bernie fell down the stairs. They later find out that Bernie has a sleeping sickness and isn't dead.

After the event has finished, Tom and Chris confess everything to the other charity board members. But when the group go back to check on Bernie, who they now believe is asleep, they find he has disappeared. They find Bernie up on the roof, furious at what had happened. He screams at Tom and Chris, telling them he knows exactly what they did to him and he won't be donating to the charity. As Bernie sits on the edge of the roof to have a cigarette, the other board members tell Chris that he has to push Bernie off the roof to avoid going to prison, and to save the charity that their jobs depend on. But Chris doesn't give in, and walks away. Brown appears on set to reassure him.

Brown speculated this might happen around two points earlier in the show when Chris stood firm and refused to follow a couple of Tom's orders. Despite some of the orders that he still conformed to throughout the evening, and the number of lessons he learned about himself as a result, Chris showed that his compliance could only be pushed so far. As Brown says, Chris showed that we can push back. But would we all do the same thing in that situation?

Can We Push Back?

At the end of the show, Brown reveals that the experiment was run four times with different participants placed in the same set-up. In the build up to the climax of the evening, like Chris, the other three participants all committed uncharacteristically unethical and immoral acts. However, unlike Chris, the other three did push Bernie from the roof (he was attached to a safety harness and dangling out of sight).

Brown reflects on the experiment from a broader social perspective, drawing attention to the influence of peer groups and ideologies in our lives, and how we give up ownership of our stories without realising:

> This experiment wasn't about who pushed and who didn't. The point was that it made the participants act in a way that went against their decent morals and values—their personalities. The point is we are all profoundly susceptible to this influence—whether it's driven by a peer group or an ideology. It's like we are handed someone else's script of how to live, but to carry out their beliefs and achieve their ambitions. By understanding this, by understanding how we can be manipulated, we can be stronger. We can say no. We can *push* back.

Our humility can be compromised in environments where we conform to authority and we lose our sovereignty. In doing so, we see less desirable traits come to the surface as we display those behaviours that we would usually deem to be beyond the potential of our decent, humane characteristics.

The darker traits that Brown attends to in *The Push* are similar to what Jung often spoke about in relation to the shadow: the ways in which we deny our potential for humanity's darkest behaviours. We suppress those least desirable tendencies that we are all capable of. Even in a fairly trivial day-to-day context, there are banal behavioural habits that see us unconsciously conforming to rules, codes and conducts of our social environments. These aren't all bad behaviours, but we should be more aware of our tendency to fall into line so easily when it's not in our best interests to do so.

Hero Mentality

Brown says that experiments like *The Push* are designed to help us develop a hero mentality, if only in the back of our minds, so that we are more willing to step out from the crowd when necessary. In an interview about *The Push*, Brown reflected on the lessons we can take from the show by explaining how our fear of not fitting in plays a major role in life. Even in situations where there might be a threat or danger to another person or the group, we can hesitate to stand up and do the right thing in the present moment.

All four participants reflected positively on their experience and have taken lessons from it that have benefited their lives. They are more self-aware and have a deeper understanding of their behaviours and vulnerabilities. The more that we can all develop this self-awareness, the more comfortable we might become in breaking those conforming tendencies and overcome the unconscious hesitation of standing out—particularly amongst peer groups or strangers.

Sam Harris raised an ethical question about *The Push*, asking whether it could have compromised the participants' wellbeing and reputation. Brown described the framing process that is used for participants to reflect on their experience and how they have been able to take those positive lessons from it. This is an important aspect happening in the background of the show beyond our viewing. Brown explains how those who pushed Bernie now feel a sense of robustness, where they are less susceptible to manipulation and social or peer pressure. Rather than exposing them as bad people, he said the show has made them more self-aware and helped them develop more robust qualities.

As Brown said earlier, we prefer heroes to Gods. People are flawed and heroism involves people struggling to overcome those flaws. However, he does not only focus on our darkest potentials to demonstrate this. Other shows have attempted to unlock the greater qualities in participants who are restricted by their inner story and can be enlightened through different experiences that their lives are not providing them with, and their inner dialogue doesn't speak to.

As Brown showed in *Apocalypse*—the show I will focus on for the rest of this chapter—transformation can be found through the familiar story of the hero's journey.[10]

Hero's Journey

In *The Hero with a Thousand Faces*, Joseph Campbell identified a *cyclical narrative pattern* that he called the monomyth.[11] This archetypal structure stimulates the formation of hero characters and the journeys they pursue in stories. Campbell states: "A hero ventures forth from the world of common day into a region of supernatural wonder: fabulous forces are there encountered and a decisive victory is won: the hero comes back from this mysterious adventure with the power to bestow boons on his fellow man."[12]

Through these stories, Campbell showed how the hero typically faced a call to adventure and would take it upon himself to initiate the quest and return home victorious with something to give back to the community. Like Jung, it was this recurring narrative and behavioural pattern that interested Campbell, especially in the way that it informed the construction of familiar and recognisable stories from so many different times and cultures.

The hero's journey is one of the most familiar narratives of mythology that we see commonly played out in fictional and non-fictional stories. We often use this narrative structure to reflect upon our own life challenges, personal experiences and journeys—sometimes misrepresenting or editing events to fit into this tidy narrative structure. As Campbell showed, heroes embody values and characteristics that are dependent upon the societies in which their stories are told. Hero narratives are dramatised and personified to reflect those core values and ideals of their culture.

Due to the familiarity of this archetype, we have become very conscious of the way that it plays out in the stories we are told about celebrities, sports stars, politicians and activists. Hero figures are almost disposable characters that can serve immediate and temporary purposes in popular culture. But what Brown tries to do is return our attention to the core function of this archetype and its resonance in a personal and transcendental sense.

If the World Ended Tomorrow

In *Apocalypse*, Brown removed a young man from his home and placed him in a hospital following a staged meteor strike that had led to the spread of a virus that caused a zombie outbreak.[13] Brown's struggling hero had to find his way home by transitioning from his youth into adulthood and discovering his potential for courage, responsibility and selflessness.

As Scott Jeffrey, a coach in transformational leadership, explains: "Neo had Morpheus. King Arthur had Merlin. Harry Potter had Dumbledore. Luke Skywalker had Obi-wan and Yoda". Jeffrey describes magicians as ritual elders who play a vital role in blessing younger generations by enabling them to grow into adulthood—fulfilling the key function of the hero's journey.[14]

In the case of *Apocalypse*, Brown plays this role in Steven's transformation. In the introduction to the show, Brown puts a question to the audience:

> If the world ended tomorrow, would you be happy with how you have lived your life? Would you have done yourself justice, or would you have just let it pass you by? … I'm going to give one unsuspecting person a second chance at life, by creating the end of the world. … Before creating the Apocalypse, I need to find the right candidate: someone who currently leads a self-centred existence and takes his friends, his life, his family, his material comforts all for granted. I'm hoping he'll be able to learn from the meticulously crafted experience I'm going to put him through. And by taking everything away from him I hope to make him recognise the value of what he has.

During auditions for a television programme on something entirely unrelated to the show, the candidate Brown found was Steven Brosnan. Steven's personality and suggestibility provided the ideal profile for Brown's crew.

According to Steven's family and friends, and by his own admission, he was selfish and lazy and took advantage of his parents. Steven lacked a sense of purpose and incentive and would never pursue any ambitions in life due to fear of failure. During the interview process, he said: "I'm lazy. I'm … irresponsible. There's no point in me trying as hard as I can and then going on to fail". This was the story Steven told himself. This story probably felt accurate when he was told he had failed the audition and would not be required to participate in the television show he thought he was auditioning for.

After the audition, using hidden cameras in Steven's home, Brown's crew spent a few weeks observing Steven's behaviour. They also interviewed those closest to him. It became clear to Brown that Steven could be selfish, lacks a sense of ambition and drive and needs to develop a sense of compassion and gratitude towards his friends and family. One day, when Steven was at work, Brown visited the house to check the state of his bedroom:

> This is the room of somebody who doesn't have a lot of control or order over their life. This is essentially the room of a teenager. Steven is in his 20s but he is the youngest in the family, so he's grown up being treated as the youngest in the family, and he hasn't quite made the move away from that now. People need to find their own role models, not authority figures. ... Steven is in my mind symptomatic of a general malaise where people feel a sense of ... entitlement. When we take things for granted we forget to desire the things we already have.

Brown was not judging Steven here. He saw a common symptom of collective psychology that signifies a deeper human problem, which the Stoics were aware of. While the show is dramatic and Brown takes elaborate, technical measures to construct a transformational experience for Steven, the core message is very simple—the opening sequence of *Apocalypse* displays a quote from Epictetus: "He is a wise man who does not grieve for the things which he has not, but rejoices for those which he has."[15]

Negative Visualisation

Brown takes us back to the Stoics who practiced a mental rehearsal of adversity in order to enhance their gratitude for what they had. This is a meditative technique known as negative visualisation—or what the Stoics called *premeditatio malorum*. In *Stoicism and the Art of Happiness*, Donald Robertson explains how modern research in psychology has shown us that if we are willing and able to accept unpleasant thoughts and feelings, without allowing them to overwhelm us, then we will be more resilient than if we always distract ourselves or replace those thoughts with positive thinking.[16]

The Stoics would visualise ill fate, death, adversity and the loss of those things they were most grateful for. This was not to be negative or stimulate anxiety, but in order to remain prepared for the inevitable adversity of life and to enhance their sense of gratitude for the things they already had. William Irvine provides examples of the Stoics regularly practice negative visualisation to remind us that we should remain grateful for those loved ones that we cherish most in life.[17]

Seneca, for example, wrote a letter to a woman called Marcia who had been grieving the loss of her son for three years without any improvement in her state of mind. After advising Marcia on how to overcome her grief he offered her guidance for the future, urging her to remember that Fortune has merely loaned us those things we value most in our lives. Fortune, Seneca explained, could reclaim those things at any moment without our permission. For this reason, Seneca said "we should love all our dear ones, but always with the thought that we have no promise that we may keep them forever—nay, no promise even that we may keep them for long".[18]

Marcus Aurelius also valued advice from Epictetus on the practice of negative visualisation. They suggest that when we kiss our children or put them to bed we should contemplate their mortality and consciously recognise our gratitude for seeing them when they wake in the morning. This meditation is not designed to torment us or fill us with fear, but should enhance our sense of gratitude for what we cherish while we have it, and make us more attentive to our loved ones rather than taking them for granted.

Likewise, Epictetus extended this contemplation to friendships and suggested we remind ourselves that when we say goodbye to a friend it could be the last time we see them. Again, this wasn't to encourage morbid thoughts, but rather a prompt that will likely mean that we take more pleasure from our friendships and we will be less likely to take our friends for granted.

Gratitude was a core principle running throughout the Stoic virtues. This enabled them to make moderate judgements, empathise with others, seek justice in society and pursue the considered life through courage and wisdom.

Brown applies the principles of negative visualisation in dramatic and experiential form to enable Steven's transformation. In other words, he uses the principles of negative visualisation to draw those divine qualities from the depths of Steven's shadow and integrate them into his conscious self. But the first thing Brown needed to do was remove his hero from his surroundings and drop him in the "other world" that heroes commonly find themselves in before they begin their journey home.

Taking Responsibility

Using methods of media and information control on Steven's phone, radio and television, Brown's crew begin to plant seeds of thought, credible threats and convincing stories about an imminent meteor strike that is about to hit earth. A staged meteor strike eventually happens on a bus travelling to a gig that Steven believes he is attending with his brother. As the meteor strike unfolds around them, Brown appears from the back of the bus and puts Steven to sleep through hypnosis. Steven is then walked away from the bus and put to bed in a hospital where he is told to sleep until the lights come on in the morning.

Steven wakes up to what he believes is an abandoned hospital on a military base. The characters he meets are all actors playing roles that are designed to bring out the best in him. As Brown explains, through these encounters Steven will learn about bravery, decision-making and compassion. As Brown puts it: "That's courage, a brain and a heart."

Steven meets a young girl called Leona who says she was taken to the hospital by her mother and is now alone. As it materialises that an infection has spread and a zombie outbreak has started, Steven and Leona face various frights, trials and tests to get to safety. Leona's role in Steven's journey is to encourage Steven to take responsibility.

At one point, Leona asks Steven to promise he will take care of her until she finds her mum. Steven responds with a gentle rub on her back and softly spoken words of reassurance for Leona. Here, the audience see the initial signs of those character traits that were suppressed by the conditions of Steven's normal life, which didn't encourage or accommodate such emotions or acts of empathy.

Steven and Leona soon meet a character called Ian, a paramedic in an ambulance who helps them escape an infected area and takes them to a compound. Ian's role is to demonstrate the leadership qualities that Steven must replicate to find his way home and, in the meantime, take care of Leona. Steven is set to leave the compound for Scotland, until he discovers that his family left a message at the hospital saying they have gone to Wales and Steven is missing. Steven is set with the task of working out how to reunite himself with his family.

It transpires that Ian has promised to wait for his wife before he leaves for Scotland. He explains that the borders to Scotland and Wales will close soon. Steven decides he has to get to a radio to call for help. Ian and Steven take the risk of passing through an area of infected people (zombies) outside the compound to get the radio. In the office containing the radio they find a man called Danny who has been hiding there for two days.

Compassion, Empathy and Leadership

Ian is reluctant to let Danny come back to the compound. His job is to make sure Steven decides whether to leave Danny or let him join them. Steven shows compassion and leadership when he insists that they cannot leave Danny and lets him come back to the compound.

Back at the compound, they spot a scratch on Danny's arm. Ian accuses Danny of being infected and tries to throw him out. Steven stops him. From behind the scenes, Brown is pulling the strings and instructs Ian (via an earpiece) to storm off since it becomes evident that Steven is starting to take charge of the situation.

Steven then uses the radio they've retrieved to send out a message to the British Army HQ. They receive a radio response confirming Steven's family are safe and well and a helicopter will be sent the next day. In this moment, we see the joy and relief in Steven's face—in contrast to the hopeless attitude and lack of self-belief he expressed during the unsuccessful audition. Steven's elation comes as a result of his actions and leadership. The group hug each other. Ian celebrates by pulling out a couple of bottles of beer. The three men enjoy this small treat from polystyrene cups, while commenting, "God that feels good".

The beers and cups are not an insignificant detail here. When Brown monitored Steven earlier on, we saw footage of him drinking beer on the sofa when he was rude to his parents, we saw him drinking excessively with his mates who said he was a liability and we saw empty beer cans lying around his messy room. The taste of this treat in the compound is Steven's reminder of normal life and friendship; a radical contrast to the environment and habitual behaviours that usually involve Steven taking things for granted and allowing small pleasantries to pass him by. This is a small connective taster back to those moments he might cherish more once they are removed from his life.

The following morning Steven's leadership continues to flourish. He gets the group to build an SOS sign for the helicopter. Ian's wife then arrives at the compound. As Ian screams with excitement and desperation to see his wife, Steven tries to calm him down to avoid attracting attention. Standing on the other side of the fence, Ian's wife reveals she is infected. Devastated, Ian insists on leaving the compound. Steven tries to stop him.

Ian tells Steven he must now take care of the others, find his family and change his life. As he leaves the compound to join his wife, Ian shouts back through the fence at Steven:

> You're the man! You're gonna take care of them and you're gonna go and see your mum, and you're gonna change your life, you're gonna change your life! Steven ... it's down to you now mate, you can do it, you can do it!

These are words and encouragement that Steven was not familiar with. "You're the man" was not a typical term of encouragement that Steven would hear as the youngest child of the family who was struggling to grow up and did not believe he was capable of achieving anything.

Ian leaves with his wife. With the remaining three left inside at the compound, Steven tells Danny he needs to be strong. Steven expresses his regret for not thanking Ian for everything. When Leona asks who is in charge now, Steven takes the lead.

Gratitude and Selflessness

Before they leave to get to the helicopter, Leona records a video message for her mum. Steven can hear Leona telling her mum about how he is taking care of her. He hears her telling her mum how grateful she is for her love and care and how she is going to be the best person she can be when she gets home. Steven tells Danny he cannot wait to get back and see his family, and that he's going to take the chance to start over and stop wasting his life.

When the helicopter arrives it lands outside the compound, which is surrounded by zombies. Danny and Leona are supposed to run to the helicopter while Steven tries to distract the zombies. But Leona is too scared and Danny goes by himself. Steven checks Leona is safe. He promises not to leave her and says he will run to the helicopter to try to get them to come closer.

When Steven gets to the helicopter he screams at Danny for leaving Leona. Danny says he is sorry, he is just a selfish person and he can't help. He tells Steven to save Leona because he believes in him. As Steven runs back to the compound, the pilot tells him they're leaving and he's on his own. He still returns to Leona and comforts her.

They now prepare to walk to Wales and set off on their journey. With the area clear, they leave the compound and walk past a mobile phone ringing on a table. Brown is on the other end and we see Steven slip into hypnosis. Steven is walked back to his house and put to bed.

When he wakes in the morning he rushes downstairs to see his family. He explains how he feels a love for them that he had never felt. He hugs his mum and won't let go. A tearful Steven is then sent through to the living room where Brown is waiting for him.

More Than Just a Dream

Brown explains to Steven: "The dream you had wasn't a dream. It did happen but it was set up—for a good reason. You've learnt a huge amount, a lot of things have changed in you, and the point of it, every second of it, was to let you find those changes. It's still you. It's just the best possible Steven Brosnan". Steven said it was reassuring to see Brown because it confirmed everything was not a dream, it really happened and his emotions were real.

After the experiment, Steven's parents described the determination, drive and confidence he had shown. Brown visited Steven a month after the show and Steven described how much happier he was about his life.

What was significant about Steven's confidence here was not a sudden sense of bravado or blind self-belief. Rather, Steven described how he felt more "engaged with life" and was willing to "take chances" without the "fear of failure". He described how his family had never been closer and he no longer wanted to waste time lazing around the house watching TV.

Since then, Brown has stayed in touch with Steven who continued to benefit from this shift in lifestyle and perspective. Brown explained to Joe Rogan that Steven has since pursued a successful career as a teacher in a special needs school and was getting married. Brown doesn't claim credit for every success in Steven's life but he does point to the transformational process that is evident in the show, which played a significant part in setting Steven on his way. A few years later, in an interview about *Apocalypse*, Steven explained how he only understood what had happened to him after the show when he had much more appreciation for the people in his life that he should be grateful for. He said he now tries to challenge himself and take as many opportunities to excel as possible.

Steven's Homecoming

Many of Steven's home comforts and securities were among the things he took most for granted. Ernst Conradie, a professor of theology and religion at Western Cape University, makes the point that only when certain boundaries are reached do we understand the journey it has taken to get there: "To develop a sense of being at home requires a journey of homecoming. The significance of the journey may become clear only by reaching the destination".[19] Through these journeys we pursue and the symbolic meanings that they reflect, we enable transcendence through the lived experiences of our stories and culture. We can individuate.

As the Jungian psychoanalyst, James Hollis explains, the individuation process is key to our personal growth through attention to our inner voice rather than those distractions from the outer world:

> The hero in each of us is required to answer the call of individuation. We must turn away from the cacophony of the outerworld to hear the inner

voice. When we can dare to live its promptings, then we achieve personhood. We may become strangers to those who thought they knew us, but at least we are no longer strangers to ourselves.[20]

Steven found that inner voice and realised what mattered most to him by seeing what life would be like if it was all taken away. His experience provided those promptings Hollis talks about. They prompted him to pull himself out of the rut he was stuck in.

Before the show, Steven was stuck in a rut. Many of us have been there at some stage or another. Even when we are stuck in dire circumstances—perhaps in a job we hate, an unhealthy relationship or a general lack of motivation for life—it can feel difficult for us to break out and do what we know is best for ourselves. In this case, it was not that Steven was a bad person or an innately ungrateful son or an inconsiderate brother. Rather, his inner dialogue was prohibiting him from realising his full potential. This is an important point because our inner stories about ourselves and those subsequent behaviours that they stimulate in daily life are somewhat addictive and self-perpetuating, even when they are not conducive to our wellbeing.[21]

We gravitate towards actions and outcomes that are not necessarily good for our wellbeing, but they are familiar and they conform to what our inner dialogue tells us about our self-worth (albeit unconsciously) and what we deserve. Steven's lack of belief and fear of failure saw his most admirable qualities suppressed—it became easier to remain at home, as the infant of the family, taking mum and dad for granted and requiring those around him to meet his needs.

As Brown points out, the transformational experience of the show meant instead that Steven had to find his heart, his courage, his ability to become a leader and use his initiative to find a way home. Steven's growth reflects an emotional grounding that the Stoics encouraged. By drawing our thoughts back to our inner dialogue through gratitude (rather than desire) and through duty to others (not only the self), we can appreciate what matters most. Steven's experience during his journey reflected the craving for home and family that Marcus Aurelius warned of: "Do not indulge in dreams of having what you have not, but reckon up the chief of the blessings you do possess, and then thankfully remember how you would crave for them if they were not yours."[22]

But this transformation was not exclusive to those Stoic practices that Brown installed in the experiment; it needed a narrative plot to turn Steven's transformation into a tangible journey for him and the audience. Such transformations are not limited to the things we say and do; they are products of our narrative building tendencies and the cyclical stories that we have been retelling for centuries. *Apocalypse* did not only reflect the archetypal structure of the hero's journey. More specifically, as Brown points, Steven lived through the plot of *The Wizard of Oz* to find his way back home.

The Wizard of Oz

In *The Wizard of Oz*, Dorothy gets swept away from her home by a tornado before landing in the magical land of Oz where she begins an adventure to find her way home. Throughout this journey, Dorothy has to endure tests and trials that challenge her spirit and resilience. These challenges confront Dorothy's shadow—those inner fears and desires of a child entering adulthood. Likewise, when Brown visited Steven's bedroom at the start of the show, he described a youngest child in the family who was struggling to make that transition to adulthood.

By defeating the Wicked Witch of the West, Dorothy's struggle and triumph teaches us that fear only has as much power over us as we allow it to. Our fears are rarely as overwhelming as we believe them to be when we face up to them. Hence, it is also unhelpful when we live in a society that constantly keeps us on high alert with ideological stories that are full of fear—fear that group, fear those people, fear that stranger, fear anything that is sold as a threat to your tribe—a point to which we shall return in the next chapter. As Ruth Wodak argues, it is not wrong to feel fear—this is a natural emotion. But social groups and political movements exploit our fear to serve ideological purposes.[23]

In his analysis of moral storytelling in *The Wizard of Oz*, George Dunn describes how Dorothy's narrative journey reflects her transformation through the process of confronting inner fears:

The optimistic outlook of the Wizard of Oz teaches us that evil isn't that powerful once you muster up enough nerve to face it down. ... In Baum's fairy tale, if you refuse to be cowed, never lose heart, and trust your native good sense and ingenuity to pull you through, success is assured. The hurdles you encounter along the way are just opportunities to discover and exercise your natural abilities and virtues. Dorothy and her companions face a host of difficult and dangerous obstacles in their journeys ... but they can always find creative solutions to their problems.[24]

Success here is not meant in the sense of material goal-setting or the blind hope of positive thinking, of course. Rather, in the psychological and philosophical parallels with Brown's work, we can see the moral sense of personal development, psychological growth, shadow integration and individuation. We can focus on our sovereignty to remain in control of our thoughts and actions to avoid the crippling fear and paralysis that is often caused by those dreaded unknowns. This is what is meant by success here—the ability to grow and cope with life's fate.

As the Stoics would say, we cannot control fate but we can control how we respond to its circumstances. Rather than screaming out with resentment and shaking our fists at misfortune, we can respond with the will to take on those challenges that we recognise for what they truly are: opportunities to learn and grow. Gratitude for whatever fate throws our way. Amor fati!

As Dunn goes on to explain, the virtues that this fairy tale reflects are both personal and social: there are the individual qualities of good character and strong will but also the collective qualities of kindness and compassion. The success of those heroes in Oz is as much about their ability to help others as it is about themselves.

Like Dorothy, Steven wakes in the morning to what was seemingly just a dream, but the lessons learnt for both characters are distinct examples of the monomyth and individuation in action. They rise from their experiences with a gratitude for life and their families. Like Dorothy, whose memories of her developmental experience fill her with hope and appreciation for the life she has ahead of her, Steven has a similar awakening.

An important theme throughout Brown's more recent work, which was central to *Apocalypse* and the transformation of Steven's life since the show, is transcendence. Brown explains how the point of Steven going through this experience was not only to become more grateful and grow as an individual but to appreciate that there is something more to life than the self. As Brown pointed out in *20 Years of Mind Control*, regardless of how we feel about the rights and wrongs of religion, one thing that they have encouraged throughout time is transcendence.[25] This is not to suggest everyone should desire a return to religious practices that have declined in modern society, but we should be aware of a problematic secular void, especially if our culture is prone to overlooking the value of introspection and transcendence.

Transcendence and Individuation

Transcendence is integral to Jung's concept of individuation. Jung conceptualised two stages of life and the individuation process.[26] The first concerns the will to establish ourselves in the world—perhaps through our early ambitions and career or building our family or home—as we pursue those external factors that mean something to our identity and place in society. The second is to invest in something beyond ourselves, something that gives us inner meaning as we transcend and appreciate the transcendental qualities of living and participating in life for the common good.

However, the order of our lives and personal growth is not straightforward. Individuation does not reflect a neat chronology of life stages per se.[27] These elements that Jung pointed to are both important, but the narrative is less tidy than we might think. As we saw in the case of Steven, he needed to transcend and invest in something beyond himself in order to kick-start that first half of his life again. Only then could he grow into the adult that he was struggling to become. By discovering Jung's second stage, he was able to revert to that stagnant first stage which had stalled his transition into adulthood.

Either way, the "stages" Jung pointed to are significant factors that play out in our lives. An equilibrium of these external and internal factors is necessary for us to grow as individuals and fulfil our duty to the collective. We do not want to be the narcissistic materialist who is only out for himself and his own gain, nor do we want to be the selfish, lazy person who is reliant on others. At the same time, we do not want to be the pushover who is enslaved to others and only out to please everyone else without any respect for our inner worth or value.

Rather, we need a robustness and inner tranquillity that enables us to find value in the common good and a sense of meaning and purpose beyond our self-serving tendencies. Our individuation is dependent on the equilibrium of those inner and outer qualities where we pursue both the inner ambitions that establish our place in the world while understanding the importance of transcendence and discovering value in things beyond the self.

Jung, Socrates and the Stoics

We can see here how a Jungian approach can accommodate and be accommodated by the Socratic method endorsed by the Stoics: we can know ourselves and we can use our reason to examine our conscious beliefs and values; we can change ourselves and we can use our reason to change our beliefs, which will change our emotions, because our emotions follow our beliefs; we can consciously create new habits of thinking, feeling and acting; and following philosophy as a way of life will enable us to live more flourishing lives.

As Steven's transformation shows us, our lives can benefit from the spirit of those Stoic virtues: courage, wisdom, justice and temperance. This is not to suggest that Steven is now a perfect person who identifies as a Stoic, but we can see how those Stoic virtues, which stem from that Socratic method, chime with the principles of Jungian individuation. Jungian psychology helps us to understand more about the depths of our minds that can make those virtues difficult to realise when we are stuck in a rut, and it shows us which narrative trajectories might help carry us forward.

Our inner dialogue determines our external relations with the world. By working on ourselves, we can do more for those around us. To individuate as individuals, we can do more to help the collective. But we also need a culture of empathy as a collective if we are to create social environments that are conducive to individual growth. The stories we tell ourselves about who we are, and the ways in which we respond to the environment in which we grow up, suppress various potential qualities and characteristics.

The political and economic circumstances we find ourselves entangled with as we become adults can pressure us into suppressing both negative and positive behavioural traits and emotions. To some extent, our culture also determines what is deemed to be positive or negative in terms of our emotional transparency.

If, for example, someone had asked me to write about my emotions and anxieties ten years ago, my response would be very different to now. That is partly due to my growth *and* circumstances: on both personal and societal levels, honesty, compassion, love and empathy are at the forefront of my ethos in a way that they weren't in the past.

Compassion, Love and Empathy

The theatrical stunts and dramatic spectacle in *Apocalypse* are not designed to suggest that we all need to go through a staged transformation hosted by an illusionist. Rather, this was a story that sought to resonate with audiences in order for us to think about the collective state of our lives. It is a reminder that we should be more grateful for the things we have in life.

Everyone has the potential for compassion, love and empathy, but our personal and cultural circumstances and the noise of everyday life get in the way; suppressing those inconvenient emotions that interrupt behavioural habits, social compliance, urges for instant gratification or the desire to control those things beyond our control.

So, the shadow is not only relevant to the individual. The collective shadow is just as important to understand. The collective shadow accommodates psychological traits that play out across entire societies in the shared stories we tell and our behaviours and beliefs as groups. This brings me to the final case study of Brown's work where I focus on another show called *Sacrifice*.[28]

Notes

1. Jung, 1938; Jung, 1959.
2. As Andrew Samuels points out (1986:53), the aim is not to eradicate the shadow but to recognise and understand it through this integration process. Shadow integration can feel uncomfortable due to its threat to our ego-consciousness, but it is a necessary process for enabling individuation.
3. Brown, 2020.
4. Jung, *The Psychology of Transference*, 2013: 28.
5. Campbell, 1949.
6. Moore and Gillette, 1990.
7. Brown, D. 2006.
8. Brown, 2018a.
9. Particularly in shows like *The Push* and *The Heist*, Brown could easily be identified as the shadow culprit here—taking advantage of his skills to exploit trust and entertain audiences at the expense of his subjects. But as he explains, he has made significant effort to counteract this dynamic and provide something positive for participants to take from their experiences. Participants are rigorously examined before and after the experiments and, as he explains, they reflect positively on what they learn about themselves.
10. Brown, 2012.
11. Campbell, 1949.
12. Ibid.: 23.
13. Brown, 2012.
14. https://scottjeffrey.com/magician-archetype/
15. Epictetus, 2012: 48.
16. Robertson, 2013.
17. Irvine, 2008:68.
18. Ibid.: 68.
19. Conradie, E., 2013.
20. Hollis, 1993: 116.
21. As Russell Brand has explained during his recovery from drug addiction, our thought patterns and stories inform habitual behaviours that are addictive—more so than we often appreciate. Brand believes that we live in an age of addiction, in a culture that encourages habitual behaviour. For Brand, addiction is not limited to drugs and those most obvious extremities of destructive behaviour. In one way or another we are all

addicted to thought patterns and stories that control our behaviour beyond our conscious reflections or critical awareness: "In a sense we rewrite our past. We change our narrative. We reprogram ourselves. There is no objective history, this we know, only stories. Our character is the result of this story we tell ourselves about ourselves, and the process of inventorying breaks down the hidden and destructive personal grammar that we have unwittingly allowed to govern our behaviour" (2017: 78–79). Steven was an example of what Brand discusses here. Our culture encourages patterns of addictive behaviour. Not only do we lose sight of gratitude, but as we saw in clips of Steven, he would be hooked on his phone, mindlessly turning the television channel with no regard for anyone else, or in a habitual cycle of getting irresponsibly drunk with his friends to the point where he was a liability. We take people for granted and we become a burden to them in the process.

22. Aurelius, 2002: 27.
23. Wodak, 2015.
24. Dunn, 2011: 155.
25. Brown, 2020.
26. Jung, 1938: 275–289.
27. For more on the complexities of individuation, see Christopher Hauke (2000).
28. Brown, 2018b.

Bibliography

Aurelius, M. (2002). *Meditations*. Penguin.
Brand, R. (2017). *Recovery: Freedom from our addictions*. Henry Holt and Company.
Brown, D. (2006, January 4). *The Heist*. Channel 4.
Brown, D. (2012, November 2). *Apocalypse*. Channel 4.
Brown, D. (2018a). *The Push*. Netflix.
Brown, D. (2018b). *Sacrifice*. Netflix.
Brown, D. (2018c). *Miracle*. Netflix.
Brown, D. (2020, August 16). *20 Years of Mind Control*. Channel 4.
Campbell, J. (1949). *The hero with a thousand faces*. Pantheon.
Condradie, E. (2013). A semiotic notion of transcendence. *Studia Hist. Ecc.* 39. http://www.scielo.org.za/scielo.php?script=sci_arttext&pid=S1017-04992013000300004

Dunn, G. (2011). The wonderful smallness of evil in Oz. In R. Auxier & P. Seng (Eds.), *The wizard of Oz and philosophy: Wicked wisdom of the west.* Open Court.
Epictetus. (2012). *Discourses and selected writings.* Penguin.
Hauke, C. (2000). *Jung and the postmodern: The interpretation of realities.* London: Routledge.
Hollis, J. (1993). *The middle passage: From misery to meaning in mid-life* (Studies in Jungian psychology by Jungian analysts). Toronto: Inner City Books.
Irvine, W. (2008). *A guide to the good life: The ancient art of Stoic joy.* University Press.
Jung, C. G. (1938). Psychology and religion. In *Psychology and religion: West and east, collected works of C.G. Jung* (Vol. 11). Routledge.
Jung, C. G. (1959). *The archetypes and the collective unconscious.* Routledge and Kegan.
Jung, C. G. (2013). *The psychology of transference.* Taylor & Francis.
Moore, R., & Gillette, D. (1990). *Magician warrior king lover: Rediscovering the archetypes of the mature masculine.* HarperOne.
Robertson, D. (2013). *Stoicism and the art of happiness.* Mobius.
Samuels, A., Shorter, B., & Plaut, F. (1986). *A critical dictionary of Jungian analysis.* Routledge.
Wodak, R. (2015). *The politics of fear: What right-wing populist discourses mean.* Sage.

6

Beyond Them-And-Us

Jung's concept of individuation is just as helpful when we reflect on the *collective* shadow. Societies need to individuate when the collective shadows of our culture are suppressed or left unaddressed over time. Sometimes we need to confront the psychology behind our group behaviours by having difficult conversations and confronting social tensions in good faith so that we can understand more about the conditions that create social tensions.

Only then can we integrate the collective shadow into public consciousness and develop a healthier awareness of what it means for our nations, communities and identities. In the same way that individuals tell themselves stories that compromise their wellbeing, societies do the same. We don't always tell stories that serve our best interests and we are not comfortable integrating those less admirable traits of our collective stories and ideologies. And we have a collective tendency to suppress those stories that don't provide particularly pleasant accounts of our pasts.[1]

The Rise of Tribalism

Larger Us makes the point that tribalism ("them-and-us thinking") is on the rise globally and is significantly compromising the health of our democracies. With fear and anxiety playing a central role in political discourse, societies are becoming increasingly polarised. This is not just detrimental to the functioning of civil society, but it also impacts upon our psychological wellbeing as individuals, the decisions we make, the stories we tell, and our sense of place and belonging in the world.

Polarisation is usually understood through attention to political, economic and cultural factors that impact upon social and ideological tensions in global democracies. However, while those factors are important, Larger Us argues that this approach tends to overlook the underlying psychology at play, especially when collective anxieties are increasingly due to the contagious nature of threat perception in politics. This is particularly the case in a politics of fear where socio-economic challenges are blamed on vulnerable groups, and communities are turned against each other as they go on the defensive.

On personal and collective levels, our fears and desires shape our stories and our stories often reinforce those fears and desires. But we can break this cycle. Brown tries to show us how powerful this shift can be if we fracture those stories that keep us locked into a dialogue that binds us and divides us into our tribes. Our affiliation to one tribe often pitches us against another who we deem to be "the problem". Our fears and desires are dependent upon multiple cultural factors that we are exposed to (or not) throughout our lives. Many of us tell different stories about the world and disagree on what we should be fearful of and why, but most humans want the same things: basic financial security, safety for our families, happiness for our loved ones, and a sense of meaning and purpose in our lives. But *how* we believe we should pursue those things triggers different ways of seeing the world.

As Jonathan Haidt argues: "People bind themselves into political teams that share moral narratives. Once they accept a particular narrative, they become blind to alternative moral worlds".[2] Our culture might steer us towards one narrative or another, but we all share the tribal tendency to take sides based on moral viewpoints—whatever those might be. We all need to be aware of the faults among our "tribes" and those things we do not speak of.

Haidt describes how our behavioural tendencies and potentials that we have as humans can bring out the best and worst of our nature:

> We also have the ability under special circumstances, to shut down our petty selves and become like cells in a larger body, or like bees in a hive, working for the good of the group. These experiences are often among the most cherished in our lives, although our hivishness can blind us to other moral concerns. Our bee-like nature facilitates altruism, heroism, war, and genocide.[3]

As Haidt puts it, our "hivishness" can bring us closer together, but it also polarises us if we work against each other in groups that pull us further apart. The latter makes us feel more isolated, more fearful, more disconnected and more powerless when things go wrong. Our collective anxieties are more likely to fuel resentments and shadow projections that blame other groups for our discontent.

In These Divided Times

In *Sacrifice* Brown conducts an experiment to see whether he can create a scenario where someone is willing to sacrifice their own life to protect a stranger (someone they believe is an illegal immigrant). Brown introduces the film as follows:

> For the past 20 years I've performed as a psychological illusionist. Now, in these divided times, I want to try and create a hero—someone who will willingly lay down their life and take a bullet … for a complete stranger. To put your life on the line, not just for a stranger, but for someone you don't identify with, requires two traits: to be *fearless* and to have *empathy*. So for those to work I have to create those qualities in my hero.

The subject selected for the show is a man called Phil—a family man and city maintenance worker from Florida.[4] Phil believes he is taking part in a documentary about cutting-edge biotechnologies that can be used to bring dramatic improvements to your life. Like Steven earlier, Phil is unaware of Brown's alternative plot that is based entirely around him at the centre of a psychological experiment.

In addition to Phil's suggestible nature, which makes him ideal for Brown's experiment, he has been selected due to his views on immigration:

> There is absolutely an immigration problem in the United States. You think, 'well you're not even supposed to be here, why do you think we should follow your religious beliefs?' ... We're still getting a lot of illegal immigrants coming through—not working—can't work because they're illegal. ... I am certainly scared they could turn our country to shit. I say kick them out, I say kick them all out. ... I've always been more biased towards white people. I am not racist. That is just how I was brought up.

Those strong views on immigration, combined with other personality traits required for the experimental conditions to work, made Phil the ideal candidate for the show.

The Politics of Fear

It is important to note again here that Brown is not critical of Phil personally and he acknowledges Phil's position as a working father who is trying to raise a family: "Raising a family is tough and much of Phil's frustration is directed at illegal immigrants who he sees as being favoured over his family." As Ruth Wodak points out in her book, *The Politics of Fear*, the stories we tell ourselves as groups within nation states often see us picturing ourselves as "homogenous people" living within a "well-protected territory".

"Our" territories are often deemed to be spaces in which "we" must *protect* ourselves from outsiders who are a threat to our livelihoods, welfare and resources. In response to those fears that shape our perceptions of social change and those threats ("out there") in the world, the politics of fear, as Wodak demonstrates, has normalised the language of nationalism, racism and xenophobia in public discourse and mainstream political rhetoric.

The likes of Phil are symptoms of that collective fear, and he reflects significant narrative traits in how we tell ourselves stories. Phil's story features something called interdiscursivity—a term used to describe the practice of drawing together multiple discourses that feed into each other to tell a story that serves ideological purposes.[5]

When someone making a point about immigration seeks to strengthen their case, for example, the story they tell will often merge together multiple topics such as national security, employment, welfare, family, religion or whatever else these anxiety-inducing stories draw upon: *they are coming here, taking our jobs, claiming benefits, disrespecting our traditions, refusing to learn our language, and putting our national security at risk with their radicalism, criminality and lack of moral values.*

In these familiar stories, multiple discourses combine to create an interdiscursive story, reflecting the many layers of fears and anxieties of the tribe who deem themselves to be the homogenous group of their nation state. We often see parts of the press and political class playing on those collective fears with stories that repeatedly draw attention to the "threats" facing the homogenous nation state, imposed by outsiders coming in.

Our stories often fracture our connection with each other as humans—particularly through the dichotomy of "them" and "us". Stories become politically divisive when they stimulate emotions such as fear and anger while suppressing other emotions such as compassion and empathy *between* social groups. These stories that bind one group (considered to be "us") versus another group (considered to be "them") stimulate collective fears and frustrations that are often symptoms of other political and economic causes—projecting them onto groups who are represented as a threat to the "tribe".

Since fear is a significant theme in *Sacrifice*, Brown's experiment is more focused on understanding Phil and transforming his perceptions and attitude rather than judging him. Like Steven in *Apocalypse*, Brown is not encouraging the audience to make moral condemnations of Phil as a person. When asked why Brown chose Phil, he explained that despite Phil's views on immigration, he was a nice guy who was likeable and faced challenges in his life—despite the fact that immigrants had become a scapegoat for his difficulties, Phil was still a good person that many people could relate to.

The aim of the experiment involving Phil is to see if a series of scenarios can radically change Phil's strongly held beliefs while also making us reflect on our beliefs and behaviours as an audience. As Brown states: "I hope to show Phil the amazing things we are capable of when we let go of the stories we think define us. ... By the end of this journey I hope to have him willingly take a bullet for someone he thinks is an illegal immigrant".

Place and Belonging

Through a combination of placebo and classical conditioning, Phil is led to believe that he is trialling a new technology that will improve his life by empowering him with a greater ability to act decisively. As part of the experiment that Phil believes he is involved in, Brown creates a scenario where Phil thinks he has a chip inserted into his neck, which is linked to an app on his phone. The app makes a sound that he associates as prompts for other actions that Brown gets Phil to perform. Brown's conditioning techniques form a series of triggers in Phil, which enhance his sense of pain management and the feeling that he has more control over his fears.

In an early stage of the experiment, Phil does not act as Brown plans. Brown hoped Phil would overcome his fear of heights by jumping into a quarry. Despite managing to walk out to the edge of the platform over the water below, Phil could not bring himself to jump. Nonetheless, Brown was confident that other techniques could still work more effectively on Phil.

In the next stage, Brown attempts to enhance Phil's feeling of empathy towards strangers and other groups: "For Phil to act heroically, it is not just about Phil acting decisively, and not just in the face of fear, but also acting out of empathy and placing another person's life before his own". At this point, the audience is reminded of Phil's strong views on immigration through another quote from the screening process: "This is not your fucking country. This is our country, and you've come in and you're alienating your hosts".

During the screening process, Phil gave a DNA test, which he was told was for the app he was using. However, as Brown reveals, this data was really gathered with the intention of revealing Phil's own heritage to help him re-evaluate his opinions. Brown reveals the results of Phil's DNA test with a map of the world laid out in front of them. Phil sees that his DNA make-up can be traced back to regions all over the world. Brown comments on the story that we are often not told about who we are: "It's amazing to think over these tens of thousands of years how people have moved around, and that story, which has led to you sitting here, is from those ancient tribes and groups just moving around, migrating and mixing."

The results that Phil is most shocked by (in a positive way, as he points out) are those regions that he least expected to have any connection to, which include Israel, Syria, Mexico and Peru. When Brown asked Phil why he was most shocked by those regions, Phil acknowledged that the places where we live have an influence on our perceptions of other places where we consider people to be different to us, and we form negative assumptions about them.

By interrupting that story, he begins to deepen Phil's empathy and rebuild his sense of connection with other groups he wouldn't typically associate himself with. This reflects an important dynamic that Larger Us points to: we need to move from perceptions of disconnection that reduce empathy and stimulate prejudice to feelings of connection and belonging that increase empathy and reduce prejudice. In other words, we need to undo the affective stimuli that a politics of fear has harnessed to disconnect us, reduce empathy between social groups and heighten our sense of differences defined by borders, identities and ethnicities.

What's important here is the subtlety of Brown's approach that is gradually shifting Phil's perception based on evidence that he is confronted with. In his book, *Shifting Stories*, Andrew Scott makes the point that people often hold on to their stories more tightly if they feel they are being undermined or prised away from them against their will—even with evidence or strong arguments against their beliefs.

In other words, there is little to gain from bashing someone over the head with moral reasons to demonstrate why their beliefs are wrong if they cannot see a different story that resonates with them. As we see in the case of Phil, he needed to *feel* his perception shifting through evidence that he found meaningful. As Phil sat and looked at the map and saw how connected he was to all these regions that he previously felt disassociated from, it reminded me of a powerful concept called The Overview Effect (also known as The Big Picture Effect).

The Overview Effect

While travelling back from the moon, an astronaut called Edgar Mitchell once described the deeply ecstatic, embodied feeling of oneness, unity and empathy that he experienced as he looked out of his shuttle window at the Earth. Mitchell describes the transformative effect it had on him as he contemplated the senseless behaviour of life on Earth as people fight and kill each other over borders and Gods.

In *Philosophy for Life*, Jules Evans recounts Mitchell's writing about the experience. Mitchell described how he tried to make sense of his experience when he was back home, in an effort to find out what had happened to him:

> I started digging through the science literature, and I couldn't find anything, so I appealed to some anthropologists over at Rice University near the space centre, and said 'Please help me try and understand what was going on'. They came back to me a short time later, and pointed out to me the Sanskrit term 'samadhi', an experience of seeing things in their separateness, but experiencing them as unity, accompanied by ecstasy. And I said, yes, that's exactly the type of experience I had.[6]

This deeply moving experience has been shared and spoken about by numerous astronauts since then and it has been taken seriously as an affective mechanism that can have a profound impact upon civilisations. Through technologies like VR, there is a growing interest in how we can replicate this experience, or take people to other places and spaces that can unlock empathy.[7]

The notion of unlocking is crucial here. These potentials that lie within us all—the light and the dark of the shadow hosts our least and most desirable traits. The experience that Brown puts Phil through should not be left as a gimmick for a television show; it is something that we should take seriously. As Mitchell states, "if we could get our political leaders to have a summit meeting in space, life on Earth would be markedly different, because you can't continue living that way once you have seen the bigger picture."[8] As Phil learns, by seeing the bigger picture we can be less prohibited by our unconscious narratives that keep us wrapped up in our own business. These stories overstate the importance of what are essentially trivial matters, or things that concern us because we are lacking the empathy required to invest in a common good.

As Larger Us points out, there are many ways of creating a sense of belonging, shared identity and mutual interest across different social groups and communities. Social contact theory is one example that has shown us how, in the right conditions, majority and minority groups within a society can develop more empathy and decrease prejudice through more contact and familiarity with each other. This bears some relevance to the next technique that Brown adopted in his experiment on Phil. As Brown points out, Phil seemed genuinely affected by the DNA results and Brown tried to build on this by further increasing Phil's sense of connection and empathy with people he would typically consider to be different to him.

Connection and Empathy

Phil has to sit face-to-face in silence with a stranger of a different ethnicity to him for four minutes. Phil is told the test is designed to help recalibrate the biotechnology he is trialling—he is still unaware of Brown's conditioning process. The exercise is based on research by Arthur Aron to provoke feelings of empathy between strangers.[9] Brown describes his use of the test:

> Pairs of complete strangers sit facing each other and are asked to silently stare into each other's eyes for four minutes. I hope that following the news about his DNA, staring into the eyes of someone from a different race will create intense emotions that I can anchor and use at the climax of this experiment.

During this test, Phil begins to cry and asks the stranger if he can give him a hug. Phil describes the experience as follows:

> It was almost like looking into his soul. And I just got this overwhelming feeling like I already knew him. ... Everything that I've ever thought about other people, the way I have been towards people, was just gone and the whole time looking at him I just wanted to give him a hug. It was overwhelming.

Combined with the impact of the DNA test beforehand, the experience that Phil has here shows how powerful these techniques can be. Phil's empathy was unlocked through a feeling of common connection with a stranger in an intimate space that momentarily suspended his stories. He was faced with someone more real than the imagination of his stories about "them".

Phil's experience also resonates with a point that Brown made more recently in *A Book of Secrets* where he refers to Luthanian philosopher, Emmanuel Levinas. Levinas saw face-to-face encounters as a fundamental feature and requirement of our social and ethical nature. Brown points to the distinction Levinas drew between the ancient Greek notion of our rational nature and what he deemed to be a truer reflection of our socio-ethical tendencies.[10]

For Levinas, face-to-face encounters stimulate a sense of responsibility towards one another. It's through these encounters—that are notably absent during increasingly common exchanges on social media or through our consumption of stories about other social groups via politicians and the press—that we develop empathy and a sense of compassion towards others.

Expanding Phil's Oikeiōsis

Through Brown's experiment, Phil's oikeiōsis—which the Stoics identified as our sense of what belongs to us and the affinity we feel with others—was expanded beyond himself and his family or familiar social groups.[11] He begins to see a connection with strangers that takes him beyond his tribe and expands his sense of empathy that was previously prohibited by his inner stories. This shows why cosmopolitanism is an important ethos in conjunction with oikeiōsis; without the former, the latter is problematic since it is prone to defining the interests of "us" at the expense of "them".

As Liz Gloyn points out in her discussion of oikeiōsis: "Stoicism argues that we are each responsible for our moral disposition and thus are fully in control of our own journey towards virtue. It is very much up to us to look at our failings and to seek to improve them by correcting any misunderstandings we might have about what virtue actually consists of". As Gloyn explains, the Stoics advocated frank introspection of ourselves and our beliefs—encouraging us to confront our perceptions and judgements of others and change them in accordance with virtue.

Brown guided Phil through that introspective process and made him question those conceits and affronts on immigrants and other groups that he had typically deemed to be a threat to him and his community. The Stoics would argue that our social oikeiōsis and sense of duty towards each other is what enables us to embrace the ethos of cosmopolitanism.

This principle is all well and good, and Phil was clearly moved by this part of the experiment, but feeling a common connection with a stranger is not the same as taking a bullet to protect an illegal immigrant. Hence, Brown conducts a series of tests in the show that are designed to persuade Phil that the chip he's had inserted is reducing his sense of fear and pain. Not all the tests work, but most of them do—even on the occasion when Phil could not overcome his fear of height by jumping into a quarry, he still came close, which enhanced his belief that the chip was helping him overcome fear and pain.

Brown's intention was that Phil's belief in the chip, an awareness of his ability to overcome pain, and his heightened sense of empathy would change his internal narrative and enable him to act heroically. As Brown states in the show: "I really hope this works—I would like everyone to see what is possible if we can just get past the narrow constraints of the stories that we tell ourselves."

At this point, Phil was told that filming for the television show was complete, and he returned home to America. Unaware that this was a placebo trial of fake biotechnology and there was no chip in his neck,

Phil described the profound effect the experience had on him: "It's been an absolute rollercoaster of emotions throughout this whole process, and it's been an experience that I can't even begin to explain how much it is going to change me moving forward. It's just been awesome".[12]

After being home for some time, Phil was led to believe that his friend had won a trip to Vegas and invited him on a free trip away. As part of the set-up, Phil was picked up by a taxi that broke down in the desert. He waits in a bar for the car to be fixed. Phil is unaware that the bar has been set up with cameras and actors for a staged scenario.

A Hero's Calling

While Phil is waiting for the car to be fixed, a group of bikers start talking to him. After a scuffle breaks out when some Mexican men try to enter the bar and the bikers kick them out, one of the gang apologises to Phil and explains why they don't like letting Mexicans into the bar. The biker shares similar views to those that Phil had at the start of the show. The bikers befriend Phil and give him a gang member's jacket to make him feel part of their group. They offer Phil a lift to get back to his taxi. When leaving the bar, they see the Mexican men vandalising the gang's bikes. They chase them down, interrogate them and find out they are illegal immigrants—at which point one biker pulls out a gun.

Phil watches the conflict escalate from the gang's van where a fake radio station is playing. Audio triggers from Brown's experiment are embedded in the radio show and played as a subconscious stimulant for Phil. Phil can see that the man is going to get shot and gets out of the van to intervene. He pleads with the gang to stop and call the police while standing in front of the man he still believes to be an illegal immigrant. The gang refuse to call the police and tell Phil to get out the way before he gets shot. Phil refuses to move and the gang member shoots his gun. Phil believes he has been shot as fake blood bursts in the jacket that the gang gave him earlier.

Brown immediately appears on set to explain what has happened as he picks Phil up and embraces him:

It's not real blood. Up you get. Look at me. This whole thing was about who we are and what we are capable of when we rid ourselves of those stories. And what you've just done is the single most heroic and extraordinary thing that any human being can do for another human being. Also, Phil, there were no other participants in this show, it was just you. This was all just you and you don't have a microchip implanted in you. You did all this on your own. I'm so proud of you! I'm so proud of you!

The show tells a hero story through Phil's transformative journey—realising his human potential beyond the restrictive parameters of the stories he was previously prohibited by. Once Phil has calmed down, he describes his experience:

Something pushed me to get out the truck. It was like a surge of energy to get out the truck. It was adrenaline because I just couldn't sit in the truck and watch it. … So something pushed me to get up out the truck … and try to stop what was happening. I did it because I wanted to help. … I need to start looking at things differently and helping where I can and changing my outlook on things. I couldn't have rightfully stepped aside and watched him get killed.

What Brown did in this experiment was fracture some of Phil's narrative building blocks that fuelled his fears and beliefs. The global map and DNA exercise interrupted that territorial perception that a politics of fear preys upon. The staring exercise reduced Phil's fear of interpersonal differences and disconnection based on his perceptions of ethnicity. It reconnected him with groups he deemed himself to be disconnected from.

Stories and ideologies are powerful; they are experiential and affect us deeply through the narratives shared in our social groups, institutions, families and personal lives. But as Phil's experience shows, there are affective mechanisms that can change those stories based on alternative experiences and insights that stimulate other emotions at the core of our humanity. There are potentials beneath the surface expressions of our storytelling that make us human—these qualities transcend political persuasions and tribal narratives. Through his transformation, Phil's deeper human qualities were unlocked through his shifting story. Instead of a story about "them" and "us", it was a story about humanity, justice and a common cause. Phil wanted to help another human and didn't want his story to feature him sitting back and allowing another man to be shot.

But *Sacrifice* is about more than Phil's transformation. There is a collective message in the show that resonates with current times. As Brown points out, our perceptions of reality are limited and misleading. We are trying to make sense of that infinite data source that can only be understood through the stories we tell ourselves based on a limited part of that data. Even our sense of self is like an illusion, partly shaped by those private hallucinations that we live in. More attention to these limitations, and an understanding that the world is so much more complicated than our stories often suggest, can increase our empathy and compassion for others. In more dialogue between groups we find more potential for human flourishing.

Dialogue Between Sides

Our minds draw on archetypal narrative structures to help us edit down the complexities of life into a simple story. Brown tries to distinguish the political role of our stories from our human qualities that precede politics. In his closing comments he says that qualities such as kindness, compassion and human flourishing are only possible if we find space for dialogue *between* political sides:

> The stories we tell ourselves dictate the corners we fight from. One story tells us to protect our group and guard against outside threat, even at the expense of the disadvantaged. The opposite story tells us to protect the disadvantaged, even at the expense of overall stability. Each side is convinced the other is mad or bad yet it's precisely in the dialogue between sides that we find truth, and humanity flourishes. We can protect our groups and maintain compassion. So this experiment wasn't to make someone switch from one narrow political story to another. I think what emerged in Phil's defining moment was something more important and more unifying, which is kindness.

As Larger Us points out, when we lose our common ground we stop responding to the difficult and most pressing challenges we face as a species. These are challenges that can only be solved through a collective effort in which we work together.

Brown discussed this tension and the importance of maintaining common ground, in a conversation with Joe Rogan.[13] He explained how the show resonates politically but it is not a political show. His aim was to show how we get constrained by political narratives, and Phil's transformation sees him coming out of his particular socio-political narrative to find what are ultimately human qualities of kindness and compassion. Brown insisted that these are not political qualities, but they tend to get politicised.

The point of *Sacrifice* wasn't about getting audiences to switch their political allegiances overnight or to judge people if they lack compassion. Neither was it a sanctimonious attempt to impose a preachy, pious tale upon the masses. Rather, it drew attention to how we form our stories and beliefs and the fact that a culture of polarisation is further disconnecting us from each other. We are losing sight of the bigger picture because we are so often pitched against each other and fearful of what "they" will do to "us". These are not the beliefs of nasty people who are beyond redemption, they are the fears of good people with jobs, homes and families.

Sacrifice provides a dramatised spectacle that plays out Jonathan Haidt's principles in practice: decent people are divided by narratives that force us apart and fracture the dialogue between sides, which we need in order to maintain a sense of common ground and mutual, collective interest.

Furthermore, *Sacrifice* shows us how our culture prohibits human qualities in our psyche. Consequently, this can see our greatest and most enlightened potentials suppressed to the shadows of our unconscious minds.

The meaning of the show is not about the grand narratives of political parties and nation states. Nor is it suggesting we should find ways of putting our life on the line for another person. It is about our daily interactions, common ground and connections with each other as humans.

While our behaviours and interactions might be influenced by socio-political narratives and ideologies, our human qualities precede politics and we all have the potential to be more kind and compassionate towards each other. These daily interactions are the things that can help us to move beyond polarisation in our personal lives regardless of what the media is telling us or how our political leaders are behaving.

I, for example, regularly drink and socialise at a working men's club in the North East of England. It would be an understatement to suggest that my political opinions are not shared by most of the people I drink with—particularly on immigration, EU membership, foreign policy and social justice. Sometimes people share reprehensible views and there are times when I feel a sense of responsibility to challenge them and tell them why I think they're wrong. But even then, I try to remind myself that these opinions are not signifiers of "bad people". Those reprehensible views rarely sum them up as people beyond those topics of conversation. Humans are complex, and so is life.

Fate and Perspective

Our stories are formed from different places, experiences and perspectives. Many of these circumstances are determined by fate and factors beyond our control from the day we are born. These aren't excuses for bad behaviour or detestable world views. But they are factors and contexts that are worth some consideration if we are to think beyond "them-and-us" by understanding more about our stories and how they are shaped by our culture.

As an example, take my own response to the September 11th attacks on the World Trade Center in 2001. When I was watching the evening the news after the attacks I saw footage of what was presented as a group of Muslim men in "another country" dancing and celebrating in the street. I was 18 years old at the time. I was naïve, and I was furious. In my eyes, whatever world leaders did in response to this atrocity was fully justified and "they" deserved whatever was coming their way.

I later learned that this specific piece of footage was taken from an entirely different context—it had happened at a different moment in time, and for different reasons, which had no relation to September 11th. It was reshown after the attacks on the World Trade Center to enforce the message that "other" parts of the world were celebrating at the expense of American deaths.

This experience was prior to university, where I studied media and journalism. Not only did university provide a life experience that transformed me as a person, but my studies taught me among other things to critically analyse news media, political rhetoric, propaganda and ideology. This changed my way of seeing the world and taught me to be more critically aware of the stories I was being told by others and how that infinite data source around me was manipulated to serve political purposes and shape my perceptions of the world.

I am not suggesting everyone needs to go to university to avoid being as naïve as I was. But that was *my* experience. That was *my* place and perspective. Much like Phil, I was partly responding to the perspective my surroundings had shaped for me. To echo Brown's point, it is not about badness or madness. A large part of our lives is a product of fate and circumstance that shapes our stories.

Beyond Madness and Badness

The ancient Greeks talked about the problem of amathia. Amathia is often translated to mean ignorance, but it is more nuanced than such a translation suggests. The English language does not have one direct word that adequately translates in this respect. As the antithesis of Sophia (wisdom), Epictetus approached amathia as a form of "anti-wisdom".[14]

Again, we should approach what Epictetus means here with caution, since amathia does not simply mean "stupidity" either—another common misconception in its translation. Amathia can be used to describe the state of mind in which an otherwise "good" person is resistant to reason and dismisses any facts that contradict their beliefs. Hence, an intelligent person can hold reprehensible views or behave abhorrently. This is, as the ancient Greeks would argue, due to amathia. They are not stupid, but they are not using their virtue to obtain or apply wisdom either.

More complex than plain ignorance and more corrupting than stupidity, amathia is a self-centred complex of the psyche that prohibits empathy, projects internal antipathies onto the external world and knowingly rejects any evidence that is contrary to one's inner dialogue. Amathia does not accommodate those moral or ethical perspectives that are conducive to knowledge and reason. Massimo Pigliucci shares what he deems to be the best definition of amathia from D.R. Khashaba, who refers back to that Socratic method I introduced earlier:

Socrates' life mission was to combat *amathia* ('ignorance') by helping his interlocutors examine themselves. *Amathia*, the evil of which the Socratic elenchus rids the soul, is not lack of knowledge: in its milder variety, it is obscure and confused thought; in its more pernicious variety, it is 'disknowledge' instilled into the soul by bad upbringing and bad education, consisting in false values and notions and beliefs.[15]

So, through Socratic reason and self-examination, the spiritually corrupting nature of amathia can be rid from the soul. But again, when Khashaba refers to bad upbringing and bad education, we are not literally blaming a person's parents or the school they attended for their beliefs. As discussed earlier, values and beliefs are products of upbringing and education in a broader sense—domestically, educationally, socially, politically and professionally. They are products of society.

When our stories serve immoral or unethical purposes, those sociological and pedagogical functions of myth that Joseph Campbell identified can be as corrupting as they might otherwise be enlightening.[16] In *Sacrifice*, Phil is clearly not a stupid person. Neither is he evil nor is he ignorant. Phil was an example of someone who was convinced that his story told the truth as a result of his environment and upbringing (in its broadest sense). His inner response to the external world suppressed some of his human qualities. The Socratic self-examination that Khashaba describes is similar to the process that Phil went through in Brown's experiment. Brown used powerful, affective techniques on a suggestible personality to interrupt Phil's stories in ways that were too persuasive for his own cognitive dissonance to go ignored.

As Phil said during the screening process, he did not see himself as racist—he saw the views he held as the "common sense" products of his upbringing. However, Brown shows that there are perceptual mechanisms that can be stimulated to interrupt those narratives, which fractured Phil's ideological lens on the world. If the focus had been about judging and condemning Phil's views rather than focusing on his potential as a human, the show would serve a very different purpose. Not only would it fail to demonstrate how Phil's moral character and virtue could be improved through the individuation process of the show, but it wouldn't send a message to the *audience*, as it does, where they are forced to think about their own stories and flaws as humans.

The Human Problem

In an essay on the concept of "stupidity", the Lutheran pastor and theologian, Dietrich Bonhoeffer described a similar problem to that of amathia during the rise of Nazi Germany. While imprisoned for his vocal opposition to Hitler, Bonhoeffer wrote a series of letters and essays in which he described how "facts that contradict one's prejudgement simply need not be believed ... and when facts are irrefutable they are just pushed aside as inconsequential, as incidental".

By "stupidity" Bonheoffer was not referring to an intellectual problem, but a human one. He deemed this to be a combination of psychological and sociological factors, stating:

> It is a particular form of the impact of historical circumstances on human beings, a psychological concomitant of certain external conditions. Upon closer observation, it becomes apparent that every strong upsurge of power in the public sphere, be it of a political or religious nature, infects a large part of humanity with stupidity. It would even seem that this is virtually a sociological-psychological law. The power of the one needs the stupidity of the other.[17]

As Bonhoeffer argued, it is not that people suddenly lose their intellect—by stupidity he was not suggesting that some people are innately "thick". Instead, he argued that when these upsurges of power occur in society (we could identify these "upsurges of power" as ideologies that gain significant public support), some people become deprived of independence and autonomy in their ability to critically assess the emerging circumstances around them. That deprivation of autonomy and independence, again, reflects the danger of disempowerment, disengagement and hopelessness that drives a politics of fear and despair.

While Bonhoeffer was talking about the rise of Nazi Germany in the 1930s, he still described a conversational dynamic that will be familiar to many of us in entirely different historical and cultural circumstances:

> The fact that the stupid person is often stubborn must not blind us to the fact that he is not independent. In conversation with him, one virtually feels that one is dealing not with him as a person, but with the slogans,

catchwords, and the like that have taken possession of him. He is under a spell, blinded, misused, and abused in his very being.[18]

While most of us have, thankfully, not experienced anything like the events Bonhoeffer witnessed prior to his execution in 1945, his account here might not be so dissimilar to some of the tribal exchanges many of us have experienced or witnessed in more recent years.

Furthermore, social media provides us with additional social and psychological factors to contend with as the complexities of our communicative practices and political discourse are reduced to limited characters, clicks, likes, shares and retweets. We lack the interactive nuances of face-to-face communication and the empathy developed through social contact. In an age where we have never been so technologically connected, we have never been so communicatively blunt and interactively void of complexity—to the point where we feel socially and personally disconnected.

We are all vulnerable to these social and psychological factors. Consequently, as Jonathan Haidt would argue, we become seduced by particular narratives that bind us to the groups we most identify with—especially when we are full of fear and despair and we seek the comfort of the tribe.[19] The Stoics were aware of these tribal tendencies and they tried to rise above them through reason and virtue. The Stoics would have little sympathy for the nationalism and identitarian populism we have seen in recent years. Instead, their cosmopolitan ethos meant they saw themselves as "citizens of the universe".[20]

Ethical Cosmopolitanism

The Stoics drew their sense of universal citizenry, in part, from Socrates. Epictetus, for example, wrote: "Do as Socrates did, never replying to the question of where he was from with, 'I am Athenian', or 'I am from Corinth', but always, 'I am a citizen of the world'."[21] Through our reason and virtue, the Stoics believed that we could rise above our tribal tendencies and approach other people as if every human belonged to an ideal city, which they called the *cosmopolis*.

In *How to Think Like a Roman Emperor*, Donald Robertson states the importance of this principle that is fundamental to the ethics of Stoicism:

"Although this social dimension of Stoicism is often overlooked today, it's one of the main themes in *The Meditations*. Marcus touches on topics such as the virtues of justice and kindness, natural affection, the brotherhood of man, and ethical cosmopolitanism on virtually every page".[22] As Robertson explains, because the Stoics saw humans as thinking creatures—that are both capable of reason in ourselves and recognising the potential for reason in others—they deemed us to be inherently social and identified the natural affection that we carry towards, for example, our loved ones.

But this affection is not limited to those closest to us; through virtue, it grows and extends beyond our immediate family and friends. The wiser we become in life, the greater our "moral considerations" become, as we foster a deeper sense of universal connection between all humans. As Robertson puts it, "Stoic ethics involves cultivating this natural affection toward other people in accord with virtues like justice, fairness and kindness".[23]

Massimo Pigliucci discussed the principles of ethical cosmopolitanism in relation to western immigration policies and the refugee crisis. Pigliucci was not suggesting that it would be practical, realistic or even necessary to abolish all borders tomorrow and implement some unfeasible system in which everyone is required to become cosmopolitan overnight. Rather, as he puts it, the Stoics provide us with an ideal to strive for, which can provide a fairer and kinder influence in the here and now. He argues that if we adopted a more cosmopolitan ethic in our political approach to immigration policy, and particularly the refugee crisis, then we would recognise our collective responsibility as developed nations to help those who are suffering:

> The Stoics were among the first advocates of cosmopolitanism, the notion that all human beings are members of one large family, the cosmopolis, and that we should act accordingly ... I do think that cosmopolitanism is an ethical standard attainable right here, right now, as difficult as it may seem given the recent tide of populism and nationalism that has swept western countries, and the utter lack of anything like that ideal in many other places in the world. ... I'm not holding my breath until the world imagined by John Lennon (or Zeno of Citium) actually materializes. But I think we

can, and should, work tirelessly toward that ideal. And a more humane immigration policy throughout the western world is a necessary first step (Pigliucci, 2020).

The politics of populism and nationalism provide the antithesis of the ethical cosmopolitanism that the Stoics advocated. The ideological role of nationalism thrives on those stories that artificially disconnect us and fragment us further away from the cosmopolitan ideal—yet in ways that can feel natural and somewhat inevitable. This is anything but true in reality: while our tribal tendencies are natural human characteristics, our ability to reason is an evolutionary trait that can be harnessed to make us wiser and experience the deeper connections between all humans, which precede politics.

As we saw in *Sacrifice*, the stories we tell in our culture and our personal lives determine whether we revert to tribal tendencies or reach out to others with kindness and empathy. Particularly through his DNA test, an awareness of historical complexity through ancestral movement around the world shifted Phil's perspective towards a more cosmopolitan mindset. The face-to-face staring session saw Phil's natural affection stimulated towards a stranger after Brown developed that sense of shared connection between Phil and those "other" groups that a nationalist mindset had conditioned him to feel threatened by and opposed to.

By fracturing a culturally learned sense of belonging to a particular group that was defined by a narrow sense of nationality, Phil's story changed. The narrative thread to his story provided a more interconnected and historically complex notion of humankind beyond the arbitrary borders and boundaries of "them-and-us" thinking.

The Quest for Complexity

When our narratives become dogmatic, we are not open to complexity or able to accommodate the inevitable ambiguities that life throws at us—socially, morally or politically. As Brown pointed out earlier on, we are obsessed with endings and our stories often provide decisive conclusions that we are convinced can explain exactly how things are in the world. But these stories are flawed and they only explain the world on our terms, through our internal, editorial machinery, and all the baggage that comes with it.

Journalist and author Malcolm Gladwell makes the point that instead of dogmatically drawing reductive conclusions to stories, we should be more dogmatic about the process that we go through to reach those conclusions. As Gladwell argues: "We have, as human beings, a storytelling problem. We're a bit too quick to come up with explanations for things we don't really have an explanation for".[24]

Gladwell believes we should be dogmatically curious and committed to understanding other people on *their* terms in order to appreciate the complexities and ambiguities that we are reluctant to account for when we jump to conclusions.[25] For Gladwell, the process of reaching a conclusion is more important than the conclusion itself—it is this process that we should have more faith in.

As the likes of Brown and Haidt argue, we can pursue truth through dialect and conversations between sides. All sides are prone to reducing the complexities of emerging circumstances down to simple slogans that "sum up" the problem concerned. If we are not careful, our ability to empathise can be paralysed by our loyalty to the tribe and those stories that we deem to be taking the moral high ground. This disconnect in political dialogue only feeds polarisation.

As narrative building machines, we should seek out transformative experiences that help us to share better stories for a better future. As individuals and collectives, Jung's individuation process never ends; it is a lifelong journey requiring constant reflection and integration that enables us to grow. We flourish when we reflect and transform.

Notes

1. Historian and writer Paul Gilroy (2004) makes the point that British society is suffering from post-colonial melancholia. Gilroy argues that aspects of British society and stories about British national identity are so entrenched in its colonial past that its collective consciousness is in a melancholic state—it has not re-mythologised what it means to be British by critically integrating its colonial past and reforming its sense

of place in the world. Hence, this melancholic state has played out in the cultural and political tensions of recent years (see Kelsey, 2017). A Jungian perspective on Gilroy's point would see this as an example of the collective shadow: a lack of cultural confrontation with the past and a common failure to understand the consequences of a colonial (and postcolonial) legacy. Consequently, our collective shadow simmers away in our culture and creates more divisions, defensiveness and resentments than it would if we integrated our past more constructively. By integrating the collective shadow, we could tell a better, more inclusive story that unites us in modern life and critically examines our place in the world through a fuller and more integrated cultural psyche. Returning to Gilroy's point, a failure to do this in British society has restricted the ability to collectively progress from the self-deserving psyche of a postcolonial power and re-mythologise British identity.
2. Haidt, 2012: xvii.
3. Ibid.: xvi.
4. Brown invited applicants to participate in a documentary about biotechnology. From thousands of applicants Brown shortlisted 100 for audition and interview to find a candidate with a strong bias against another group and appropriate personality traits to make them susceptible to the conditions of the experiment.
5. Wodak and Meyer, 2001; Kelsey, 2015.
6. Evans, 2013: 104.
7. https://scholar.google.com/scholar?hl=en&as_sdt=0%2C5&q=virtual+reality+and+empathy&btnG=
8. Ibid.: 105.
9. Aron et al., 1991, 1992, 1997.
10. As Brown (2021: 128) states: "In this mind, the history of philosophy has failed to appreciate the essentially social nature of our existence. We are neither fundamentally rational creatures, as the Greeks thought and we have continued to think more or less ever since, nor should we be reduced to the result of physical processes or swirling clouds of atoms. We are essentially *ethical*, because everything starts with the particular relationship between two individuals, and this entails a fundamental obligation".
11. See Gloyn (2017) for more on Seneca's approach to oikeiōsis in family life.
12. Gloyn, 2018.

13. Brown, 2018.
14. See Pigliucci, 2019.
15. https://howtobeastoic.wordpress.com/2016/01/19/one-crucial-word/
16. Campbell's four functions of mythology were the metaphysical (or mystic) function, the cosmological (or cosmic) function, the sociological function and the pedagogical function. As Kelsey (2017: 6) explains: "Campbell was a comparative mythologist and anthropologist who spent decades researching stories and rituals of different cultures and communities around the world. He identified what he saw as four common functions of myth. These functions explain the social and psychological levels through which we use myths to help make sense of the world. There is no need to interpret these functions rigidly or use them to [rigidly] categorise [stories]. ... Rather, the intertextual complexities of storytelling and current affairs will often contain overlapping layers of mythological functions. These complexities show us how multiple archetypes are developed through the affective dynamics and recurring functional traits of mythology". (For further examples of how these functions operate in modern life, see Kelsey, 2017: 6–10.)
17. Bonhoeffer, 2010: 23.
18. Ibid.: 23.
19. Haidt, 2012: 335.
20. Robertson, 2019: 41.
21. Epictetus, 2008.
22. Robertson, 2019: 41.
23. Transcript - Introduction to Stoicism: https://learn.donaldrobertson.name/courses/245573/lectures/3869620
24. Gladwell, 2005: 69.
25. Gladwell, 2020.

Bibliography

Aron, A., Aron, E. N., & Smollan, D. (1992). Inclusion of other in the self scale and the structure of interpersonal closeness. *Journal of Personality and Social Psychology, 63*, 596–612.

Aron, A., Aron, E. N., Tudor, M., & Nelson, G. (1991). Close relationships as including other in the self. *Journal of Personality and Social Psychology, 60*, 241–253.

Aron, A., Melinat, E., Aron, E. N., Vallone, R., & Bator, R. (1997). The experimental generation of interpersonal closeness: A procedure and some preliminary findings. *Personality and Social Psychology Bulletin, 23*, 363–377.
Bonhoeffer, D. (2010). 'After Ten Years'. *Letters and papers from prison* (Dietrich Bonhoeffer Works/English, vol. 8). Fortress Press.
Brown, D. (2018). Joe Rogan & Derren Brown – The idea of happiness. *The Joe Rogan experience #1198*. https://www.youtube.com/watch?v=E3DigsvZCXo
Brown, D. (2021). *A Book of Secrets: Finding Solace in a Stubborn World*. London: Penguin.
Epictetus. (2008). *Discourses and selected writings*. London: Penguin.
Evans, J. (2013). *Philosophy for life: And other dangerous situations*. Rider.
Gilroy, P. (2004). *Post-colonial Melancholia*. New York: Columbia University Press.
Gladwell, M. (2005). *Blink: The power of thinking without thinking*. Little Brown.
Gladwell, M. (2020). *The Adam Buxton Podcast*. E.118. Malcolm Gladwell. https://www.adam-buxton.co.uk/podcasts/tag/MALCOLM+GLADWELL.
Gloyn, L. (2017). *The ethics of the family in Seneca*. University Press.
Gloyn, L. (2018). Stoicism and the family by Liz Gloyn. *Modern Stoicism*. https://modernstoicism.com/stoicism-and-the-family-by-liz-gloyn/
Haidt, J. (2012). *The righteous mind: Why good people are divided by politics and religion*. Penguin.
Kelsey, D. (2015). *Media, myth and terrorism: A discourse-mythological analysis of the 'Blitz Spirit' in British newspaper responses to the July 7th bombings*. Palgrave.
Kelsey, D. (2017). *Media and affective mythologies: Discourse, archetypes and ideology in contemporary politics*. Palgrave.
Pigliucci, M. (2019). One crucial word. *How to be a Stoic: An evolving guide to practical stoicism for the 21st century*. https://howtobeastoic.wordpress.com/2016/01/19/one-crucial-word/
Pigliucci, M. (2020). Immigration, borders, and the thorny issue of cosmopolitanism. https://medium.com/lotus-fruit/immigration-borders-and-the-thorny-issue-of-cosmopolitanism-4ba4e1897d00
Robertson, D. (2019). *How to think like a Roman emperor*. St Martin's.
Wodak, R., & Meyer, M. (2001). *Methods of critical discourse analysis*. Sage.

7

Reflections and Transformations

From the moment I started writing this book, it was all about transformation. I was moving into a transformative state myself as I embraced the opportunity to adjust my inner dialogue and live a healthier, happier and more considered life. As I explained earlier, my discovery of Brown's work was serendipitous: it featured new areas of philosophy that resonated with my psychological journey and treatment at the time; and there were other shared interests between Brown's work and my own research and teaching on storytelling, mythology and collective psychology.

This book has focused on a collection of Brown's work that reflects those connections. This has by no means been an exhaustive account of everything that Brown has done over the past 20 years or so—that was not my aim. Rather, I have focused on a particular collection of work that unfolded through Brown's own transformative journey—where he, by his own admission, had moved into a new stage of his career and his act had transformed over time. It had become less about the magic and more about the meaning.

As Brown has explained, meaningful magic is relevant to the time and place in which it is performed: it needs to resonate with its audience beyond the trick or the self-applauding ego of the magician. With this ethos in mind, Brown encourages us to think about our potentials as humans: from our dangerous and darkest traits through to the transformative, heroic and divine qualities that we often struggle to realise.

As we have seen, stories can bind us together and pull us apart; they can show us the light, but they can cover us in darkness. In our personal and collective lives, stories can often be the determining factor between our greatest and most destructive potentials. Stories can determine whether we are happy or suffering—or sometimes a bit of both. Stories can lead us down the path to enlightenment or walk us through the shadows of humanity. Some collective reflection on our stories can help us to understand what state we are in personally and as a society.

Collective Reflections

Before reflecting on the journey we have been on in this book and what this means moving forward, let's consider the key psychological transitions that we need to make in response to our inner and outer crises. Larger Us states those transitions as follows:

> *From fight-or-flight to self-awareness.* When fear and anxiety become central to politics, polarisation is the result. So we need to be able to manage our states so that we can choose how to react to events instead of sliding into triggered fight-or-flight responses.
>
> *From powerlessness to agency.* Feelings of powerlessness—in our lives at home and at work, in communities, in politics—make us unhappy, and prevent us from tackling real world injustices that undermine mental health. So we need to build agency in our lives, and the ability to organise to shape our collective future.
>
> *From disconnection to belonging.* Our epidemic of loneliness isn't just disastrous for health. It also undermines empathy and makes us vulnerable to extremism. So we need to feel like we belong to a larger collective, but one that's radically inclusive, rather than defined in terms of in-group versus out-group.[1]

All three of these transitions are important to individuals and collectives. They are conducive to psychological wellbeing in people and they enable democracies to flourish. The stories and meanings discussed throughout my exploration of Brown's work resonate with these core principles of our collective psychology and show us how popular culture can produce meaningful entertainment that reflects the spirit of these transitions. Popular culture can be undervalued and overlooked as a space for meaningful storytelling, which can speak to individuals and collectives about the times in which we live and how we can create the social and environmental conditions for a better future.

Brown addresses those underlying psychological dynamics at play in our minds and culture—especially in relation to our increasing levels of anxiety and the contagious nature of threat perception in politics. We saw some stand-out examples in Brown's attention to the politics of fear and polarisation, personal circumstances that exacerbate feelings of hopelessness and disempowerment, and problematic messages from the self-help industry that create unhealthy expectations of ourselves and our surroundings. Furthermore, Brown's attention to our individual and collective shadows focused on those psychological dynamics we are less likely to confront in our personal and societal dialogue.

Democracies can only function healthily if enough of us can stay self-aware, feel empathy for each other and share a sense of common identity. From individual agency and empowerment through to the social conditions that might help us to overcome the paralysis of polarisation and tribalism, Brown encourages us to find deeper connections within ourselves and with each other through a transcendental sense of common interest. Much of this is done through his oscillation between personal and collective storytelling.

I began this book, for example, with a personal perspective that found resonance and reassurance in Brown's writing. But I soon reached a point where I recognised that Brown's performative work in recent years has been speaking to our collective psychology on a deeper and more meaningful level than the mere spectacle of magic. For me, the connective thread in Brown's work is not only about our stories and beliefs, it is about transformation. We can be more enlightened when we shed some light on our shadows.

Getting to Know Our Shadows

Attention to the shadow took us beyond the helpful grounding that the Stoics provided in Chap. 3 to consider those emotions and perceptions that Stoicism might help us to navigate and control. But depth psychology also teaches us that we are not always aware of the inner stories that we are telling ourselves and humans are not so well accomplished when it comes to distinguishing what is within and beyond our control. Our inner dialogue often skews our perceptions and we need to dig a little deeper to integrate those aspects of the shadow that are difficult to confront.

When we integrate the shadow, confronting those inner complexes and unconscious authorship of our stories, we can take back more control of ourselves as narrative building machines. We can understand ourselves better on a personal level, which enables us to connect more compassionately with others on a social level. In other words, we can individuate in the way that Jung described. If we live in a culture that encourages this personal growth, then collective individuation becomes a realistic possibility.

As people and societies we are capable of growth, greatness, compassion and empathy. But we are also capable of destruction, selfishness and monstrosity. Through Brown's shows, the audience receives a stark reminder from Jung; in every person there is another one of us whom we do not know and, thus, confronting someone with their shadow means showing them their own light. As Jung points out, the shadow is a moral problem that is relevant to all individuals and partly influenced by the circumstances of our culture.

To work on our shadows as individuals and collectives, we need a more critically reflective culture of introspection to understand how we live in the present and how we might live differently in the future. This introspection is necessary on multiple levels from our personal lives through to our professional and institutional cultures and our society as a whole.

Introspection and Transformation

I became a manager for the first time just after my daughter was born. Those first few years as a team leader and a father coincided with my own developmental journey in CBT, which provided me with ideal toolkits to fix my stories. But CBT also has its fair share of critics. It is often accused of being too focused on fixing the individual rather than the environmental and cultural factors that compromise our mental wellbeing. There are some valid critiques that shouldn't be overlooked here, but we shouldn't underestimate the advantages of CBT either. I see CBT as a toolkit that can help us either manage our responses to those environmental factors that are causing problems beyond our control, or shift our perceptions of problems that we are unnecessarily concerned by because of the stories we have told ourselves. Whether our problems are real or imagined, we can only control our thoughts and actions.

But CBT is only one contributory component available to support our wellbeing, and it's not always the answer. There are environmental, social and professional factors that impact hugely on our mental health and we need to keep those elements in check. We must avoid lazy occupational cultures of CBT provision in which institutions overlook their own working conditions and responsibilities; sending an employee off for some introspective therapy that provides no acknowledgement of the legitimate causes of stress in the workplace. There is little point in workplaces providing access to counselling and wellbeing services if institutions themselves are systematically causing employees to be unnecessarily stressed, disillusioned or disempowered at work. Institutions require collective introspection and transformative leadership that supports their employees in order to reduce the necessity for counselling and undue pressure on wellbeing services.

That said, these collective and institutional responsibilities do not warrant us to completely dismiss the validity of CBT. Individuals can and should help themselves too. For me, I needed to fundamentally rethink the way I lived and what stories I told myself about life—personally and professionally. Yes, there were cultural, educational and professional factors that influenced my inner dialogue and perceptions of the world, and there were institutional pressures and influences that had understandably filled me with self-doubt and anxiety. Some of those factors needed to change, and some of them have. However, some of my personal struggles needed to be fixed, and no amount of finger pointing or projection would solve the problem.

Either way, many of the factors causing me stress were beyond my control and I needed to tell myself healthier stories in response to them. I needed that robustness and resilience that would help me function better and attend only to those factors that were within my control. Particularly at work, there were environmental factors that I could help to change. As a manager I decided it was my duty to put fairness, empathy and collegiality at the centre of our ethos as a team. CBT helped me reach this point and develop the confidence to be a team leader who could encourage positive change. Having helped myself, I could help others and create a fair and supportive environment for my team.

With the help of CBT and Stoicism, I began to embrace the opportunities I had as a leader and a father, to invest in something beyond myself with a sense of gratitude and responsibility, rather than hesitance, fear, self-doubt and anxiety. Holiday and Hanselman suggest that fear is a self-fulfilling prophecy. They quote Seneca to make this point: "Many are harmed by fear itself, and many have come to their fate while dreading fear."[2]

At times, when that imposter voice creeps in, or those obsessive thought patterns seek to construct some sense of impending doom, a bit of negative visualisation is helpful: "Yes", I tell myself, "You could lose everything tomorrow; fate could throw something cruel your way. So be grateful for what you have in this moment and exercise the autonomy you have in your personal and professional life. Have a positive impact on the world, and be a positive influence in your duty of care to others. You won't be here forever, there's work to be done, get on with it!"

When I first became an academic I told myself I would try to avoid taking on any leadership responsibilities as much as possible—a management role was the last thing I wanted as a distraction from my teaching and research. But the experience of becoming a manager was the antithesis of what I expected and became part of my transition away from exclusively individualistic goal-setting and sense of investing in a collective ethos beyond my own aims and ambitions. In doing so, combined with the teaching and research that I already adored, I found a sense of meaning and responsibility that increased my enthusiasm and sense of purpose in my career.

When I began my leadership role, we were a new team that had been assembled following a restructure within our school. Change is always difficult in a large organisation and there were tensions and anxieties throughout the group. It was only by reducing the prohibitive side of my ego that I could find the empathy, patience and compassion that was necessary to gain the trust of a large academic department. This team was full of individuals with their own stories—plenty of which were based on negative past experiences in our institution.

One Team, Many Stories

One of our professional coaches at Newcastle University, Andrew Scott, makes the point that being a team leader is not so much about managing people, but actually managing stories.[3] This is true. A key part of managing those stories is about creating positive changes and influencing people's perceptions so that they have *good reasons* to tell a different story. In my team, I needed to understand why a lack of trust was shaping the stories of some individuals and I needed to tell my stories with those experiences in mind.

My aim was to build a narrative about us as a team that was both positive and *true*. This meant negotiating, compromising and communicating with people who I sometimes disagreed with. This was challenging, and still is at times, but it was the most rewarding aspect of being a leader when I learnt how to connect with colleagues who I had previously struggled to get along with—moving together on a journey where we understood each other and could collaborate with a sense of common purpose and collective interest.

The team flourished and have had many great stories to tell. But the team's story couldn't be told through spin and manipulation; it was told through evidence and action that had a positive impact on collective wellbeing and a sense of collective purpose. And a touch of Brown's strategic pessimism has been necessary at times: we know a rainy day is beyond our control, we know that things might go wrong at times, but we understand that sometimes it is okay to fail. When we don't win, we learn. There are many positives to take from constructive failure, where we reflect and fix things together as a team. As the journalist and podcaster, Elizabeth Day argues, understanding why we fail makes us stronger, and learning how to fail teaches us how to succeed.[4]

A transformative team ethos cannot be solely created or imposed on a team by a manager. These stories must consist of more than words and strategies. They need to be experienced, practiced and felt on the ground by as many people in the team as possible. When success and growth is experienced across a team, everyone has a shared interest, common ground and a sense of belonging in the collective effort. With those positive conditions of collective psychology in mind, individuals can feel responsible, engaged, empowered, connected and autonomous—rather than having those negative feelings of hopelessness, bewilderment, disengagement and powerlessness.

Our team did this through our actions and the story we wrote for ourselves. More staff had more reasons to tell better stories. Over time, some of the historical baggage and stories from the past were replaced (or at least accompanied) by stories about growth, success and optimism. A transitional journey was what we experienced as a team within a large and complex institution.

Institutions must seek to create a collective ethos in which people can see that their voice is heard and their input might sometimes influence decisions and create positive change. Feelings of powerlessness are often a cause of fear and anxiety in our personal, domestic, professional and social lives. This is important since it is not only the biggest stories in global politics that affect us. How we feel within the institutions where we work, or how we communicate in our professional and personal lives, impacts upon our personal and collective wellbeing.

Speaking as President of the mental health charity Mind, Stephen Fry has shared his optimism about the growing attention in our culture to our minds and mental health and what it means to be human. As a guest on Fearne Cotton's podcast, Fry shared his belief that this will become an increasingly prominent focus of society and will produce collective forms of work and inquiry—replacing what we have long considered to be the inevitable, manual nature of human work. Fry hopes that the increasing presence of Artificial Intelligence (AI) might take some of the manual work away from us.[5]

The Changing World of Work

Fry believes our work as humans could become more focused on our humanity, mental wellbeing and our duty of care to each other. He sees a world in which the machines will do more of the mechanical, repetitive and difficult work that we have been used to since the industrial revolution, and we will find other ways of working that will require greater attention to how we feel and how we relate to each other.

As Fry points out, the industrial work that we have been used to for the past 200 years is not an inevitability and hasn't always been the norm. These cultures of work often feel natural and inevitable because it is the only story we know about what it means to work and participate in society. But other ways are possible and inevitable as we grow and evolve as humans and societies. Fry makes the point that making things better for ourselves does not mean we have to make them perfect. Better is fine. If we can progress to a point where the environments in which we live, work and play are better for our collective wellbeing, then those new ways of thinking, talking and behaving are worthwhile.

By Fry's own admission, despite his optimism he is a terrible prophet and he doesn't encourage us to take his words so literally that we envisage a utopian world without the problems and challenges that humans have a tendency to create for themselves. But if Fry is right and the machines do most of the hard graft, we will need to focus on our collective psychology more than ever, as we work out our sense of meaning, purpose and place in the world.

While Fry has spent many years being openly critical about religion, he is equally full of praise for mythology and its importance in our lives.[6] With this sense of meaning, purpose and place in mind, we need to keep an eye on that "myth gap" and how we might fill it if our collective theology continues to decline to the detriment of our cultural mythologies and the sense of collective meaning they have traditionally given us. One concern is the growing secular void in which we have underestimated the importance of communal, ritualistic and meaning-making practices that transcend those inner and outer worlds.

A Secular Void?

Larger Us acknowledges the historical role of religion in its capacity to transcend those inner and outer worlds: "At their best, religions offer a treasury of techniques for navigating and transforming our inner worlds: from meditation or prayer through to shared myths that provide entire societies with meaning, identity, and purpose."[7] Of course, religion has also been exploited to create division and harm, but that is not to suggest it has only served this purpose.

Larger Us suggests that the most significant shifts around the role of religion, which have impacted upon its capacity to accommodate a robust culture of collective psychology, have occurred in two ways:

> First, religion has over recent centuries retreated steadily from the public sphere in the west and become seen as a purely private concern (a shift that Karen Armstrong argues is ground zero for the very modern phenomenon of fundamentalism). Second, more recently, religiosity itself has been in steep decline in most developed countries, especially among the young. The result of these two epochal shifts is that, almost unnoticed, one of our most important spaces for the practice of collective psychology, over thousands of years, has been eroding steadily, leaving a vacuum in its wake.[8]

This is not to suggest that we reverse this decline and return to the past, but the vacuum is the concern. Some will disagree and will see the decline of religion as a welcome absence in modern life. Either way, whether our current collective void (or myth gap) is due to the decline of religion or not, it needs filling.

Filling the Secular Void

Given the increasing attention to mental health in public discourse, there is a growing awareness that we need to work on both our inner and outer worlds to create a better society for present and future generations. As Brown explained in *20 Years of Mind Control*, for all the problems and faults that we often point to in religion, one thing that it was always trying to do was encourage transcendence.[9] Collective ritual and a connective community ethos was fundamental to those theistic societies and stories that people relied upon for meaning, morals, values and a sense of greater purpose beyond the self.

The duty of the individual was both required for the benefit of the community while individuals were equally dependent upon the support of the community itself. And so, in response to the secular void that Alex Evans and the Larger Us team are concerned with in modern life, perhaps we are finding our way towards what will become a primary focus in collective consciousness: a greater understanding and nurturing of our minds, brains and humanity through a nexus of cultural tools available to us in the stories of science, religion, philosophy and spirituality.

Evolutionary biologist, Bret Weinstein makes the point that while religions might be declining in their popularity, we should not lose sight of their value since they contain stories that might seem untrue when taken literally, but that contain deeper truths when understood metaphorically. He argues that stories containing these deeper meanings about our humanity can transcend political persuasions and offer us core values and belief systems that we can share and believe in regardless of our political differences.

Reflecting on the current state of polarisation, Weinstein states the importance of finding those core values and common ground that make us human:

> We find ourselves unfortunately stuck in an archaic argument about policy; frankly the left and right are both out of answers and they should team up on the basis that they agree at a values level about what a functional society should ideally look like.

This is not a proposition for some centrist utopia—Weinstein does not advocate for this. Rather, he is suggesting that we can only find ways forward through negotiations of different social and political interests if we agree on some fundamental truths in our humanity; truths that can accommodate more transformative belief systems that are conducive to our evolutionary interests.

Weinstein believes that the growing perception of religion as a "brain disease" in some militant atheist dogma is prohibiting us from connecting with these universal truths of what it means to be human. Instead, Weinstein argues that we should see religions as products of our evolution, reflecting those belief systems that have flourished because they have accommodated the survival interests of humans.

Weinstein is not suggesting that the structural, institutional or ideological uses of religion are always positive or serving our best interests—we know that our belief systems can be tribal and destructive, especially during times of social adversity or financial austerity. But belief systems can also be ethical, progressive and conducive to further advances in human evolution.

By understanding the literal and metaphorical truths of our stories, we can understand more about our existence than ever before. But we need to find the right stories, and we need the right mindset to do so. As we have seen in Brown's work, we sometimes need to go back to the wisdom of our ancient past to find some lessons that are worth relearning for the benefit of living modern life.

Transformative Philosophy

Despite being an atheist himself, Massimo Pigliucci shares Weinstein's frustration with the militant atheism of recent times. He explains how the Stoics "believed that the universe is structured according to what they called the Logos, which can be interpreted either as God or simply what is sometimes termed 'Einstein's God': the simple indubitable fact that Nature is understandable by reason". It doesn't matter whether a practicing Stoic is theistic or atheistic; it is a philosophy that can offer meaningful principles in either context.[10]

7 Reflections and Transformations

Pigliucci describes Stoicism as a rational and science-friendly philosophy that is open to revision and eminently practical for daily life. As he points out, it does not matter if one believes the Logos is God or Nature, what we need is a shared recognition that a good human life requires the nurturing of one's character and a sense of duty to others. Through our concern for others and our respect for Nature, the Stoics believed that we could moderate our attachment to worldly goods, and cultivate a deeper sense of gratitude for what matters most in life.

With or without religion, the Stoics would argue that we can pursue collective virtues of justice, wisdom, courage and temperance. How we transform our daily practices in accordance to those virtues requires collective support and individual responsibility. As *The Daily Stoic* states: "No matter your age, sex, religion, or social status, you can build a Stoic practice and build a better life for yourself." This is an ideal philosophy to advocate with our collective psychology in mind.

After all, Stoicism was not designed for the political benefit of any particular elite or the interests of one social class of people. It has been adopted by the richest and poorest people in history, and it was taught on the streets to help people cope with everyday life. As Pigliucci explains, Stoicism may not appeal to everyone since it can be demanding and its practices can be surprisingly difficult to apply with discipline and perseverance. But philosophy can help to transform how we think, act, feel and live.

What attracted a scientist like Pigliucci to Stoic philosophy was the Stoics' openness to considering sound challenges to their ideas and a willingness to adapt them accordingly. Pigliucci describes Stoicism as "an open-ended philosophy, ready to incorporate criticism from other schools ... as well as new discoveries". The Stoics saw neither themselves nor their predecessors as the holders of all truth or wisdom. On this point, Pigliucci quotes Seneca: "Men who have made these discoveries before us are not our masters but our guides. Truth lies open for all; it has yet been monopolized. And there is plenty of it left even for prosperity to discover". In response to Seneca, Pigliucci states: "In a world of fundamentalism and hardheaded doctrines, it is refreshing to embrace a worldview that is inherently open to revision."

Without committing to either of the extremes that Pigliucci points to here, we do need to understand what elements of religion or ancient philosophy are significant to our collective wellbeing. In other words, the metaphorical truths, mythological functions and ritualistic meditations of religion combined with ancient philosophies for life might teach us some lessons on how to make new myths for current times.

Another problem we currently face as a society is loneliness and social disconnection.[11] Loneliness damages our stories because the more disconnected we become, the less empathetic we are towards others, and the more susceptible we are to "them-and-us" thinking that drives us further apart. Loneliness makes people more self-centred, more socially resentful towards other groups and susceptible to radicalisation. Our narrative building machinery suffers under such conditions and prohibits the storytelling required for more connected and unified communities. We need to get connected.

Communal Connections

In Johan Hari's book, *Lost Connections: Why You're Depressed and How to Find Hope*, he shows that we have typically understood depression and anxiety as problems related to brain chemistry, which can be managed with prescription drugs.[12] However, as the scientific evidence has grown, and the drugs that people are prescribed often fail to provide the long-term benefits that patients hope for, we are learning that depression and anxiety are not only about brain chemistry. Hari does not doubt that antidepressants can help people in many cases, but it has become increasingly clear that the state of our mental health is significantly influenced by the social and environmental factors involved in how we live than we previously thought.

Jonathan Gottschall makes the point that despite living in an age of Prozac and other antidepressant drugs, it is interesting how the most common way that people seek help for depression is through a therapist. This is because therapists help us to understand our stories and guide us to tell better stories for our wellbeing. Gottschall refers to the psychologist, Michele Crossley who explains how depression can often be linked to a patient's incoherent inner dialogue, inadequate narratives of the self, and other awry life stories that have lost their way.[13]

These points are important because societies are reliant upon healthy individuals who can connect and relate to each other as a collective. Individuals need strong community connections, but those collective interests also suffer without robust individuals. Larger Us makes the point that it is becoming increasingly evident that democracies can only function properly if we are self-aware and empathetic towards others, with a sense of common interest and identity.

Without this approach at the forefront of our collective thinking, the internal and external crises we experience are amplifying and reinforcing each other. Larger Us suggests that if we are to reverse this dynamic, then healing the world will mean we need to heal ourselves *and* each other.[14]

Transformative Mythologies

In Brown's work we are reminded that our stories, shadows and projections are, in part, conditional to our cultural environments *and* human characteristics. We are encouraged to recognise that we are all prone to getting caught up in narrative allegiances that can blind us to alternative moral worlds. Nonetheless, we can transcend political differences to produce more stable foundations for negotiating social change. Better stories about our humanity can enable us to do this. Our stories provide the binding, ritualistic and transpersonal qualities required for us to foster shared values and cohesive belief systems.

However, the old myths that we have lived by for so long might need some rethinking. The monomyth (hero's journey), for example, is usually about the individual who undergoes the individuation process—confronting the shadow, overcoming trials and tribulations and returning home with something in return for the community.

These hero stories are retold time and again in popular culture to convey particular meanings, values, ideals and ideologies of our times. Hero stories often resonate with us collectively because they metaphorically reflect the individuation process at the core of us growing and flourishing as individuals and investing in a greater cause beyond ourselves. We saw this in Brown's work. But this was not a simple case of regurgitating archetypal storytelling for the sake of mere drama and entertainment.

These stories were told and understood in relation to the times, spaces and places in which we live. Therefore, we should think carefully about the role of classical mythologies and the purpose they serve in society. That is not to suggest they are wrong, but I am suggesting they might need refining. After all, as Joseph Campbell showed, all societies using the monomyth have refined it to suit the culture in which the story was told.

Towards a Modern Monomyth

While the monomyth clearly applies to *Sacrifice* and *Apocalypse*, Brown's shows make an important point by not reducing the meaning of the transformation down to the individual. The message is collective. And if we are to make the monomyth work in modern times, we need to find ways of adapting its archetypal role for current and future generations. If we are to think more about our "hivish" behaviour and how it influences what we do (for better or worse), then we need to think about what the monomyth means for *our* journey, not only as individuals but as a collective.

Brown's work shows why we should not lose sight of the individual journeys we need to pursue through our own lives and stories—pursuing those individuation processes that enable us to integrate our shadows and transform for the benefit of the collective (the hero returns home with something to give back to the community). This is the developmental cycle that the monomyth has historically reflected. But we cannot lose sight of the fact that collectives need to help their individuals and we are all better off when we work together.

Responsible, empathetic and compassionate individuals make for more connected and unified collectives. Those collectives shape the environment, culture and development of individuals. This is a symbiotic cycle that we need to recognise if we are to envisage an entirely new story for the benefit of future generations. If more considered communities foster compassion, tranquillity and robustness, then societies can flourish. But we need to get collective. Humans get things done when we work together.

The Collective Journey

Collectives are eclectic. Our differences are what can help us thrive and flourish. Some scholars have recently urged us to rethink the narrative role of archetypes such as the monomyth. Maya Zuckerman, for example, calls for us to draw inspiration from Campbell's monomyth by creating our own variations to the Hero's Journey—like those he spotted across every culture he looked at:

> Joseph Campbell gave us an amazing model from which our [human] journey can draw inspiration. ... The 'simple' story no longer represent[s] who we are as a people. Our modern civilization is very different, but the narrative is just starting to change. ... The Collective Journey is a nonlinear, multiplatform, physical and digital experience and story of several diverse people, groups, tribes, cultures, networks, coming together for a higher purpose and a common cause. In their journeys, they move beyond their own individual experiences to a cohesive collective that is both the sum of all individuals and also a new entity entirely.[15]

As Zuckerman explains, archetypes are not static forms—their narrative roles are partly determined by the cultures in which they appear. We need to find ways, as Zuckerman suggests, of using the monomyth for a new collective story that takes us on a journey and tells us a story that will save our future. This enables us to transcend from the individual narrative into one with a global perspective of humanity, incorporating diverse communities and perspectives while continuing to support individual growth and fulfilment of potential.

We can see how Brown's work applies in both contexts here. The monomyth is still crucial to self-development and individuation. Equally, it is through empathy, kindness and dialogue that we can serve collective interests, together on a journey that pursues the common good for all humanity. Zuckerman argues that an evolved form of the monomyth in "The Collective Journey" is a story that can help us move towards a greater narrative with a global perspective of humanity:

> Stories have always been a part of what makes us human, and new narratives are important in times of great transformations. The ancient stories cannot contain and serve us as we are embarking on changes at a planetary level. We need The Collective Journey as a teaching tool for the masses to come together to work on our most pressing matters. The Collective Journey can become a tool for social movements, climate change groups, and empower groups to change political narratives in geographical areas. These are stories of empowerment that are accepting of all voices and can bring forth positive change.[16]

This is about the healthy and necessary integration of individuals and communities for the benefit of collective individuation—creating a better world for a better future.

After all, as Zuckerman points out, we are more connected and aware of each other than ever in our history. As we stand at the threshold of a future that is dependent on how we use these connections and communication, we need a story that celebrates a collective journey in the same way that we have mythologised individual heroism. As narrative building machines, we need to transform ourselves and our stories need to transform with us.

That said, we don't always have to be heroes, and we are not seeking to pursue one grand goal via one grand narrative. Our actions do not always require us to pursue triumphant milestones for humanity. But we all need to do our bit. This won't always be glamorous. We need to think about a larger us through a deeper sense of empathy and common purpose in our smaller actions and our private stories. As Ryan Holiday points out, it is not what we read, say or write that matters most, it is *how* we live our daily lives that determines our character—small moments teach us big lessons.[17]

We need to get on and take those steps forward, however small they might be. To quote Marcus Aurelius: "Don't go on discussing what a good person should be. Just be one".[18] When we apply temperance in our pursuit of justice we have to accept that the small steps we take in the passing moments of daily life are as crucial as any grand story for humanity.

Stories to Save the World

Michael Meade is a distinguished storyteller and author who utilises his knowledge in mythology, anthropology and psychology to improve community relations. His organisation, Mosaic Multicultural Foundation, helps to inspire creative and ceremonial activities in communities of need—fostering cross-cultural alliances, community healing, personal growth and mentorship through educational events and connections to meaningful traditions.

With some distinct traits of the archetypal magician in his own persona, Meade's public profile describes his ability to combine "hypnotic storytelling" with "street-savvy perceptiveness" and "spellbinding interpretations" of ancient myths and cross-cultural rituals.[19] Through his work, Meade shows how we can synergise these disciplines by reconnecting with our ancestral wisdom and applying it to the stories we are living today.

When Meade appeared on Russell Brand's *Under the Skin* podcast, Brand asked Meade to share a story that might help us to understand the current crises that we find ourselves in.[20] Accounting for the interconnected, social and environmental crises we face, Meade told a story that resonates with the prudent self-awareness and realistic expectations we need to have of ourselves—individually and collectively—when we try to fix the problems we face.

Meade shared a native American story about a cave that contains all the knowledge that everybody's been looking for but nobody ever goes to. Inside the cave is an old woman weaving the most beautiful garment anyone has ever seen. Every so often the old woman has to walk to the back of the cave where there is a cauldron hanging over an ancient fire. The cauldron contains the seeds of all the plants, trees, grains, fruits and flowers in the world, which will die if the seeds burn, so the woman has to stir the cauldron. As she moves slowly towards the back of the cave, a black dog appears next to her garment. The dog sees a loose thread and pulls on it until the entire garment is unravelled.

When the lady returns from the cauldron, she sees that the beautiful garment has been unravelled into chaos. As she sits down, she picks up a loose thread and begins to weave again. This time, her vision of the garment is even more beautiful than the one she had made before. Meade says that when the elders are telling the children this story, one of the children would typically say, "Damn that black dog!"

But the elders point out that if it wasn't for the black dog she would have finished the garment and it would have been perfect (meaning it would be over and done with, which is connected to death). Rather than cursing circumstances she cannot control, she takes the chance to start again on something even greater than she had before.

As Meade explains, the elders tell the children that the story means we should be grateful for what unravels the world because the world unravels only to be rewoven out of threads. In response to the current crises we face, Meade compares us to the old woman as we stare at the chaos unfolding in the world. He explains that it is neither our job to fix it all, nor should we collapse into fear and worry. It is our job to pick up a thread like the woman does and begin with the new vision.

Meade finishes this story by referring to an old Irish myth. He says: "When the world falls apart the pieces are laying in the margins and our job is to pick up a piece from the margin and pull it back to the middle." He relates this to the woman in the cave by making the point that if everyone brings their thread forward we can reweave the garment of the world from our individual threads. Nobody has to be a hero. We all just have to be dedicated to weaving.

Collective Weaving Machines

We are not perfect. We cannot expect to fix everything now. But we cannot afford to collapse into fear and worry or, worse still, extinction. We are not pursuing perfection or extinction, but we are trying to make things better. As Stephen Fry said earlier, better is fine. Those Stoic virtues can be applied through our collective weaving as we build a better world. We can pursue justice for humanity by weaving our wisdom, courage and temperance together through a collective story that pursues a better vision for a better future.

While our modern adaptation of the monomyth might have its part to play in our story moving forward, that story needs to be collectively realistic and progressively possible. We don't always need individual heroics and we are not working towards a grand finale. The journey we pursue will require collective weaving that requires us all to bring our thread to the garment. Meade's story reminds us to avoid a grand narrative that leads us down the collective blind alley of pursuing utopia. Humans will always create and find problems for themselves. Humanity's shadow contains its greatest and darkest potentials, and keeping this shadow in check will never be a simple task.

Chaos can always descend from order, but order can always be re-established if we are collectively robust enough to pick up our loose ends and start weaving again. The lessons we learn increase the wisdom we apply in our pursuit of justice. As we avoid collapsing with fear, we can use our collective courage to support each other. Our temperance can keep our egos in check as we remember that we cannot fix everything ourselves, but we can be part of a collective story that weaves together something meaningful. A magical story to enlighten us.

Brown reminds us that life is an evolutionary miracle, and one we should cherish:

> Here's another miracle: the fact that you are sat there right now ... One of your father's 12 trillion sperm with half your name on it just happening to collide with one of your mother's thousands of eggs with the other half of your name on it. ... You are undeniably at one end of your very own perfect unbroken ancestral chain that starts with you and goes right back to the very first single celled organism seven billion years ago. That is a miracle. And we can remember that when we tell ourselves we are a bit fat or our lives are a bit rubbish. This is our one life and the one body we have. We can tell ourselves a different story about it at least.[21]

Through our stories we can be kinder to ourselves and others. So, let's start our story with a call for kindness. After all, as Brown once said: "The single most valuable human trait, the one quality every school child and adult should be taught to nurture, is, quite simply, kindness".[22]

Notes

1. Larger Us, 2018: 3–4.
2. Holiday and Hanselman, 2016: 47.
3. Andrew Scott, 2016.
4. https://www.elizabethdayonline.co.uk/podcast
5. Fry, 2018a.
6. Fry, 2018b.
7. Larger Us, 2018: 14.
8. Ibid.: 14.
9. Brown, 2020.
10. For an example of Stoicism applied in modern Christian living, see: Kevin Vost, 2015. For a discussion of Al-Kindi's work on Stoicism and Islam, see: Robertson, 2020. For a discussion of parallels between Hindu and Stoicism, see: Bishop, 1970. For discussions on Stoicism and Buddhism, see: Chen, 2020; Wright and Pigliucci, 2017.
11. Larger Us, 2018; Hari, 2018.
12. Hari, 2018.
13. Gottschall, 2012: 175.
14. As the Larger Us report (2018: 2) states, we need to focus on creating the breakthrough scenario that steers us away from the prospective catastrophes of a background scenario: "Our future is pitched as a choice between two scenarios: one's the breakdown scenario. Climate chaos, extinction, scarcity, inequality, tribalism, collapse. This paper's about how we get to the other one: the breakthrough scenario. A future of safety, restoration, and flourishing, for us and for the world. Whether we make it there depends primarily on what goes on inside our minds. Whether we're able to manage our mental and emotional states, at a moment of extraordinary turbulence. Whether we reach for the right stories to explain what's happening at this moment in history. Whether enough of us see ourselves as part of a Larger Us instead of a them-and-us, or just an atomised 'I'".
15. Zuckerman, 2016.
16. Ibid.
17. Holiday, 2020.
18. Aurelius, 2002.

19. Meade's profile page at Mosaic Voices can be found here: https://www.mosaicvoices.org/about
20. Meade, 2020.
21. Brown, 2018.
22. Brown, 2011: 91.

Bibliography

Aurelius, M. (2002). *Meditations*. Penguin.
Bishop, D. (1970). Parallels in hindu and stoic ethical thought. *Studies in Comparative Religion, 4*(2). http://www.studiesincomparativereligion.com/Public/articles/browse_g.aspx?ID=135
Brown, D. (2011). *Confessions of a conjuror*. Transworld.
Brown, D. (2018). *Miracle*. Netflix.
Brown, D. (2020, August 16). *20 Years of Mind Control*. Channel 4.
Chen, G. (2020). *The striking similarities between stoicism and Buddhism*. https://thestoicsage.com/stoicism-and-buddhism/
Fry, S. (2018a). *Happy Place Podcast*. https://open.spotify.com/episode/6MNOV4A8QjOnTOuSsqa5YV?si=93V22YIhRN2A_k1xosESaA&dl_branch=1&nd=1
Fry, S. (2018b). *Mythos: The Greek myths retold*. Penguin.
Gottschall, J. (2012). *The storytelling animal: How stories make us human*. Mariner.
Hari, J. (2018). *Lost connections: Uncovering the real causes of depression – And the unexpected solutions*. Bloomsbury.
Holiday, R. (2020). It's the little moments that make the big lessons. *Ryan Holiday: Meditations on strategy and life*. https://ryanholiday.net/study/
Holiday, R., & Hanselman, S. (2016). *The Daily Stoic: 366 meditations on wisdom, perseverance, and the art of living*. Penguin.
Larger Us. (2018). *A larger us*. file:///C:/Users/Admin/Downloads/A%20Larger%20Us%20(2).pdf.
Meade, M. (2020, August 3). A story to save the world. *Russell Brand: Under the skin podcast*. https://www.youtube.com/watch?v=1VaEKZRa1rQ
Robertson, D. (2020). Stoicism and Islam: Al-Kindi's device for dispelling sorrows. https://medium.com/stoicism-philosophy-as-a-way-of-life/stoicism-and-islam-53a46f3f3e4d

Scott, A. (2016). *Shifting stories: How changing their stories can transform people*. Troubador.

Vost, K. (2015). *The porch and the cross: Ancient Stoic wisdom for modern Christian living*. Angelico Press.

Wright, R. and Pigliucci, M. (2017). Buddhism vs. Stoicism. *The Wright Show*. https://www.youtube.com/watch?v=qcEiF6_Uevo.

Zuckerman, M. (2016). Transformative media: From the hero's journey to our collective journey. *Kosmos Journal*. Online at: https://www.kosmosjournal.org/article/transformative-media-from-the-heros-journey-to-our-collective-journey/. Last accessed 8 Apr 2020.

Postface: Collective Growing

Stoicism is not a magic bullet. One does not need to identify as "a Stoic". As Brown points out, Stoicism is something to lean into when we need it; it can provide us with some grounding and clarity during troubled times, and it offers alternative advice to those unhelpful messages we often receive in our noisy lives.[1]

There are times when a Stoic approach can keep us on track or give us the nudge that we need. But this doesn't mean we live in perfect harmony with nature—like the ideal of a Stoic sage—seamlessly void of anxiety, anger, loneliness or other emotional blips. As discussed earlier, by the time Brown finished writing *Happy* he had grown to appreciate the value of some disturbance in our lives and the important signals that anxiety sends us about the situations we find ourselves in.[2]

If we pay attention to those signals and understand what they are really telling us, they provide opportunities for growth—especially when we reach out to seek help.[3] Even Marcus Aurelius can reassure us here: "Don't be ashamed of needing help. You have a duty to fulfil just like a soldier on the wall of battle. So what if you are injured and can't climb up without another soldier's help?"[4] Reaching out doesn't make us weak. It makes us stronger, and it's our duty to support each other. As the courageous Helen

Keller once said, "Walking with a friend in the dark is better than walking alone in the light".[5] It takes courage to help and be helped.

For Brown, the problem is not that we experience the burdensome weight of daily life and the anxieties that it brings—nor should we use our Stoic toolkits to completely avoid disturbances either. The problem is that we often think we are the only ones suffering. If we were all a little more open about the innate disturbances of being alive we might feel a little less isolated. We would realise that pretty much everybody is experiencing similar feelings in one way or another.

Shortly after I finished writing this book, Brown published *A Book of Secrets: Finding Solace in a Stubborn World*. Here, Brown considers how we might recognise the commonality of negative emotional states and use them as opportunities for consolation, compassion and connection. Brown suggests we should sometimes just allow these negative states to come and go as a shared and common part of life in our collective psychology—understanding what these states say about the human condition and growing through those experiences that we share *together*.

Everybody is working through their own struggles in one way or another—it is *how* we respond to those struggles that matters. Too often we have a tendency to think, "But nobody around me really feels like *this*". When we tell ourselves a story that suggests everybody else is happier, more confident and content (because their Instagram feed suggests so), we fail to appreciate how life's burdens and uncertainties are what actually connect us most in our shared experiences of living. And it is this connection that Brown has recently turned his attention to.

At the time of reading *A Book of Secrets*, I was looking forward to a post-lockdown date night with my wife—we had tickets to see Brown's latest stage show, *Showman*. In an unfamiliarly full theatre, which felt peculiarly 'normal' after lockdown, Brown was making us, as an audience, feel a little more connected than we had been for some time.

But he wasn't the God-like figure on stage; true to form, he was the mentor, the wise old man, guiding us on our way as we all tried to settle back into life and social participation. The archetypal magician was communicating with his audience, using his knowledge and skillsets to enlighten people, helping the community to discover new possibilities, shedding light on who we are, and helping us grow after the collective suffering of a global pandemic. Brown was helping us discover things about ourselves—helping us *feel* the way that we edit our stories and make sense of the world, while reminding us that we are all in this together.

Soon, with a stack of notes and examples from this new material, I had a dilemma: the initial temptation was to go back through my book and ensure that Brown's latest works featured throughout each chapter wherever relevant points occurred. However, other than a few notes and quotes here and there, I decided against this.

This book was never meant to be an examination of Brown's entire career. Rather, it has paid rigorous attention to a collection of works that resonated with me due to a performative turn in Brown's career and a meaningful moment in my life. Brown also asked audiences not to give away any details on what happens in his latest show, since it would compromise future performances for other audiences. So I won't take any risks in this respect either.

While Stoicism has been incredibly useful and now plays a practical role in my daily life, there are still times when I realise that no amount of ancient wisdom can pull me from the depths of anxiety or uncertainty that come and go through recurring episodes. That's fine. We never stop learning and growing.

When I was trying to publish this book, I was anything but Stoic: constantly checking for emails from publishers; hoping and wishing for outcomes I couldn't control; worrying about how a reviewer or editor might interpret my work; doubting whether I would ever get the book published; preoccupied with frustration and bruised by rejections. Rather than resisting or hopelessly trying to avoid the self-indulgent fears and frustrations of publishing, I had to let them sit, but I also had to *notice* what was happening.

Rather than becoming overwhelmed and all-consumed by anxiety (as I would have in the past), I used my toolkits to understand it. I noticed that some of this stemmed from unreasonable elements of my ego, impatience caused by my emotional investment in this project, and typical insecurities stemming from the common anxieties of writing and publishing.

Meanwhile, I noticed that other frustrations were understandable responses to concerns and circumstances beyond my control. I couldn't banish those feelings, but I could curtail the discomfort they would otherwise cause me. I told myself this negative state would pass and shifted focus in my daily activities to accommodate my temporary divergence of mindset.

That state did pass—events played out and life took care of itself. I was fine with this because my personal growth had enabled me not to permanently avoid anxiety, but to sit with it, understand it, learn something from it, and allow it to move on. This was not a crisis. Everything was absolutely fine. Previously, I would have been much more agitated, unreflective and challenging to be around. This time, I was just a bit annoying.

My writing of this book had already been rudely interrupted by a global pandemic. The universe had reminded me that it couldn't care less about what my plans were. Writing was put on hold, research time was non-existent, the lockdowns were challenging for everyone, and working in a university posed multiple pressures and uncertainties—as it did for so many of us in our personal and professional lives. None of us knew what would happen, and I am grateful that my personal circumstances were extremely fortunate compared to many.

Professionally, the Stoics proved to be useful at this time: courage, justice, wisdom and temperance were at the forefront of my ethos as a team leader who was trying to reassure, support and lead my colleagues by example. Personally, the pandemic taught us all to be grateful for things that we often take for granted – family, security, nature, life, friends and colleagues.

Ataraxia—that sense of tranquillity that the ancient Greeks spoke of—can be found in a sense of gratitude for what matters most. Only through gratitude for what really matters can we pursue the right course for justice in the world.

Love what you have. You never know when it might disappear. Cherish the moment.

Amor fati. Memento mori. Carpe diem.

Postface: Collective Growing 177

Portrait by Leanne Pearce. www.leannepearce.co.uk. Instagram: @leanne_pearce_artist

Notes

1. Brown, 2018.
2. Ibid.
3. Brown 2021a, b.
4. Holiday, 2021c.
5. Keller had lost her sight and hearing when she was 19 months old, but she went on to become the first deaf-blind person to graduate from university with a Bachelor of Arts degree, and became a leading voice for human rights and social justice.

Bibliography

Brown, D. (2018). Joe Rogan & Derren Brown – The idea of happiness. The Joe Rogan experience #1198. https://www.youtube.com/watch?v=E3DigsvZCXo

Brown, D. (2021a). *A book of secrets: Finding solace in a stubborn world*. London: Penguin.

Brown, D. (2021b, September 11). *Showman*. Empire Theatre.

Holiday, R. (2021c). *Don't be ashamed to ask for help*. https://dailystoic.com/dont-be-ashamed-to-ask-for-help/

Bibliography

Abram, D., & Sheldrake, R. (2015, August 6). *What is magic? A dialogue with David Abram*. At Hollyhock Leadership Learning Centre. https://www.sheldrake.org/audios/what-is-magic-a-dialogue-with-david-abram

Aron, A., Aron, E. N., & Smollan, D. (1992). Inclusion of other in the self scale and the structure of interpersonal closeness. *Journal of Personality and Social Psychology, 63*, 596–612.

Aron, A., Aron, E. N., Tudor, M., & Nelson, G. (1991). Close relationships as including other in the self. *Journal of Personality and Social Psychology, 60*, 241–253.

Aron, A., Melinat, E., Aron, E. N., Vallone, R., & Bator, R. (1997). The experimental generation of interpersonal closeness: A procedure and some preliminary findings. *Personality and Social Psychology Bulletin, 23*, 363–377.

Aurelius, M. (1998). *Meditations*. University Press.

Aurelius, M. (2002). *Meditations*. Penguin.

Aurelius, M. Collier, J., Dacier, A., & Gataker, T. (1726). The emperor Marcus Antoninus: His conversation with himself.

Barthes, R. (1993). *Mythologies*. Vintage.

Bassil-Morozow, H. (2018). *Jungian theory for storytellers: A toolkit*. Routledge.

Blavatsky, H. (1877). *Isis unveiled*. Theosophical University Press.

Bochner, A. (1997). It's about time: Narrative and the divided self. *Qualitative Inquiry, 3*(4), 418–438.

Bochner, A., & Ellis, C. (1992). Personal narrative as a social approach to interpersonal communication. *Communication Theory, 2*(2), 165–172.

Bonhoeffer, D. (2010). 'After Ten Years'. *Letters and papers from prison* (Dietrich Bonhoeffer Works/English, vol. 8). Fortress Press.

Brand, R. (2017). *Recovery: Freedom from our addictions*. Henry Holt and Company.

Brinkmann, S. (2017). *Stand firm*. Polity Press.

Brown, D. (2006, January 4). *The Heist*. Channel 4.

Brown, D. (2011a). *Confessions of a conjuror*. Transworld.

Brown, D. (2011b, April 25). *Miracles for Sale*. Channel 4.

Brown, D. (2012a, November 2). *Apocalypse*. Channel 4.

Brown, D. (2012b). *Apocalypse Q&A*. https://derrenbrown.co.uk/apocalypse-qa/

Brown, D. (2012c). *Steven and Karl*. https://www.youtube.com/watch?v=AqAqhaa0DhE

Brown, D. (2016a). *Happy: Why more or less everything is absolutely fine*. Penguin.

Brown, D. (2016b). New Derren Brown "Happy" book interview. *BBC Breakfast*. https://www.youtube.com/watch?v=ay7IyqQLjtg

Brown, D. (2016c). Derren Brown: 'Performers can be shy and despite my dramatic stunts, in reality, I truly do not like the attention'. *The Belfast Telegraph*. https://www.belfasttelegraph.co.uk/entertainment/news/derren-brown-performers-can-be-shy-and-despite-my-dramatic-stunts-in-reality-i-truly-do-not-like-the-attention-35064763.html

Brown, D. (2017). *Renowned illusionist Derren Brown on stoicism and why more or less everything is absolutely fine*. https://dailystoic.com/derren-brown/

Brown, D. (2018a). Joe Rogan & Derren Brown – The idea of happiness. *The Joe Rogan experience #1198*. https://www.youtube.com/watch?v=E3DigsvZCXo

Brown, D. (2018b). *The Push*. Netflix.

Brown, D. (2018c). *Sacrifice*. Netflix.

Brown, D. (2018d). *Miracle*. Netflix.

Brown, D. (2018e). #143 Keys to the mind: A conversation with Derren Brown. *Making sense with Sam Harris*. https://samharris.org/podcasts/143-keys-mind/

Brown, D. (2019a, May 31). Desert Island Discs. *BBC Radio 4*. https://www.bbc.co.uk/programmes/m0005dyb

Brown, D. (2019b). An illusionist reacts to movies and TV shows about illusions. *Vulture*. https://www.vulture.com/2019/08/derren-brown-reacts-to-movies-and-tv-shows-about-illusions.html

Brown, D. (2019c). Derren Brown: The magician's secrets. BBC World Service: Outlook. https://www.bbc.co.uk/programmes/w3csyhj9

Brown, D. (2019d). *The Adam Buxton podcast*. Ep.110: Derren Brown. https://www.adam-buxton.co.uk/podcasts/17

Brown, D. (2020a). *The path to less stress? Strategic pessimism.* | Derren Brown | Big Think. https://www.youtube.com/watch?v=wKfUK1Gd6YM

Brown, D. (2020b). Derren Brown's new book offers advice on overcoming anxiety. *Sky News*. https://www.youtube.com/watch?v=lKqwl4hb-ew

Brown, D. (2020c, August 16). *20 Years of Mind Control*. Channel 4.

Brown, D. (2021a). *A book of secrets: Finding solace in a stubborn world*. London: Penguin.

Brown, D. (2021b, September 11). *Showman*. Empire Theatre.

Byrne, R. (2006a). *The secret*. Atria.

Byrne, R. (2006b). *The secret*. Prime Time Productions.

Campbell, J. (1949). *The hero with a thousand faces*. Pantheon.

Chen, G. (2020). *The striking similarities between stoicism and Buddhism*. https://thestoicsage.com/stoicism-and-buddhism/

Clay, R. (2020). 21st-century mythologies with Richard Clay. *BBC Four*. https://www.bbc.co.uk/iplayer/episode/m000p9t7/21stcentury-mythologies-with-richard-clay

Condradie, E. (2013). A semiotic notion of transcendence. *Studia Hist. Ecc.* 39. http://www.scielo.org.za/scielo.php?script=sci_arttext&pid=S1017-04992013000300004

Couser, G. T. (1997). *Recovering bodies: Illness, disability, and life writing*. University of Wisconsin Press.

De Botton, A. (2013). *Religion for atheists*. Penguin.

Deflem, M. (2016). *Lady Gaga and the sociology of fame: The rise of a pop star in an age of celebrity*. Palgrave.

Dennett, D. (2017). The illusion of consciousness. *TED Talk*. https://www.youtube.com/watch?v=fjbWr3ODbAo

Denzin, N. (1989). *Interpretive biography*. Sage.

Dunn, G. (2011). The wonderful smallness of evil in Oz. In R. Auxier & P. Seng (Eds.), *The wizard of Oz and philosophy: Wicked wisdom of the west*. Open Court.

Ehrenreich, B. (2010). *Bright-sided: How positive thinking is undermining America*. Picador.

Ellis, C., Adams, T., & Bochner, A. (2011). Autoethnography: An overview. *FQS Journal, 12*, 1. https://www.qualitative-research.net/index.php/fqs/article/view/1589/3095

Epictetus. (2007). *Art of living: The classical manual on virtue, happiness, and effectiveness.* HarperCollins.

Epictetus. (2012). *Discourses and selected writings.* Penguin.

Evans, A. (2017). *The myth gap: What happens when evidence and arguments aren't enough.* Eden Project Books.

Evans, J. (2013). *Philosophy for life: And other dangerous situations.* Rider.

Evers, C. (2006). How to surf. *Journal of Sport & Social Issues, 30*, 229–243.

Farnsworth, W. (2018). *The practicing Stoic: A philosophical user's manual.* Godine.

Farnsworth, W. (2021). *The socratic method: A practitioner's handbook.* Godine.

Flood, C. (2002). *Political myth.* Routledge.

Freud, S. (2017). *Studies in hysteria.* Penguin.

Fry, S. (2018a). *Happy Place Podcast.* https://open.spotify.com/episode/6MNOV4A8QjOnTOuSsqa5YV?si=93V22YIhRN2A_k1xosESaA&dl_branch=1&nd=1

Fry, S. (2018b). *Mythos: The Greek myths retold.* Penguin.

Giles, D. (2020). A typology of persona as suggested by Jungian theory and the evolving persona studies literature. *Persona Studies, 6*(1), 15–29.

Gladwell, M. (2005). *Blink: The power of thinking without thinking.* Little Brown.

Gladwell, M. (2009). *Talking to strangers: What we should know about the people we don't know.* Little Brown.

Gloyn, L. (2017). *The ethics of the family in Seneca.* University Press.

Gloyn, L. (2018). Stoicism and the family by Liz Gloyn. *Modern Stoicism.* https://modernstoicism.com/stoicism-and-the-family-by-liz-gloyn/

Goto-Jones, C. (2016). *Conjuring Asia: Magic, orientalism and the making of the modern world.* University Press.

Gottschall, J. (2012). *The storytelling animal: How stories make us human.* Mariner.

Graver, M. (2007). *Stoicism and emotion.* University Press.

Haidt, J. (2012). *The righteous mind: Why good people are divided by politics and religion.* Penguin.

Harari, Y. N. (2014). *Power and imagination.* http://www.ynharari.com/topic/power-and-imagination/

Hari, J. (2018). *Lost connections: Uncovering the real causes of depression – And the unexpected solutions.* Bloomsbury.

Harris, S. (2019). #150 – The map of misunderstanding. *Making sense with Sam Harris.* https://samharris.org/podcasts/150-map-misunderstanding/

Hay, L. (1984). *You can heal your life*. Hay House.
Hierocles. (2015). *Ethical fragments*. Penguin.
Hill, N. (1937). *Think and grow rich*. The Ralston Society.
Holiday, R. (2014). *The obstacle is the way: The ancient art of turning adversity into advantage*. Profile.
Holiday, R. (2016). *The ego is the enemy: The fight to master our greatest opponent*. Profile.
Holiday, R. (2019). *Stillness is the key: An ancient strategy for modern life*. Profile.
Holiday, R. (2020a). Daily Stoic Sundays: 10 of the most Stoic moments in history. *The Daily Stoic Podcast*. https://dailystoic.com/daily-stoic-sundays-10-of-the-most-stoic-moments-in-history/
Holiday, R. (2020b). It's the little moments that make the big lessons. *Ryan Holiday: Meditations on strategy and life*. https://ryanholiday.net/study/
Holiday, R. (2020c). *7 benefits of adopting a Stoic practice in 2020*. https://dailystoic.com/benefits-stoicism/
Holiday, R. (2021a). *Courage is calling: Fortune favours the brave*. Profile.
Holiday, R. (2021b). *You have to see both*. https://dailystoic.com/you-have-to-see-both/
Holiday, R. (2021c). *Don't be ashamed to ask for help*. https://dailystoic.com/dont-be-ashamed-to-ask-for-help/
Holiday, R., & Hanselman, S. (2016). *The Daily Stoic: 366 meditations on wisdom, perseverance, and the art of living*. Penguin.
Hollis, J. (1993). *The middle passage: From misery to meaning in mid-life* (Studies in Jungian psychology by Jungian analysts). Toronto: Inner City Books.
Houdini. (1953). George Marshall. Paramount Pictures.
Illusionist, The. (2006). Neil Burger. Yari Film Group / Freestyle.
Inwood, B. (2018). *Stoicism: A very brief introduction*. University Press.
Irvine, W. (2008). *A guide to the good life: The ancient art of Stoic joy*. University Press.
Irvine, W. (2020). *Stoicon 2020. William B. Irvine*. https://www.youtube.com/watch?v=QfdvrY731yc
Johannsen, D., & Otto, B. (2021). *Fictional practice: Magic, narration, and the power of imagination*. Brill.
Jung, C. (2014). *The collected works of C.G. Jung*. University Press.
Jung, C. G. (1938). Psychology and religion. In *Psychology and religion: West and east, collected works of C.G. Jung* (Vol. 11). Routledge.
Jung, C. G. (1959). *The archetypes and the collective unconscious*. Routledge and Kegan.

Jung, C. G. (2013). *The psychology of transference*. Taylor & Francis.
Kahneman, D. (2012). *Thinking, fast and slow*. Penguin.
Kaufman, B. (2020). *Transcend: The new science of self-actualization*. Penguin.
Kelsey, D. (2015). *Media, myth and terrorism: A discourse-mythological analysis of the 'Blitz Spirit' in British newspaper responses to the July 7th bombings*. Palgrave.
Kelsey, D. (2017). *Media and affective mythologies: Discourse, archetypes and ideology in contemporary politics*. Palgrave.
Kelsey, D. (2018). Affective mythology and 'the notorious' Conor McGregor: Monomyth, mysticism, and mixed martial arts. *Martial Arts Studies, 5*, 15–35.
Kelsey, D. (2020). Psycho-discursive constructions of narrative in archetypal storytelling: A discourse-mythological approach. *Critical Discourse Studies*. https://doi.org/10.1080/17405904.2020.1802766
Kuhn, G., Amlani, A., & Rensink, R. (2008). Towards a science of magic. *Trends in Cognitive Sciences, 12*(9), 349–354.
Kuhn, G., Olson, J., & Raz, A. (Eds.). (2016). The psychology of magic and the magic of psychology. *Frontiers in Psychology*. https://doi.org/10.3389/fpsyg.2016.01358
L'illusionist. (2010). Sylvain Chomet. Warner Bros.
Lamont, P., & Wiseman, R. (2005). *Magic in theory: An introduction to the theoretical and psychological elements of conjuring*. University Press.
Larger Us. (2018). *A larger us*. https://larger.us/ideas/?report
Leddington, J. (2016). The experience of magic. *The Journal of Aesthetics and Art Criticism, 74*(3), 253–264.
Lule, J. (2001). *Daily news, eternal stories: The mythological role of journalism*. Guilford Press.
Manson, M. (2016). *The subtle art of not giving a fuck*. HarperOne.
Marshall, D. (2014). *Celebrity and power: Fame in contemporary culture*. University Press.
Marshall, D. (2016). *The celebrity Persona pandemic*. University Press.
Marshall, D., Moore, C., & Barber, K. (2015). *Celebrity Studies, 6*(3), 1–18. https://doi.org/10.1080/19392397.2015.1062649
Marshall, D., Moore, C., & Barber, K. (2019). *Persona Studies: An introduction*. Wiley.
Maslow, A. (1971). *The farther reaches of human nature*. Penguin.
McGregor, C. (2020). *Conor McGregor on UFC 246, Khabib, Mayweather | extended interview*. Ariel Helwani's MMA Show https://www.youtube.com/watch?v=0lzbKIwLc8k.

McLeod, S. (2018). Carl Jung. *Simply Psychology*. https://www.simplypsychology.org/carl-jung.html.

Meade, M. (2020, August 3). A story to save the world. *Russell Brand: Under the skin podcast*. https://www.youtube.com/watch?v=1VaEKZRa1rQ

Messerly, J. (2013). *The meaning of life: Religious, philosophical, transhumanist, and scientific perspectives*. Darwin & Hume Publishers.

Moore, R., & Gillette, D. (1990). *Magician warrior king lover: Rediscovering the archetypes of the mature masculine*. HarperOne.

Moro, P. A. (2017). Witchcraft, sorcery, and magic. In *The International Encyclopedia of Anthropology*. https://doi.org/10.1002/9781118924396.wbiea1915

Mulford, P. (1910). *Your forces and how to use them*. F. J. Needham.

Nartey, M. (2021). Yvonne Nelson and the heroic myth of Yaa Asantewaa: A discourse-mythological case study of a Ghanaian celebrity. *Critical Studies in Media Communication, 38*(3), 255–268. https://doi.org/10.1080/15295036.2021.1907429

Nissim, M. (2011, June 2). Derren Brown: 'Lottery twist was banned'. *Digital Spy*. https://www.digitalspy.com/showbiz/a322800/derren-brown-lottery-twist-was-banned/

Peale, N. V. (1952). *The power of positive thinking*. Vermilion.

Pigliucci, M. (2017). *How to be a Stoic: Ancient wisdom for modern living*. Rider Books.

Pigliucci, M. (2019). One crucial word. *How to be a Stoic: An evolving guide to practical stoicism for the 21st century*. https://howtobeastoic.wordpress.com/2016/01/19/one-crucial-word/

Polaschek, B. (2018). The dissonant personas of a female celebrity: Amy and the public self of Amy Winehouse. *Celebrity Studies, 9*(1), 17–33. https://doi.org/10.1080/19392397.2017.1321490

Robertson, D. (2013). *Stoicism and the art of happiness*. Mobius.

Robertson, D. (2019). *How to think like a Roman emperor*. St Martin's.

Robertson, D. (2020a). The difference between stoicism and Stoicism. https://medium.com/stoicism-philosophy-as-a-way-of-life/the-difference-between-stoicism-and-stoicism-907ee9e35dc5

Robertson, D. (2020b). Stoicism and Islam: Al-Kindi's device for dispelling sorrows. https://medium.com/stoicism-philosophy-as-a-way-of-life/stoicism-and-islam-53a46f3f3e4d

Routledge, C. (2018). *Supernatural: Death, meaning and the power of the invisible world*. University Press.

Samuels, A., Shorter, B., & Plaut, F. (1986). *A critical dictionary of Jungian analysis*. Routledge.

Scott, A. (2016). *Shifting stories: How changing their stories can transform people*. Troubador.

Seneca. (2004). *Letters from a Stoic*. Penguin.

Sherman, N. (2021). *Stoic wisdom: Ancient lessons for modern resilience*. University Press.

Sikka, T. (2021). The Neoliberalization of sleep: A discursive and materialist analysis of sleep technologies. *Journal of the Swiss Anthropological Association, 26*, 105–121.

Steenberg, L. (2019). Bruce lee as gladiator: Celebrity, vernacular stoicism and cinema. *Journal of Global Media and China, 3*, 4. https://journals.sagepub.com/doi/full/10.1177/2059436419874625

Storr, W. (2019). *The science of storytelling: Why stories make us human and how to tell them better*. Abrams.

Sturges, F. (2018, October 13). Derren Brown: Sacrifice – Have the illusionist's party tricks lost their shine?. *The Guardian*. https://www.theguardian.com/tv-and-radio/2018/oct/13/derren-brown-sacrifice

Tannen, R. (2007). *The female trickster the mask that reveals: Post-Jungian and postmodern psychological perspectives on women in contemporary culture*. Routledge.

Thorndike, L. (1905). *The place of magic in the intellectual history of Europe*. University Press.

Vost, K. (2015). *The porch and the cross: Ancient Stoic wisdom for modern Christian living*. Angelico Press.

Weinstein, B. (2018). The evolution of religion: Why belief systems are literally false and metaphorically true. *The Big Think*. https://bigthink.com/thinking/bret-weinstein-how-evolution-explains-religion/

Willis, D. (2017). Magic and witchcraft. In A. Kinney & T. Hopper (Eds.), *A new companion to renaissance Drama*. https://doi.org/10.1002/9781118824016.ch13

Wittman, T. (2020a). *Justin Gaethje's coach Trevor Wittman reacts to Khabib weighing in and previews UFC 254 card*. https://www.youtube.com/watch?v=Hzaev5R6uBM

Wittman, T. (2020b). *UFC 254: Trevor Wittman pre-fight interview*. https://www.youtube.com/watch?v=B3V2Wz9LY68

Wodak, R. (2015). *The politics of fear: What right-wing populist discourses mean*. Sage.

Wodak, R., & Meyer, M. (2001). *Methods of critical discourse analysis*. Sage.
Wright, R. and Pigliucci, M. (2017). Buddhism vs. Stoicism. *The Wright Show*. https://www.youtube.com/watch?v=qcEiF6_Uevo.
Zuckerman, M. (2016). Transformative media: From the hero's journey to our collective journey. *Kosmos Journal*. Online at: https://www.kosmosjournal.org/article/transformative-media-from-the-heros-journey-to-our-collective-journey/. Last accessed 8 Apr 2020.

Index[1]

A
ABC model of emotions, 6, 13n14
Academic, 42, 154, 155
Achievement, ix, 78
Actions, 7, 27, 28, 42–49, 51–53, 56, 57, 61, 66, 77, 78, 82, 83, 85, 99, 100, 109, 113, 115, 128, 153, 155, 156, 166
Actor, 29, 30, 49, 62, 99, 100, 108, 134
Addiction, 119n21
Affect/affective, x, xii, 6, 36n5, 44, 56, 63, 68n2, 82, 129, 130, 135, 140, 147n16, 156
Amathia, 139–141
Ambition, 47, 50, 64, 77, 102, 105, 106, 116, 117, 155
America(n), 74, 79, 133, 138, 167
Amor fati, 54, 115
Ancient, x, 6, 9–11, 13n2, 33–35, 35n2, 41–43, 52, 54, 82, 129, 132, 139, 160–162, 166, 167
Animal, 4
Anthropology/anthropologist(s), 130, 147n16, 167
Antidepressant, 162
Anti-self-help, 73
Anxiety, ix, 44, 49, 50, 52, 55, 56, 61, 65, 66, 75, 77, 81, 82, 88, 107, 118, 124, 125, 127, 150, 151, 154–156, 162
Apatheia, 60
Apathy, 47, 78
Apocalypse, The, 105
Apocalypse (television show), 11, 12, 30, 103–106, 112, 114, 115, 118, 127, 164

---

[1] Note: Page numbers followed by 'n' refer to notes.

© The Author(s), under exclusive license to Springer Nature Switzerland AG 2022
D. Kelsey, *Storytelling and Collective Psychology*,
https://doi.org/10.1007/978-3-030-93660-0

Index

Archer, 48
Archetype/archetypal, xi, 3, 5, 10, 11, 13, 14–15n22, 16n27, 16–17n28, 21–35, 35–36n2, 36n4, 36n5, 74, 80, 82, 90, 97, 103, 104, 114, 136, 147n16, 163–165, 167
Aron, Arthur, 131
Art, xi, 2
Artificial Intelligence (AI), 157
Aspire/aspiration, 47, 89
Ataraxia, 54, 75, 76
Atheism/atheist, 92n26, 160
Athens/Athenian, 10, 35, 41, 43, 67n1, 142
Audience(s), xi, 7, 11, 23–30, 38n18, 80, 84, 86, 89, 90, 96, 97, 105, 108, 114, 118, 119n9, 127, 128, 137, 140, 149, 152
Aurelius, Marcus, x, 42, 44, 55–57, 61, 66, 88, 89, 107, 113, 166
Autoethnography, 15n23, 36n5

B

Barthes, Roland, 2
BBC, 4, 29
Beck, Aron, 6
Belonging, 8, 124, 128–131, 144, 150, 156
Big Think, 47
Blame, 61, 62, 78, 80–82, 96, 125
Blavatsky, Helena, 80
Bonhoeffer, Dietrich, 141, 142
Book of Secrets, 14n20, 37n8, 91n11, 132
Brand, Russell, 119–120n21, 167
Brave/bravery, 108
British, xii, 4, 14n22, 145–146n1
Burley, Kay, 50, 52

C

Campbell, Joseph, 103, 104, 140, 147n16, 164, 165
Carpe diem, 54
Celebrity, xi, 14n22, 22, 30, 36n5, 73, 80, 83–84, 89, 90, 104
Channel 4, 11
Charlatan, 27, 30, 82
Child(ren), ix, 24, 62, 82, 99, 107, 110, 114, 168
Christian(ity), 79
Citizen, 142
Civic, 42, 43
Clay, Richard, 2
Cognitive Behavioural Therapy (CBT), x, 6, 7, 13n14, 32, 59, 153, 154
Collective journey, xi, 165–166
Collective unconscious, 16n27
Community, xiii, 1, 26, 57, 83, 104, 123, 124, 131, 133, 147n16, 150, 159, 162–167
Compassion, 61, 106, 108–110, 115, 118, 127, 132, 136, 137, 152, 155, 164
Conjuring/conjure, x, xi, 1, 92n26
Conjuror, xi, 4–5
Conscious, 9, 16n27, 27, 37–38n14, 43, 57, 67, 89, 95, 104, 108, 117, 120n21
Consciousness, 4, 9, 16n27, 23, 33, 37n6, 57, 67, 123, 145n1, 159
Cosmopolitanism, 133, 142–144

Cotton, Fearne, 156
Courage, 43, 46, 52, 66, 80, 85, 99, 105, 107, 108, 113, 117, 161, 168, 169
Creatures, 1, 143, 146n10

D

The Daily Stoic, 44, 75, 161
Daughter, x, 46, 62, 63, 153
Day, Elizabeth, 156
De Botton, Alain, 10, 42, 68n7
Dead/death, 37n8, 54, 92n26, 101, 107, 138, 168
Dennett, Daniel, 4
Depression, 38n18, 162
Desert Island Discs, 4
Dialogue, 32, 35, 55, 59, 63–65, 77, 87, 103, 113, 117, 124, 136–139, 145, 149, 151–153, 162, 165
Dichotomy (of control), 44–46
Discourse, 15n22, 124, 126, 127, 142, 159
Divided, ix, 125–126, 137
DNA, 129, 131, 132, 135, 144
Drama, 90, 96, 97, 163
Dream, x, 74, 75, 77, 111–112, 115
Duty, 42, 46, 61, 67n1, 80, 113, 116, 133, 154, 157, 159, 161

E

Earth, 108, 130, 131
Ego, 25, 27–29, 37–38n14, 49, 52–54, 57, 69n27, 83, 85–87, 97, 149, 155, 169
Ehrenreich, Barbara, 73, 79, 80

Ellis, Albert, 6, 13n14
Emotion, 6, 13–14n14, 32, 34, 37n14, 41, 43, 44, 46, 48, 49, 52, 54, 55, 58–61, 68n2, 87–89, 108, 111, 114, 117, 118, 127, 131, 134, 135, 152
Empathy, 12, 61, 96, 108–110, 117, 118, 125, 127–133, 136, 139, 142, 144, 150–152, 154, 155, 165, 166
England, 4, 98, 138
Epictetus, x, 6, 13n14, 44, 45, 55, 106, 107, 139, 142
Ethics/ethical, 12, 28, 63, 65, 78, 103, 132, 139, 142–144, 146n10, 160
Ethos, 7, 10, 12, 22, 30, 34, 42, 43, 51, 87, 118, 133, 142, 150, 154–156, 159
Eudaimonia, 42
Eupathieai, 60
European Union (EU), 138
Evans, Alex, xii, xiii, 8, 159
Evans, Jules, 6, 13n14, 42, 43, 130
Evers, Clifton, 15n23
Evil, 45, 96, 115, 140
Evolution, 58, 99, 160
Experiencing self, 30–33
Exploit, 27, 82, 114, 119n9

F

Failure, 14n19, 50, 57, 74, 77, 79, 81–82, 89, 105, 112, 113, 146n1, 156
Faith healing, 27, 38n18
Family, 1, 12, 47, 64, 65, 78, 89, 95, 105, 106, 109–116, 124–127, 132, 135, 137, 143, 146n11

Index

Fate, 11, 44, 49, 50, 52–54, 56, 57, 79, 81–83, 85, 92n26, 107, 115, 138–139, 154
Fatherhood, 65
Fear, ix, x, 3, 50, 66, 82, 95, 102, 105, 107, 112–115, 124, 126–129, 133, 135, 137, 141, 142, 150, 151, 154, 156, 168, 169
Flourish(ing), 7–9, 35, 42–44, 54, 63–67, 110, 117, 136, 145, 151, 155, 160, 163–165, 170n14
Foreign, 138
Fortune, 45, 52, 67n1, 73, 75, 80, 81, 83, 87–90, 107
Fraud, 27, 30, 38n18
Freud, Sigmund, 75
Fundamentalism, 158, 161
Future, xii, xiii, 8, 9, 12–13, 33–35, 46, 49, 50, 53, 58, 62, 63, 83, 107, 145, 150–152, 159, 164–166, 168, 170n14

G

Gillette, Douglas, 22, 36n4, 74, 97
Gladwell, Malcolm, 145
Gloyn, Liz, 47, 133
Goals, 53, 73–75, 77–79, 166
God, 22, 27, 38n18, 96–97, 103, 130, 160, 161
Gottschall, Jonathan, 13n2, 162
Gratitude/grateful, x, 26, 42, 54, 64–66, 89, 106, 107, 110–113, 115, 116, 118, 120n21, 154, 161, 168
Graver, Margaret, 69n42
Grow(th)/growing, 12, 21, 46, 50–51, 62, 64, 73, 75, 112, 113, 115, 116, 118, 130, 152, 156, 158–160, 163, 165, 167
Guardian, 29

H

Haidt, Jonathan, 12, 124, 125, 137, 142, 145
Hallucination(s), 3–4, 136
Happy/happiness, x, 6, 29, 33, 35, 35n2, 42, 45, 55, 67, 73–79, 81, 100, 105, 124, 150
Harari, Yuval Noah, 1
Hari, Johann, 162
Harris, Sam, 6, 32, 103
Heist, The (television show), 11, 98, 119n9
Help, ix–xiii, 2–4, 9, 10, 12, 13, 13n2, 21, 22, 25, 33–35, 41, 42, 48, 50, 52, 54, 58, 60, 63, 65, 66, 68n7, 75, 76, 97, 100, 102, 108, 109, 111, 115, 117, 129–131, 135–137, 143, 145, 147n16, 150–154, 161, 162, 164, 165, 167
Hero(es)/Heroic, ix, 11, 21, 96–97, 102–104, 108, 112, 115, 125, 134–136, 150, 163, 164, 166, 168, 169
Hero's Journey, 103–105, 114, 163, 165
The Hero with a Thousand Faces (Joseph Campbell), 103
Hindsight, x, 66–67
History/historical/historian, 1, 2, 14n22, 17n28, 24, 79, 120n21, 141, 144, 146n10, 156, 158, 161, 166, 170n14
Holiday, Ryan, x, 43, 51–53, 59, 69n27, 89, 166

Index

Hollis, Jame, 112, 113
Home, 58, 104–106, 108, 109, 111–114, 116, 130, 133, 134, 137, 150, 163, 164
Houdini, 25

I

Identity, xi, 1, 2, 30, 32, 33, 37–38n14, 63, 95, 116, 123, 129, 131, 145–146n1, 151, 158, 163
Ideology, 63, 99, 102, 123, 135, 137, 139, 141, 163
Illusion, 4, 13n6, 23, 35n2, 136
Illusionist, x, 3, 7, 24, 25, 30, 118, 125
Illusionist, The, 24
Immigrant(s)/immigration, 125–128, 133, 134, 138, 143, 144
Individuation, 95, 96, 112, 115–117, 119n2, 123, 140, 145, 152, 163–166
Injustice, 46–48, 57, 80, 150
Inner dialogue, 32, 35, 55, 59, 64, 65, 77, 103, 113, 117, 139, 149, 152, 153, 162
Institution, 1, 63, 78, 135, 153, 155, 156
Introspective, 57, 133, 153
Irvine, William, x, 33, 88, 107

J

The Joe Rogan Experience, 6
Journalism, 138

Journey(s), ix, xi, 3, 4, 9, 21, 30, 64, 66, 88, 91, 96, 97, 103–105, 108, 111–115, 128, 133, 135, 145, 149, 150, 153, 155, 156, 163–166, 169
Jung, Carl Gustav, 7, 8, 14n19, 14n20, 16n27, 17n28, 21, 37n14, 57, 60, 62, 69n27, 75, 95, 96, 102, 104, 116–118, 123, 145, 152
Justice, 12, 42, 43, 46, 47, 52, 66, 67, 80, 99, 105, 107, 117, 135, 138, 143, 161, 166, 168, 169

K

Kahneman, Daniel, 30–33, 61
Kaufman, Scott, 37n6
Keller, Helen, v, 167–168
Kelsey, Darren, 14–15n22, 16n23, 16n28, 146n1, 147n16
Kind(ness), 42, 60, 76, 115, 136, 137, 143, 144, 165, 169

L

Laverne, Lauren, 4, 5, 27
Law of Attraction, 80–85, 89
Leadership, 105, 109–110, 153–155
Learn(ing), 6, 9, 30, 41, 49–51, 64, 75, 97, 156, 162
Lessons, xiii, 5, 7, 9, 11, 25, 27, 49–52, 66, 76, 82, 97, 101–103, 115, 160, 162, 166, 169
Levinas, Emmanuel, 132

Index

Life/living, 1–3, 6, 7, 9–12, 16n23, 22, 23, 26, 32–35, 41–43, 45, 46, 49–57, 60, 63–67, 68n10, 73–77, 80, 84, 87–90, 97, 99, 102, 104–108, 110–113, 115–118, 125–128, 130, 131, 136–138, 143, 144, 146n1, 146n11, 147n16, 149, 153, 154, 158–162, 166, 167, 169
L'illusionist, ix–xi, 24
Logos, 160, 161
Loneliness, 150, 162
Love, ix, 54, 64, 86, 107, 110, 111, 118

M

Machines, 1–13, 145, 152, 157, 166, 168–169
Magical thinking, 74
Magician/magic, x, xi, xiii, 3–5, 10, 11, 13, 17n32, 21–35, 35n2, 43, 54, 90, 96, 97, 149, 151
Making Sense with Sam Harris, 6
Martial arts, xi, 51, 84
Maslow, Abraham, 37n6
McGregor, Conor, 11, 84–90, 92n28
Meade, Michael, 167–169
Meaning/meaning-making, 1, 6, 7, 21–23, 25, 30, 75, 77, 92n26, 97, 116, 117, 124, 137, 149, 155, 157–159, 164
Meditations, 42, 143
Memento Mori, 54
Memory, 16n23, 30–32, 37n14, 58, 115
Mentor(s)/mentoring, 50, 97
Metaphysics, 42
Miracle, 27, 169

Miracle (Netflix), 10, 16n26, 27, 34, 78
Miracles for Sale (television show), 38n18
Mitchell, Edgar, 130, 131
Mixed martial arts (MMA), 11, 51, 84
Moderation, 42, 43
Modern, ix, x, 11, 22, 33, 42, 52, 61, 77, 106, 116, 146n1, 147n16, 158–160, 164, 165, 169
Monomyth, 103, 115, 163–165, 169
Moore, Robert, 22, 36n4, 36n5, 74, 97
Moral(s)/morality, xi, 2, 12, 21, 25, 43, 57, 63, 102, 114, 115, 124, 125, 127, 129, 133, 139, 140, 143, 145, 152, 159, 163
Morale, 49
Mother, 62, 63, 108, 169
Murder, 99, 100
Mystical/mystic, 23, 73, 81, 83–85, 90, 147n16
Mythology/myth/mythmaking, 2–3, 14n22, 23, 37n8, 104, 140, 147n16, 149, 157, 158, 167, 168

N

Narrative, xi–xiii, 1–13, 14–15n22, 16n27, 17n28, 22, 25, 26, 33, 37n8, 46, 55, 62, 63, 65, 78, 82–87, 90, 96, 104, 114, 116, 117, 120n21, 124, 127, 131, 133, 135–137, 140, 142, 144, 145, 152, 155, 162, 163, 165, 166, 169

National identity, 145n1
Nationalism, 126, 142–144
Nature, 1, 5, 14n20, 16n27, 33, 37n6, 45, 55–57, 76, 96–98, 124–126, 132, 140, 141, 146n10, 151, 157, 160, 161
Negative visualisation, 106–108, 154
Nero, 88, 89
Neuroscience, 13n2
Neurosis, 14n19, 75
News, 86, 131, 138, 139
Noun, 76, 91n11
Nurmagomedov, 86
Nyman, Andy, 62, 63

O

Oikeiōsis, ix, xi–xiii, 12, 17n30, 47, 132–134, 146n11
Other/othering, 4, 9–12, 17n28, 17n32, 21, 22, 24–29, 31–35, 36n5, 37n6, 46, 47, 53, 54, 56, 57, 59–61, 63–66, 69n27, 74, 78, 81–83, 86, 87, 89, 95, 100, 101, 103, 107–111, 124–133, 135–139, 141–145, 149, 151, 152, 155, 157, 161–163, 166, 169, 170n14
Outcomes, 46–51, 54, 67, 77, 78, 81, 84–86, 113
Outer world, xii, 2, 8, 14n19, 22, 23, 55–58, 83, 87–89, 96, 112, 158, 159
Overview effect (Big Picture Effect), 130–131

P

Parents, 10, 62–64, 89, 105, 110, 111, 140
Past, xii, 5, 9, 11, 26, 30, 33–35, 36n4, 42, 53, 62, 63, 73, 79–80, 89, 111, 118, 120n21, 123, 125, 133, 145–146n1, 149, 155–158, 160
Penn and Teller, 96
Persona, xi, 7, 10, 11, 15n22, 16n23, 17n28, 22–26, 28, 30, 36n5, 59, 84, 86–88, 90, 167
Personality, 10, 11, 17n28, 22, 41, 102, 105, 126, 140, 146n4
Pigliucci, Massimo, x, 139, 143, 161
Place, 1–3, 37n8, 42, 50, 56, 91n11, 92n26, 100, 116, 117, 124, 128–130, 138, 139, 143, 146n1, 149, 157, 164
Planet, xii, 12, 83
Podcast(s), x, 4, 6, 156, 167
Polarisation, xii, 11, 124, 137, 138, 145, 150, 151, 159
Politics, xi, xii, 14n22, 124, 126–129, 135–137, 141, 144, 150, 151, 156
Populism, xi, 142–144
Positive thinking, 73–75, 77, 79–81, 83, 85, 106, 115
Positive visualisation, 80, 81, 84, 85, 89
Power(s), 21, 24, 27, 44, 46, 56, 73, 75, 80–82, 89, 97, 104, 114, 141, 146n1
Premeditatio malorum, 106
Present, 32–35, 42, 49, 53, 54, 77, 78, 89, 92n26, 103, 152, 159
Pride, 48

Index

Projection (shadow Jung), 95, 96, 125, 154, 163
Protestant, 11, 73, 79–80
Psyche, 8, 11, 16n27, 17n28, 23, 38n14, 44, 60, 61, 63, 66, 73, 75, 90, 95, 137, 139, 146n1
Psychic, 16n27, 17n28, 27
Psychoanalysis, 75
Psychoanalyst, 41, 61, 75, 112
Psychodiscursive, 14–15n22, 36n5
Psychotherapy, 6, 23
The Push (Netflix), 11, 98–100, 102, 103, 119n9

R

Reflections, 12, 15n23, 21, 50, 52, 59, 66–67, 120n21, 132, 145, 149–169
Relationships, 22, 56, 78, 113, 146n10
Religion, 37n8, 112, 116, 127, 157–162
Remembering self, 30–33
Research, x, xi, xiii, 5, 7, 9, 14–15n22, 15n23, 30, 31, 33, 36n5, 61, 64, 84, 106, 131, 149, 154, 155
Resilience/resilient, 66, 68n7, 106, 114, 154
Responsibility, x, 7, 12, 46–48, 61, 76, 80, 83, 105, 108–109, 132, 138, 143, 153–155, 161
Ritual, 23, 105, 147n16, 159, 167
Robertson, Donald, x, 41, 60, 76, 106, 142, 143
Rogan, Joe, 7, 112, 137

S

Sacrifice (Netflix), 11, 12, 29, 118, 125, 127, 136, 137, 140, 144, 164
Schopenhauer, Arthur, 76
Science, 15n22, 43, 61, 130, 159
Secret, The (Rhonda Byrne), 73, 80–84, 89, 91n18, 92n26
Secrets, 28, 73
Self-esteem, 63
Selfish, 52, 69n27, 105, 106, 111, 117
Semiotics, 14n22, 15n22
Seneca, x, 44, 45, 58, 88, 107, 154, 161
Serendipitous/serendipity, x, 6–7, 149
Shadow, 8, 9, 11, 14n20, 21, 26–30, 37n8, 57, 60, 74, 80, 82, 90, 95, 96, 102, 108, 114, 115, 118, 119n2, 119n9, 123, 125, 130, 137, 146n1, 150–152, 163, 164, 169
Shadow magic, 27, 30, 38n18, 74, 90
Shadow magician, 27–29, 82
Sherman, Nancy, 41, 60
Sikka, Tina, 15n23
Social compliance, 98–100, 118
Social justice, 138
Socrates/Socratic, 6, 15n23, 42, 43, 54, 67n1, 68n10, 117–118, 139, 140, 142
Sophia, 139
Spirit, 6, 14n22, 37n8, 42, 43, 45, 53, 80, 114, 117, 151
Spiritual, 21–23, 96

Stage, x, xi, 4–6, 10, 12, 23–25, 27, 30, 34, 35n2, 43, 50, 66, 78, 113, 116, 128, 149
Stephen, Fry, 156, 168
Stoa Poikile, 41
Stoic archer, 48
Stoic Sage, 47
Storr, Will, 1, 3
Strangers, 99, 100, 103, 113, 114, 125, 128, 131–133, 144
Strategic pessimism, 75–76, 156
Success, ix, 48, 50, 73, 83, 85, 89, 90, 112, 115, 156
Suffering, xii, 55, 76, 143, 145n1, 150
Summum bonum, 43
Supernatural, 92n26, 97, 104
Support, 12, 31, 37n8, 66, 69n55, 141, 153, 159, 161, 165, 169

T

Teaching, xi, 12, 42, 67n1, 149, 154, 155, 166
Team, xiii, 8, 65, 124, 153–157, 159
Television, 4, 11, 28, 30, 35n2, 38n18, 96, 105, 108, 120n21, 131, 133
Temperance, 42, 43, 46, 47, 52, 57, 66, 99, 117, 161, 166, 168, 169
Tennis, 48
Therapy/therapist, x, 7, 32, 64, 65, 153, 162
Transcend(ence), 22, 24, 34, 37n6, 97, 112, 116–117, 135, 158, 159, 163, 165

Transform(ation), 4, 6, 12, 21, 26, 97, 103, 105, 107, 114, 115, 117, 118, 135–137, 145, 149–169
Tribe/tribal(ism), 11, 47, 114, 124–125, 127, 129, 133, 135, 142, 144, 145, 151, 160, 165, 170n14
Tricks, 3–5, 7, 23–25, 27–29, 34, 35n2, 54, 80, 97, 149
Trickster(s), 27

U

UFC, 51, 84–87, 92n28
Unconscious, 6–8, 16n27, 17n28, 34, 35, 57, 61–63, 67, 90, 95–98, 103, 131, 137, 152
Unhappiness, 75
University, 46, 64, 65, 69n55, 78, 138, 139

V

Verb, 76–79, 91n11
Virtual Reality (VR), 130
Virtue, 12, 37n8, 41, 43, 44, 46, 47, 51, 52, 55, 60, 66, 67n1, 89, 100, 107, 115, 117, 133, 139, 140, 142, 143, 161, 168

W

Weinstein, Bret, 159, 160
Wisdom, ix, 2–4, 11, 13, 21, 27, 29, 34, 35n2, 43, 44, 46, 52, 60, 66, 67n1, 80, 89, 99, 107, 117, 139, 160, 161, 167–169

Wise old man, 97
Wittman, Trevor, 51
Wizard of Oz, 114–116
Wodak, Ruth, 114, 126
World, ix, xii, xiii, 1, 2, 5, 6, 8, 13, 14n19, 22–24, 30, 34, 35, 38n18, 42, 46, 50, 51, 53, 55–58, 61–63, 74–76, 79, 80, 82–85, 87–90, 92n26, 96, 97, 99, 104–106, 112, 116, 117, 124, 126, 129, 136, 138–140, 143, 144, 146n1, 147n16, 150, 153, 154, 157–159, 161, 163, 166–168, 170n14
Worry, ix, x, 7, 45, 46, 54, 65, 75, 168

Z

Zeno of Citium, 41, 143
Zuckerman, Maya, 36n4, 165, 166